Backpacker Tourism

PEFC
PEFC/16-33-111
CATG-PEFC-052
www.pefc.org

TOURISM AND CULTURAL CHANGE
Series Editors: Professor Mike Robinson, *Centre for Tourism and Cultural Change, Leeds Metropolitan University, Leeds, UK* and Dr Alison Phipps, *University of Glasgow, Scotland, UK*

Understanding tourism's relationships with culture(s) and vice versa is of ever-increasing significance in a globalising world. This series will critically examine the dynamic inter-relationships between tourism and culture(s). Theoretical explorations, research-informed analyses, and detailed historical reviews from a variety of disciplinary perspectives are invited to consider such relationships.

Other Books in the Series
Irish Tourism: Image, Culture and Identity
    Michael Cronin and Barbara O'Connor (eds)
Tourism, Globalization and Cultural Change: An Island Community Perspective
    Donald V.L. Macleod
The Global Nomad: Backpacker Travel in Theory and Practice
    Greg Richards and Julie Wilson (eds)
Tourism and Intercultural Exchange: Why Tourism Matters
    Gavin Jack and Alison Phipps
Discourse, Communication and Tourism
    Adam Jaworski and Annette Pritchard (eds)
Histories of Tourism: Representation, Identity and Conflict
    John K. Walton (ed.)
Cultural Tourism in a Changing World: Politics, Participation and (Re)presentation
    Melanie K. Smith and Mike Robinson (eds)
Festivals, Tourism and Social Change: Remaking Worlds
    David Picard and Mike Robinson (eds)
Tourism in the Middle East: Continuity, Change and Transformation
    Rami Farouk Daher (ed.)
Learning the Arts of Linguistic Survival: Languaging, Tourism, Life
    Alison Phipps
Tea and Tourism: Tourists, Traditions and Transformations
    Lee Jolliffe (ed.)
Tourism, Culture and Development: Hopes, Dreams and Realities in East Indonesia
    Stroma Cole

Other Books of Interest
Music and Tourism: On the Road Again
    Chris Gibson and John Connell
Shopping Tourism: Retailing and Leisure
    Dallen Timothy
Film-Induced Tourism
    Sue Beeton
Tourist Behaviour: Themes and Conceptual Schemes
    Philip L. Pearce
Tourism Ethics
    David A. Fennell
Tourism and Climate Change: Risks and Opportunities
    Susanne Becken and John E. Hay

For more details of these or any other of our publications, please contact:
Channel View Publications, Frankfurt Lodge, Clevedon Hall,
Victoria Road, Clevedon, BS21 7HH, England
http://www.channelviewpublications.com

TOURISM AND CULTURAL CHANGE 13
Series Editors: Mike Robinson and Alison Phipps

Backpacker Tourism
Concepts and Profiles

Edited by
Kevin Hannam and Irena Ateljevic

CHANNEL VIEW PUBLICATIONS
Clevedon • Buffalo • Toronto

Library of Congress Cataloging in Publication Data
Backpacker Tourism: Concepts and Profiles/Edited by Kevin Hannam and Irena
Ateljevic.
Tourism and Cultural Change: 13
Includes bibliographical references and index.
1. Backpacking. 2. Backpacking–Social aspects. 3. Sports and tourism.
I. Hannam, Kevin. II. Ateljevic, Irena III. Title.
GV199.6.B315 2007
796.51–dc22   2007022922

British Library Cataloguing in Publication Data
A catalogue entry for this book is available from the British Library.

ISBN-13: 978-1-84541-078-0 (hbk)
ISBN-13: 978-1-84541-077-3 (pbk)

Channel View Publications
An imprint of Multilingual Matters Ltd

UK: Frankfurt Lodge, Clevedon Hall, Victoria Road, Clevedon BS21 7HH.
USA: 2250 Military Road, Tonawanda, NY 14150, USA.
Canada: 5201 Dufferin Street, North York, Ontario, Canada M3H 5T8.

The policy of Multilingual Matters/Channel View Publications is to use papers that
are natural, renewable and recyclable products, made from wood grown in
sustainable forests. In the manufacturing process of our books, and to further support
our policy, preference is given to printers that have FSC and PEFC Chain of Custody
certification. The FSC and/or PEFC logos will appear on those books where full
certification has been granted to the printer concerned.

Typeset by Datapage International Ltd.
Printed and bound in Great Britain by MPG Books Ltd.

Contents

Preface. vii
Acknowledgements viii
Contributors ix

1 Introduction: Conceptualising and Profiling Backpacker
Tourism
Kevin Hannam and Irena Ateljevic 1

Part 1: Conceptualising Backpacker Tourism
2 Suspending Reality: An Exploration of Enclaves and
the Backpacker Experience
Julie Wilson and Greg Richards 9
3 The Social Psychological Interface of Tourism and
Independent Travel
Petri Hottola 26
4 Sustainability Research and Backpacker Studies:
Intersections and Mutual Insights
Phillip Pearce 38
5 Are Backpackers Ethical Tourists?
Clare Speed 54
6 The Lonely Planet Myth: 'Backpacker Bible' and
'Travel Survival Kit'
Peter Welk 82
7 Challenging the 'Tourist-Other' Dualism: Gender,
Backpackers and the Embodiment of Tourism Research
Erica Wilson and Irena Ateljevic 95

Part 2: Profiling Backpacker Tourism
8 'Van Tour' and 'Doing a Contiki': Grand 'Backpacker'
Tours of Europe
Jude Wilson, David Fisher and Kevin Moore 113
9 Uncovering the International Backpackers to Malaysia
Lee Tze Ian and Ghazali Musa 128

10 Exploring the Motivations of Backpackers: The Case of
    South Africa
    Christine Niggel and Angela Benson 144
11 Study Backpackers: Australia's Short-stay International
    Student Travellers
    Jeff Jarvis and Victoria Peel 157
12 Women as Backpacker Tourists: A Feminist Analysis of
    Destination Choice and Social Identities from the UK
    Linda Myers and Kevin Hannam 174
13 The Backpacking Journey of Israeli Women in Mid-life
    Darya Maoz 188
14 Intracommunity Tensions in Backpacker Enclaves:
    Sydney's Bondi Beach
    Julie Wilson, Greg Richards and Ian MacDonnell 199
15 Perceptions of Backpacker Accommodation Facilities:
    A Comparative Study of Scotland and New Zealand
    Jenny Cave, Maree Thyne and Chris Ryan 215

16 Conclusion: Towards a Critical Agenda for
    Backpacker Tourism
    Irena Ateljevic and Kevin Hannam 247

References 257

Index 282

Preface

This is the second volume of the ongoing research programme on backpacking developed by the Backpacker Research Group (BRG) of the Association for Tourism and Leisure Education (ATLAS). The BRG aims to act as a platform for the discussion and debate between researchers of backpacker travel worldwide. It follows on from the success of the first volume *The Global Nomad* (Richards & Wilson, 2004) and seeks to further shape this relatively new area of tourism research.

The idea for the book was initiated at a meeting at Kasetsart University in Bangkok in September 2005 attended by 31 members of the BRG including researchers from the UK, Germany, Spain, the Netherlands, Finland, Australia, New Zealand, Japan, Korea, Israel and Malaysia. Drafts of the chapters contained in this volume were presented at this three-day meeting and these generated continued discussion and updates on the nature, meaning and significance of backpacker tourism. The meeting also enabled feedback to be given to the contributors to this volume and helped to develop the concept of the book.

This book, however, is not an exhaustive account of backpacker tourism research and nor is it meant to be. There are clear areas of theoretical, methodological and geographical research on backpacker tourism still to be covered and we point to this in the concluding chapter of the volume. Furthermore, at the time of writing new meetings of the BRG are being planned in Malaysia and India. Information about the ATLAS BRG activities can be found on the Internet (www.atlas-euro.org).

Kevin Hannam and Irena Ateljevic
Amsterdam and Sunderland, November 2006

Acknowledgements

A large number of individuals and organisations were involved in the various activities that have made the publishing of this volume possible. Specifically we would like at the outset to thank Jeff Jarvis for his enthusiasm for the project. We would also like to thank Greg Richards and Julie Wilson, who, in editing *The Global Nomad*, gave us valuable inspiration for the current volume and a tough act to follow. They have also been active in the development of the BRG from its inception and continue to provide guidance. The continued development of the BRG owes much to the support of Leontine Onderwater of ATLAS, who provides much needed administrative and organisational support. The BRG meeting in Bangkok at Kasetsart University was of course crucial to the development of this book and our thanks go to Nirundon Tapachai, who organised and supported this in Thailand, as well as the Tourism Authority of Thailand for its sponsorship. We would also like to thank James Johnson, a research assistant at the University of Sunderland, for his help in formatting the book and to other colleagues in our respective departments for their warmth and support in our many endeavours.

Finally, this book would not have been possible without the hard work of the members of the BRG and all of those that attended the meeting, even if their work is not represented in this volume.

Kevin Hannam and Irena Ateljevic
Amsterdam and Sunderland, November 2006

The Contributors

Dr Irena Ateljevic, Associate Professor, Wageningen UR, Wageningen University Landscape Centre, Socio-Spatial Analysis, Building no. 358/ De Hucht, Generall Foulesweg 13, 6703 BJ Wageningen, The Netherlands. e-mail: Irena.Ateljevic@wur.nl

Angela Benson, Centre for Tourism Policy Studies (CenToPS), University of Brighton, Darley Road, Eastbourne BN20 7UR, UK. e-mail: a.m. benson@brighton.ac.uk

Jenny Cave, Waikato Management School, The University of Waikato, Private Bag 3105, Hamilton, New Zealand. e-mail: CAVEJ@waikato.ac.nz

Dr David Fisher, PO Box 84, Lincoln University, Canterbury, New Zealand. e-mail: Fisherd@lincoln.ac.nz

Professor Kevin Hannam, Head of Tourism, University of Sunderland, School of Arts, Design, Media and Culture, Priestman Building, Sunderland SR1 3PZ, UK. e-mail: kevin.hannam@sunderland.ac.uk

Dr Petri Hottola, Senior Assistant Professor, The Finnish University Network for Tourism Studies (FUNTS), University of Joensuu, Centre for Tourism Studies, P.O. Box 78, FIN-57101 Savonlinna, Finland. e-mail: petri.hottola@joensuu.fi

Lee Tze Ian, Graduate School of Business, Faculty of Business and Accountancy, Level 4, Block C, City Campus, University of Malaya, Jalan Tun Ismail, 50480 Kuala Lumpur, Malaysia. e-mail: bp_universityofmalaya@yahoo.com

Jeff Jarvis, Graduate Tourism Program, National Centre for Australian Studies, Monash University, Clayton, Victoria 3168, Australia. e-mail: Jeff.Jarvis@arts.monash.edu.au

Ian MacDonnell, University of Technology, Sydney, PO Box 123, Broadway, NSW 2007, Australia.

Dr Darya Maoz, The Hebrew University of Jerusalem, 34 Charlap St., Jerusalem 92342, Israel. e-mail: daryariva@pob.huji.ac.il

Dr Kevin Moore, PO Box 84, Lincoln University, Canterbury, New Zealand. e-mail: moorek@lincoln.ac.nz

Ghazali Musa, Graduate School of Business, Faculty of Business and Accountancy, Level 4, Block C, City Campus, University of Malaya, Jalan Tun Ismail, 50480 Kuala Lumpur, Malaysia. e-mail: bp_universityofmalaya@yahoo.com

Linda Myers, PhD Student, University of Sunderland, School of Arts, Design, Media and Culture, Priestman Building, Sunderland SR1 3PZ, UK. e-mail: linda.myers@sunderland.ac.uk

Christine Niggel, Sperberweg 1, 72119 Ammerbuch, Germany. e-mail: chrissi2006@gmx.net

Professor Phillip Pearce, Tourism Program, James Cook University, Townsville, Queensland, Australia. e-mail: Philip.Pearce@jcu.edu.au

Victoria Peel, Tourism Research Unit, Monash University, Caulfield East, Victoria 3145, Australia. e-mail: vicki.peel@arts.monash.edu.au

Dr Greg Richards, Tourism Research and Marketing, Gran de GrÁcia 183 (4-1), 08012 Barcelona, Spain. e-mail: greg@tram-research.com

Professor Chris Ryan, Waikato Management School, The University of Waikato, Private Bag 3105, Hamilton, New Zealand. e-mail: CARYAN@waikato.ac.nz

Clare Speed, The Scottish Hotel School, University of Strathclyde, Curran Building, 94 Cathedral Street, Glasgow, UK. e-mail: c.speed@strath.ac.uk

Dr Maree Thyne, Aberdeen Business School, The Robert Gordon University, Garthdee Campus, Aberdeen AB10 7QG, Scotland. e-mail: m.thyne@rgu.ac.uk

Peter Welk, c/o George Taran, 14 Confederate St, Red Hill, Queensland 4059, Australia. e-mail: petewelk@yahoo.com.au

Dr Erica Wilson, Lecturer, School of Tourism and Hospitality Management, Southern Cross University, PO Box 157, Lismore, NSW 2480, Australia. e-mail: ewilson@scu.edu.au

Jude Wilson, PO Box 84, Lincoln University, Canterbury, New Zealand. e-mail: wilsonj2@lincoln.ac.nz

Dr Julie Wilson, University of the West of England, Bristol, UK. e-mail: Julie.Wilson@uwe.ac.uk

Chapter 1
Introduction: Conceptualising and Profiling Backpacker Tourism

KEVIN HANNAM and IRENA ATELJEVIC

Academic interest in backpacker tourism research has grown in recent years. Publications focusing on the phenomenon include the recent *Global Nomad* collection edited by Richards and Wilson (2004a) and the recent special issue of *Tourism Recreation Research* (2006). In the introduction to the *Global Nomad*, Richards and Wilson (2004a: 3) argued that: 'Backpackers are to be found in every corner of the globe, from remote villages in the Hindu Kush to the centres of London and Paris'. Hence, the present collection builds on and develops the analysis of backpacker tourism geographically by providing new material on backpacker tourism in India, Malaysia and South Africa amongst other countries. Conceptually, the present collection is perhaps not as profoundly groundbreaking as *The Global Nomad*, however we feel that it offers some new insights and examples. The relatively simple title of this collection, *Backpacker Tourism*, was arrived at after much debate and advice and reflects the fact that while backpackers themselves, as well as many academics, have conceptualised the backpacker phenomenon as a form of travel rather than tourism, nevertheless backpacking is increasingly part and parcel of the wider mainstream tourism industry in the 21st century and has arguably become normalised and institutionalised through increased mobilities (see Noy, 2006; O'Reilly, 2006; Sørensen, 2003 for more on these debates).

While it is not the aim of the present collection to provide a comprehensive literature review of the research to date on backpacker tourism (see Ateljevic & Doorne, 2004; Cohen, 2004), this introduction firstly seeks to outline some of the other work that has been published on backpacker tourism since the *Global Nomad* was published in 2004 in order to provide a conceptual background. Secondly, this introduction

1

provides a summary of the varied contributions in the present collection, *Backpacker Tourism*, which we have organised on the basis of their conceptual or empirical significance. In the conclusion to this volume, meanwhile, taking note of Carr's (2006) review of *The Global Nomad*, we again discuss the work that still needs to be done to fully understand the global backpacker phenomenon and call for a theoretical engagement with recent work on mobilities (Hannam *et al.*, 2006).

Recent Conceptual Developments in Backpacker Research

Recently a great deal of new research on backpacker tourism has been published. Conceptually much of this has taken a qualitative methodological approach in order to analyse the identities of various backpacker tourists (see for example, Sørensen, 2003). Concern with analysing the sociocultural identities of backpackers has of course been a long-term interest of researchers ever since the days of Cohen's (1973) early publication. More recently, however, work by Desforges (2000), Sørensen (2003), Noy (2004a) and O'Reilly (2006) in particular has examined backpacker tourists' self-reflexive narratives in different contexts. Maoz (2006a) meanwhile has broadened these horizons by examining Israeli backpackers' host–guest interactions in India and has called for more studies of locals' perceptions of backpacker tourists and the ensuing power relationships. Similarly, Cohen (2006: 11) also notes the ongoing power dynamics between backpackers and hosts in the backpacker enclave of Pai, Northern Thailand where 'it is not the native Shan people, but rather different kinds of in-migrants to the community, who primarily benefit from backpackers'. Such power relations are also evident in the research process itself. Based upon his autoethnography of backpacking, Muzaini (2006: 156) makes the important point that being an Asian backpacker in South-East Asia means that, 'looking local also means that sometimes, one gets subjected to discrimination that other locals experience...' Drawing upon postcolonial conceptual literature, Teo and Leong (2006: 126–127) develop this analysis and argue that: 'Social relations of power also inflect Asian perceptions of Asian backpackers. ... Asian backpackers are caught in between and betwixt.'

Such power relations will be picked up again in the conclusion, however we now move on to outline the chapters that contribute to the ongoing debates over backpacker tourism that are of concern in this volume.

Structure of this Volume

There is a wider a range of contributors, theoretically and geographically, in *Backpacker Tourism* compared with the previous volume *The Global Nomad*. Again there is an evident divide between chapters that contribute more theoretical observations and those that present more empirical data. However, there are some blurrings, as some chapters evidently produce both. The aim of the volume though is to draw together both sides in order to provide a synopsis of the present state of research into backpacker tourism, however we have for organisational purposes divided chapters into two sections that focus primarily but not exhaustively on conceptual backpacker matters and empirical profiles, respectively.

Following this introduction, in Chapter 2, Wilson and Richards examine the spatial development of backpacker enclaves theoretically. They argue that in spite of the rapidly changing nature of the backpacker scene and the shifts taking place in backpacker enclaves, research has tended to lag behind these changes. They note that research has tended to focus on the individual backpacker, rather than the 'scene' as a whole, or the individual enclaves in which the scene is (re)produced. They go on to suggest that more attention needs to be paid to the role of the enclave, as a social and cross-cultural space in which the gap between ideology and practice in backpacker travel is not only created, but also reconciled for (and by) the participants of the scene. Similarly, Hottola, in Chapter 3 discusses the ways in which backpackers search for in-group membership in such enclaves or metaspatial retreats such as hotel rooms, holiday resorts and other physically or behaviourally segregated places that can function as important psychophysical safe havens in tourism, much the same way our home acts as a place of rest and recovery in the everyday. He argues that by travelling between tourist metaspaces and public spaces backpacker tourists manage the stressful part of their intercultural experience and notes that similar behaviour has been well documented among migrants.

In an attempt to marry sociological and market-orientated backpacker research, Pearce, in Chapter 4, outlines the potential for sustainability research and backpacker studies to influence one another. He questions how backpacker research contributes to sustainability discussions and how can sustainability analysis shape research into backpacking. In particular, he notes that more studies of the impacts of backpacker behaviour and more studies of the corporate sustainability status of backpacker businesses would be useful new research directions.

Following on from a discussion of sustainability, Speed, in Chapter 5, attempt to discover the extent to which backpacker tourists' behaviour exemplifies that of an ethical tourist. They argue that backpacker tourism has sometimes been characterised as 'good' tourism, in comparison with mass-market packaged tourism. They consider the meaning of ethical tourism and investigate the extent to which backpackers consider themselves to be ethical tourists in the choices they make whilst travelling.

In a turn towards material considerations, Welk, in Chapter 6, goes on to consider the considerable influence of the backpacker phenomenon on the development of *Lonely Planet* and vice versa. The impact both have had on each other is so significant that their interdependencies as well as the peculiarities of *Lonely Planet*'s history are worthwhile studying in order to begin to understand the relationship between backpacker literature and backpacker tourism.

In the final chapter in this section of the book, Wilson and Ateljevic develop a conceptual framework to discuss the gendered embodiment of backpacker research. By developing a gendered perspective their chapter aims to challenge the frequently assumed dualisms surrounding the conceptualisation of the backpacker tourist experience. Moreover, like Elsrud (2005), they seek to enhance backpacker research by engaging with broader theoretical discussions of tourism as a contemporary cultural and social practice through which power relations, social identities and multiple subjectivities can be addressed.

In the second section of this volume we offer a number of chapters that profile empirically different aspects of backpacker tourism whilst also highlighting other important theoretical insights. In Chapter 8 Wilson, Fisher and Moore argue that, while a range of studies and market reports have variously addressed the 'youth' or the 'student' travel market, most have considered Europe as a *source* of outbound backpacker travellers and not as a destination *per se*. They go on to discuss 'outbound' Australasian backpackers on their tours of Europe.

Ian and Musa, in Chapter 9, consider the empirical impact of international backpackers in Malaysia and uncover important economic findings. Drawing upon Pearce (this volume), they argue that the insights gained about backpacker tourists may enable the Malaysian authorities to deal objectively with the dilemma of planning for small-scale tourism developments in a more sustainable way. Chapter 10, meanwhile, offers us a new insight into the motivations of backpacker tourists in South Africa. Since South Africa became a democracy in 1994, it has become a popular backpacker destination with a developing infrastructure to meet the needs of backpacker tourists (Visser, 2004). Based upon their empirical data, Niggel and Benson argue that there are specific push and pull motivations for backpackers to visit South Africa in comparison to other destinations worldwide. Again, based upon a large empirical survey, Jarvis and Peel, in Chapter 11, profile the travel patterns and motivations of the growing short-stay international student segment in Australian universities. Their research argues that short-stay students to Australia can be better understood as 'study backpackers', a subsegment of the international backpacker market, who have responded to the increasing commercialisation of the industry in Australia by seeking a method of visitation that gives a greater perceived cultural contact with the host society.

In Chapter 12 Myers and Hannam offer new conceptual and empirical insights by drawing upon feminist theory in order to analyse the perspectives of female backpackers from the UK of different generations who have visited various destinations over their own life-courses. Based upon qualitative empirical evidence from the UK, they argue that female backpackers' tourism experiences, like their leisure behaviour, is frequently constrained by male-dominated cultural values and attitudes. However, they also argue that, conversely, women's backpacker travel in particular contexts can also be a potentially liberating experience for some women as they gain the freedom to express their often hybrid identities in new ways. Maoz, in Chapter 13, similarly makes the point that gender and age are important factors in the study of contemporary backpacker research. Hers is a study of the backpacking journey of Israeli women in mid-life who travelled in India as backpackers for more than a month. Most of the women travellers interviewed by Maoz experienced a 'mid-life crisis', and the backpacking journey to India was perceived as a chance for transformation, overcoming fears and difficulties, and finding a new meaning to life.

The penultimate chapter (14) in this section, by Wilson, Richards and MacDonnell, is an empirical examination of a backpacker tourism enclave in Sydney, Australia. They note that Australia has gained a competitive advantage in the global backpacker market because of its rapid and extensive institutionalisation and commercialisation of backpacker travel. Moreover, the Australian tourist industry, local employers and communities looking for alternative sources of economic development have generally welcomed backpackers. Sydney, the largest and best known of Australian cities, in particular has experienced the greatest growth in backpacker tourism, and the tourist enclave of Bondi Beach arguably the most problems. Wilson and Richards argue that the expansion of backpacker enclaves in the city has arguably had positive impacts in terms of employment and income for local businesses. Nevertheless they also note that it has conversely also caused many problems for local residents living near backpacker hostels, and for local authorities who have to deal with the increased financial and administrative burden of the additional temporary residents. In extreme cases, this has led to anti-backpacker attitudes on the part of Bondi residents, which contrast greatly with the positive view espoused by the national government and backpacker interest groups.

The final chapter in this section, Chapter 15, meanwhile, develops a comparative empirical analysis of backpacker accommodation in Scotland and New Zealand. Again in a conceptual blurring of older stereotypes of backpacker tourism, their research indicates that backpacker profiles may be evolving towards a wider age-inclusive demographic and use by short-break users, in a market that was once typified as the preserve of youthful, international travellers. Their comparisons also enable contrasts to be drawn between a developing destination in need of a clearer understanding of the attitudes of this market in Scotland and the more developed 'backpacker' destination of New Zealand.

In the concluding chapter to this volume, Ateljevic and Hannam attempt to draw together the key themes of the book and identify some new research directions for the future. We hope that this will be another enjoyable backpacker tourism research read.

Part 1

Conceptualising Backpacker Tourism

Chapter 2

Suspending Reality: An Exploration of Enclaves and the Backpacker Experience

JULIE WILSON and GREG RICHARDS

Introduction

The backpacker 'scene' has become an essential part of the tourism economy in recent years, particularly in certain major traveller or backpacker 'enclaves'. However, this growth has itself been accompanied by a number of changes in the nature of backpacker tourism and the supply of facilities. These include spatial changes, such as the growth of enclaves, which Richards and Wilson (2004a) have signalled as a major development that deserves further research.

In spite of the rapidly changing nature of the backpacker scene and the shifts taking place in the structure(s) and role(s) of backpacker enclaves, research has tended to lag behind these changes. One of the reasons for this is the continuing division between research encompassing anthropological and managerial traditions. Both of these traditions have tended to focus on the individual backpacker, rather than the 'scene' as a whole, or the individual enclaves in which the scene is (re)produced. Some studies have also begun to point towards the growing gap between the ideology and practice of backpacker travel, and the fact that the experiences which backpackers aspire to are rarely attained. This produces a stark contrast between anthropological perspectives, which tend to focus on individual aspiration, and quantitative surveys, which are better at capturing activity patterns.

In this exploratory chapter we suggest that more attention needs to be paid to the role of the enclave, as a social and cross-cultural space in which the gap between ideology and practice in backpacker travel is not only created, but also reconciled for (and by) the participants of the scene. Enclaves are not necessarily sites of pure reversal or extension, but

9

rather a suspension between these two extremes; metaspaces that provide the possibility for backpackers to combine familiarity and difference in appropriate circumstances.

Previous Approaches to the Study of Backpacking

The 'gap' between backpacker theory and practice, or between desire and experience, noted by Cohen (2004), can arguably be traced to differing research traditions in the field. In broad terms, backpacker research has tended to be divided between anthropologically based and market-based approaches (Richards & Wilson, 2004a). This division is mirrored in terms of theory, methodology, the research subject and newly emergent discourses.

Anthropological studies tend to focus on qualitative, ethnographic studies of the individual backpacker (e.g. Binder, 2004; Cederholm, 1999; Sørensen, 2003; Welk, 2004) that attempt to understand the meaning of backpacking from an emic perspective. Such studies are often undertaken in the field by researchers who themselves are 'backpackers'. This tends to produce a geographic focus on popular backpacker destinations, particularly in 'exotic' locations in South East Asia and India (e.g. Hottola, 1999; Johnsen, 1998; Maoz, 2004). The predominant anthropological paradigm of such studies has tended to produce a focus on a limited range of dimensions of backpacker experience. These include issues of alienation, rite de passage/moratorium, ritual, extension/reversal, the search for authenticity and distinction or cultural capital.

The predominance of analytical dichotomies in such studies in turn tends to polarise the discussion of backpacking. The idea that backpackers tend to struggle against the growth of tourism in order to preserve their lifestyle is also contained in the narratives of loss that are common in tourism literature as well as academic studies of backpacking (Richards & Wilson, 2004b). For example, studies of identity tend to be based on externalising the 'other' traveller, where inclusive membership of one community meets the exclusion of others: to be an 'x' means 'not being a "y"' (Sollors, 1989, cited in Welk, 2004). This is often echoed within the backpacker scene, with some of those who might be externally labelled as 'backpackers' tending to define themselves in terms of their *not* being backpackers. This form of 'backpacker angst' mirrors earlier trends towards 'tourist angst' (Welk, 2004) which, according to many studies, is prevalent among older, more experienced independent travellers lamenting the loss of their pioneering travel-styles due to the changing nature not only of tourism but also of backpacking. Other commentators have implicated those researching backpackers as being often guilty of such backpacker angst in their research perspectives (e.g. wilderness.com's [2004] dismissal of these narratives of loss among 'well-backpacked' researchers as 'the whingeing of purists').

Such anthropological perspectives on the backpacker 'neotribe' (Maffesoli, 1995) contrast sharply with market- or policy-based studies, which are largely based on the economic potential offered by attracting more backpackers to a specific destination. There is less concern for the nature of the 'scene', but more interest in the decision-making processes, expenditure, activities and information sources of the backpackers. These studies of the characteristics of independent/backpacker travel are usually aimed at improving the marketing or management of backpacker destinations (e.g. Loker, 1993a; Pearce, 1990). This type of research has been particularly prevalent in Australia, where the 'backpacker industry' has grown rapidly in recent years. The major limitation of this tradition tends to be a lack of theoretical basis. Instead of linking to theories about backpacker travel developed from a more anthropological tradition, the theoretical content is usually limited to a review of the findings of previous positivist–empiricist backpacker studies. Another limitation is that backpackers are usually studied in relation to other types of tourists (age groups or travel styles), which also tends to underline the apparent coherence of the group. Definitions are usually externally derived, and the 'backpackers' themselves are rarely asked if they see themselves as backpackers or not.

The polarisation of theoretical perspectives is also linked to a methodological divide, with anthropological studies being concerned to use qualitative and ethnographic methods to uncover the 'meaning' of backpacking, whereas the market studies almost invariably use quantitative survey techniques to uncover the volume and impact of backpacker flows and expenditure.

Arguably, this methodological divide has meant that backpacker studies have not generally taken a holistic view of the backpacker scene. Anthropological studies, usually based on in-depth interviews with backpackers by backpackers, tend to have set ideas about who qualifies as a backpacker, to the exclusion of other independent travellers with similar destinations and behaviour. The emphasis tends to be on the so-called 'real' backpacker, who is usually seen as somebody travelling independently for several months and only staying in budget accommodation. Such studies are usually unable to capture the changing nature of backpacking, as the largely predetermined view of who is a 'backpacker' tends to preclude newcomers to the scene or those utilising new backpacker products. The focus on a backpacker 'archetype' also tends to emphasise the individual at the expense of the group, generally avoiding the issue of intragroup diversity. As we show later in this chapter, however, the 'backpackers' themselves tend to differ greatly on the issue of backpacker identity.

The theoretical gap between the ideology and practice of the 'scene' is therefore largely reproduced in the emic/etic divide in previous research. There is some evidence that this divide is now beginning to soften, as some studies attempt to combine traditions (e.g. Westerhausen, 2002) and new case study areas emerge, such as the increasing body of European-, Asian- and Central and South American-focused studies – in terms of destinations and participants (Anderskov, 2002; Prideaux & Shiga, 2007; Speed & Harrison, 2004). However, a number of problems remain with the analyses that currently derive from the two traditions, which have created gaps in the analysis of backpacker experience and the enclaves that support them.

This indicates a need to develop new theoretical approaches to the study of backpacker-style travel that broaden current perspectives and recognise the important spatial dimensions of the phenomenon. Because most of the theory related to backpacking is derived from anthropology, most analysis is limited to backpackers as the participants, rather than the wider field of the social construction of backpacking, which includes the producers, residents and other non-participants who help to create and define the 'scene' (see Cohen, 2004).

Here we support a new conceptual approach to the study of enc- laves which attempts to move away from previous dichotomies towards a more holistic view of the backpacking experience. This takes into account not just the views of backpackers as consumers of experience, but also the backpacker role as experience producer, as well as the roles of other actors, including the local residents and service industry workers.

We argue that studies of enclaves as sites of production, reproduction and consumption of backpacker travel need to come to terms with the spatial consequences and the social reproduction of the phenomenon. It is suggested that rather than analysing backpacker travel and backpacker enclaves as either extensions or reversals of conventional tourism and of life back at home, they should be viewed as a more complex mixture of experiences, which can help to mediate between the ideology and practice of backpacker travel.

Traveller Enclaves as Spaces of Suspension

The term 'enclave' has been applied to a wide range of tourism phenomena, ranging from backpacker destinations to conventional tourism places (such as the Costas of Spain, see O'Reilly, 2003) to cruise ships (Weaver, 2005) to the tourist bubble (Judd, 1999). What tends to link these different concepts of enclaves is the idea of relative uniformity, or their role as 'homogeneous' tourist spaces (Edensor, 1998). In the case of backpacker enclaves, however, this idea of homogeneity is challenged by the sheer variety and diversity of such spaces.

Enclaves may be located at crossroads or intersections; meeting points where backpackers rub shoulders with locals. They can be found in chaotic commercial districts (Jalan Jaksa, Jakarta and Banglamphu, Bangkok) or rural paradises with low accessibility (Ubud, Bali) or scenes of subcultural gatherings (such as Goa's trance music scene, see Saldanha, 2002). They can also be temporary enclaves – punctuation marks in well-trodden festival circuits (Glastonbury Festival, San Fermín in Pamplona, Oktoberfest in Munich) or on the work trail (Harvest Trails in Australia). The key difference between backpacker enclaves and more traditional concepts of enclaves tends to be their permeability. Locals are not excluded, and visitors are not totally protected from the world outside. The penetration of the enclave is actually welcomed by the visitor searching for contact with 'real' locals, on the basis that the security of 'home' is close at hand. In fact, there is often a whole infrastructure that is created with the aim of maintaining this balance.

The idea of the function of the enclave as maintaining some form of stasis for the backpacker is a theme that has been addressed recently in the work of Hottola (2005). Hottola analyses backpacker enclaves as 'safe havens' travellers can retreat to in order to increase their level of control and counter the 'culture confusion' that reigns outside. The pressure of the host culture forces backpackers to congregate in enclaves that provide company, support and information from fellow travellers. Hottola underlines the fact that the expressed desire of backpackers to experience local culture is often not fulfilled, as the problems involved in making real contact with local people are often too great. The other backpackers in the enclave provide a surrogate cultural experience of difference that is more akin to the home culture of the traveller. Similarly, Westerhausen (2002: 69) refers to enclaves as 'a cultural home away from home' where a temporary social world comes into existence, generally with English as the lingua franca (although this is not to suggest that the inhabitants of this temporary social world are by any means homogenous).

In a pioneering study of Vietnam's urban traveller cafés, Lloyd (2003: 355) argues that the café zones (synonymous with backpacker areas, or enclaves) function as oases from which to escape Ho Chi Minh City and Hanoi's busy streets: 'catering to mainly Western backpacker clientele, traveller cafés form a safe bubble from which travellers can gaze out at the unfamiliar, while surrounded by comforts from home'. Similarly, Hottola sees the backpacker enclaves as examples of 'metaworlds' in which the visitors can exert more actual or perceived control over their situation. He emphasises, however, that backpackers differ greatly in their motivations and their ability to handle difference. This effectively means that the spaces of the enclave are also differentiated according to the degree of control required, from the 'private' spaces offered by the hostel room, to the communal 'traveller only' spaces in hostels and spaces where locals are restricted by entry charges or other barriers, such as bars, restaurants and tourist attractions.

Hottola's analysis of backpacker enclaves as metaspaces is a significant advance in the analysis of the backpacker phenomenon. It moves beyond the individual backpacker, or even the idea of a coherent backpacker group, towards the relationship between structure and action. In our view, the gap between desire and fulfilment in the consumption of difference is a crucial part of this dialectic relationship, helping to explain some of the peculiarities of backpacker behaviour as well as the spaces of backpacker consumption.

However, we would argue that this shift away from the individual backpacker needs to go even further, to consider other actors who help to construct the notion of backpacking and who can influence the degree of control exerted by backpackers in the metaworlds of the enclave. Extending the analysis to provide a more holistic view of the process of experience creation in the enclave (and on the road as well) is particularly necessary because of the relative permeability of backpacker enclaves compared with other types of tourist 'bubbles'.

The enclave experience

The experience of the enclave is highly differentiated, depending, as Hottola suggests, not just on the level of control exerted by the traveller, but also their needs and desires for experience. Many backpackers want to experience it all; they want to be away from it all *and* at the heart of things, they want to be a part of local *and* global culture, they want to be here *and* there. These often contradictory desires create tensions for backpackers in their search for experience, which are often revealed in the gap between the ideology and practice of backpacker travel. Not only is the backpacker journey shaped by such tensions, but the enclave is too. As the enclave develops through a process of interaction between 'locals' and 'backpackers', this interaction is shaped by the nature of the enclave space, but the enclave space is also reshaped by that interaction. So for example, the private and communal backpacker spaces are shaped by the demand that individuals have for privacy and interaction, and the availability of such spaces in turn makes more and different interactions possible. This dialectic relationship between space and experience begins to shape a specific type of enclave experience that we have termed 'suspension' (Richards & Wilson, 2004a).

Rather than being totally isolated or totally immersed in local culture, many backpackers who inhabit backpacker enclaves tend to be in fact 'suspended' between local and global culture, between a totally tourist culture and a totally local culture, in a space that is neither homogeneous nor totally heterogeneous. It may be the case that many modern backpackers are not so much engaged in either reversal or a strict extension of everyday life, but rather a suspension of it.

Instead of seeing the enclave as a homogeneous space, we would prefer to see backpacker enclaves as the product of dynamic forces that are constantly changing. The backpacker enclave is not so much a tourist space (an extension of home for the tourist) or a local space (a reversal of tourist experience), but rather a space suspended in the field created by a series of apparently opposing forces. Some of these basic forces or parameters of the spaces in which suspension takes place might include:

REST – LEISURE – WORK
TEMPORARY – SEMI-PERMANENT – PERMANENT
RURAL – SUBURBAN – URBAN
DEVELOPED – NEWLY INDUSTRIALISING – DEVELOPING
EAST – HYBRID – WEST
TRADITIONAL – CONTEMPORARY – POST-TOURISM
CORE – MARGINAL – PERIPHERAL

HARD EDGE – SOFT EDGE – NO EDGE
LOCAL OWNERSHIP DOMINATES – MIXED OWNERSHIP – FOREIGN OWNERSHIP DOMINATES

We would not argue that suspension represents a clear mid-point between a series of opposites. Rather the moment of suspension for each visitor will depend on their own motivation and desires as well as the opportunities and limitations offered by the enclave. Rather than see backpacking as one extreme or the other of a continuum, we have tried to adopt a more dialectic approach that posits the integration of such opposites as essential elements of the whole.

As spaces, backpacker enclaves provide customised spaces catering for (predominantly young) visitors, which often appear to have little connection with their local surroundings. Often they provide many of the 'home comforts' that visitors seem to demand, as well as the increasingly essential means of contacting home (particularly through Internet cafes). Backpackers, supposedly driven by desire to experience something different from their home environment, often end up surrounded by the extended familiarity of home even in the most remote and exotic destinations. The people that supply both the exotic and the familiar in the enclave are also effectively suspended together with their guests. In Bangkok, for example, Banglamphu has become a 'Western' leisure area of interest to locals as well as backpackers (Richards & Wilson, 2004a). What underpins the suspension of backpacker enclaves, as opposed to the homogeneous nature of other types of enclave, is the permeability of these spaces, which allows apparently opposing forces to interact to produce a state of suspension.

At present, there is relatively little consideration of such processes in the backpacker literature. We would argue that there are a number of interesting dimensions of suspension that should be worthy of further analysis:

Spatial suspension (enclaves; touristic metaspatiality)

In spatial terms the Western backpacker may be suspended between two cultures in a backpacker enclave that combines elements of the 'West' and the 'Other' in digestible doses and is, as Noy (2004b) suggests, neither 'here' nor 'there'. Backpackers cannot be 'here' because the 'real' experience is outside the enclave, but they are also not 'there', because they are surrounded by the familiarity of the enclave.

This makes it very important to think about the spatial context of the enclave, because this will condition the relativity of 'here' and 'there' as well as the influence of the difference actors on the enclave experience. Bangkok and Sydney, for example, are very different types of enclaves, even though the backpackers using them may at first seem very similar. This underlines the importance of studying enclaves in their wider local, regional or national context. Each enclave can have a different role on each of these scales.

Temporal suspension (changing routine)

The backpacker journey as conceptualised by Hottola involves a series of encounters and periods of culture confusion interspersed by periods of retreat to the metaworld of the enclave. The enclave is therefore a period of leisure, contrasted with the 'cultural work' undertaken on the road and the 'real work' waiting at home. For each person, the relationship between periods of cultural 'work' and 'leisure' will be different. Most backpackers can opt into a leisure experience or a 'Western' tempo again, simply by reaching for an American Express card (Binder, 2004). The trip may therefore involve multiple periods of suspension, as periods of roughing it are interspersed with periods of more expensive accommodation, air conditioning and other 'home comforts'.

It could be interesting to study the temporal rhythms within the enclave as well as the enclave as part of the rhythm of a whole trip (see Amin & Thrift, 2002). The 'normal' notions of time tend to be suspended in the enclave, both for the backpackers who try and avoid 'Western' notions of time (by discarding their watches, for example) and for the locals, whose rhythm often becomes attuned to that of the travellers. Again, there seems to be a need to study the rhythms of the enclave in the context of the rhythms of its surroundings.

Behavioural suspension (hybrid identities; adaptive behaviour)

Suspension becomes a means of managing personal contradictions that emerge from shifting identities. The enclave provides a social space that is suspended between intimacy and anonymity – anonymous intimacy – in which relationships are more fluid. At 'home' the backpacker is constrained by set patterns of behaviour, norms and meaning. Entering the 'host' culture replaces individual identities with stereotypes of the 'tourist'. In the enclave, suspension provides a space in which new identities can be forged, based on the shared lifestyles of fellow backpackers, who at the same time maintain the distance of strangers. Backpackers may engage in behaviour that challenges the norms of their home environment, such as the use of drugs or hanging around 'doing nothing', but at the same time they conform not so much to the norms of the host culture they are visiting, but to those of the backpacker subculture they are suspended in.

Similar opportunities are also available to locals, who can use the enclave as a space in which the norms of the locality are tempered by the presence of the backpackers. Suspended environments also provide a relatively neutral space in which the cultural knowledge of the host can be offered as a gateway to the 'authentic' experiences outside the enclave. This creates a position of power for certain brokers within the enclave who provide this cultural intermediary function (Dahles & Bras, 1999).

This dynamic relationship between the 'locals' and their guests may also apply to enclaves where the cultural distance is not that great. In Western-style cities, the factors that attracted the backpackers to a certain enclave, such as the edginess of inner city areas, or the cheapness of the rents may also eventually become attractive to other users of the space. It is no coincidence that the backpacker enclaves in Sydney, such as Glebe, have been subject to gentrification processes in recent years, whereas in other districts the backpacker presence was felt after gentrification processes had been set in motion. In this way the processes of development kicked off by the backpackers may become an economic springboard for local residents as well.

The enclave may also be a space that allows the illusion of a contemporaneous existence of reversal and extension. Instead of finding communitas (Turner, 1973) through submersion in the host culture, perhaps backpackers find a similar experience through the communal spaces of the enclave – areas in which cultural difference is clearly present, but not in the form imagined when leaving home. An exploration of the role of narrative in supporting the gap between theory and practice and in forming a surrogate communitas would be an interesting line of enquiry.

All of these potential realms of suspension could yield fruitful areas for further research. As an illustration of what could be done, the following section presents a small-scale empirical study of backpackers, residents and service providers in Bangkok and Sydney.

The 'Gap' Between Ideology and Practice in Backpacker Enclaves

The development of a more holistic understanding of backpacker experience and how this produces and is produced by back-packer enclaves requires the application of methodologies that can bridge the methodological divide in backpacker studies. As we have argued elsewhere (Richards & Wilson, 2004c), Q methodology is a potentially useful tool, as it combines qualitative and quantitative methods.

In our study of backpacker enclaves in Bangkok (Banglamphu) and Sydney (Kings Cross/Darlinghurst, Bondi, Glebe) Q methodology was used to develop a series of statements (constructs) related to the social construction of the notion of backpacking, which were then used to conduct surveys with a significant qualitative element. The surveys covered around 250 respondents, including visitors, local residents, policy makers and service providers. The fieldwork was conduct in July and August 2002, and further details of the methodology can be found in Richards and Wilson (2004c).

When looking at the motives for travel, the things that the visitors are most likely to be seeking are cultural difference, excitement, learning and relaxation. Those calling themselves 'backpackers' were particularly likely to be motivated by exploring other cultures and searching for knowledge and excitement (Richards & Wilson, 2004a).

In general, the backpackers in the enclaves of Bangkok and Sydney think that they are better equipped than other visitors to make contact with local people, learn about local culture and contribute more to the local community (Figure 2.1).

Backpackers and other visitors also perceive 'backpackers' as different, which tends to confirm the classic anthropological concepts of travel

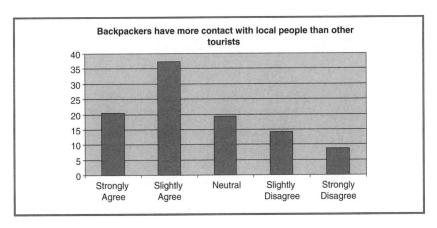

Figure 2.1 Visitor reactions to the statement 'Backpackers have more contact with local people than other tourists'

as a source of identity as well as the idea of 'backpacker angst' among other visitors (Figure 2.2).

One of the things that was also evident from the research was the relatively fluid nature of backpacker identity. Relatively very few of the visitors interviewed saw themselves solely as 'backpackers', even though a more etic analysis might tend to characterise them as such. Instead of a clear division between 'backpackers', 'travellers' and 'tourists', more interesting divisions emerged between 'purists' who identified with a single travel style, and the 'hybrids', who identified with two, three or more labels (Table 2.1).

Although 'backpacker' was the single most popular label, the 'hybrids' made up nearly 40% of the visitor sample. This indicates that for many, the label is not as important as the ability to change identity, perhaps in moving in and out of the enclave. One 'hybrid' commented 'after seeing a lot of backpackers who got stuck in foreign countries, because they liked [the feeling of being] someone "special" for the local people as a backpacker, so much I avoid trying to be a "real backpacker" because if you [exceed] your limits the only thing you are is ridiculous.'

Asked to respond to the statement 'backpackers spend most of their time with other backpackers', visitors tended to agree, pointing to a mismatch between the desire to experience the local and their actual degree of contact with local culture (Figure 2.3). There seems to be some contradiction between the general agreement that backpackers stick together and the idea that they also have more contact with locals than

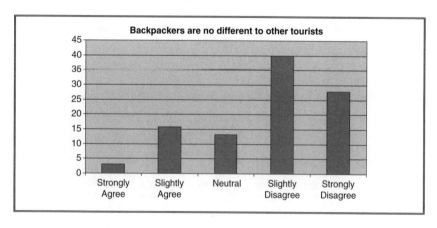

Figure 2.2 Visitor reactions to the statement 'Backpackers are no different to other tourists'

Table 2.1 Self-designation by travel style

Self-designation/label	%
Backpacker (purist)	30.7
BP/traveller/tourist (hybrid)	22.9
Traveller (purist)	21.7
BP/traveller (hybrid)	7.8
Tourist (purist)	6.0
None	6.0
BP/tourist (hybrid)	2.4
Traveller/tourist (hybrid)	2.4

other tourists. In fact, most of the comments made on this statement indicated that backpackers 'sometimes' spend more time with other backpackers, suggesting that there is a feeling that from time to time contacts are made with locals. It seems that the experience of 'other cultures' that backpackers get in enclaves is actually related to the cultures of other backpackers, rather than the local culture. In spite of this, the idea that backpacking provides more contact with local culture remains strong, indicating that backpackers are able to see themselves as experiencing more local culture primarily in relation to other visitors.

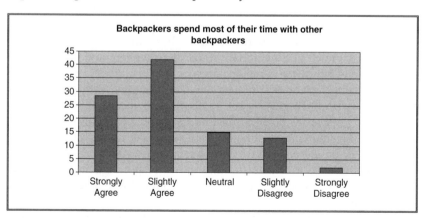

Figure 2.3 Visitor reactions to the statement 'Backpackers spend most of their time with other backpackers'

Respondents had divided opinions about the extent to which back-packers experience more of local culture than other visitors. One visitor respondent commented that 'it is nonsense to say that backpackers learn more' about the countries they visit, while another argued that back-packers do learn more about local culture 'because they spend longer in the country'. A 35-year-old Dutch airline pilot 'traveller' said 'between the age of 20 and 30 we were backpacking, travelling very basic through countries which were just "opening up". Nowadays it looks like there are not [so many] countries to discover, unless they are dangerous (e.g. Afghanistan). So backpacking nowadays is becoming so easy and accessible even for naïve travellers. So backpacking has become travelling for most people coming to Thailand... the real "edge" from fifteen years ago is gone.' So in the view of the nostalgic backpacker, the growth of enclaves and travel infrastructure between them has reduced the opportunity for 'real' travel, and also helped to push the enclave into a state of suspension.

One of the important functions of the enclave, therefore, is to provide a basis for comparing the behaviour of backpackers with other visitors. This applies not just to the visitors themselves, but also to local residents and travel industry staff. For example, in response to the statement 'backpackers are no different to other tourists', one local resident commented 'yes, they play a bigger part in our community', while a backpacker supplier said 'backpackers stay longer – it comes down to money'. For the backpackers, however, the difference tends to be underlined by travel style: 'tourists stay in resorts and do towns, backpackers do as they please'. This idea of backpacking as a relatively unstructured, 'free' form of travel is common in the backpacker community, but tends to be undermined by the institutionalisation of backpacker travel. As the responses also show, the *Lonely Planet* is the 'backpackers bible', and eventually tourists, travellers and backpackers all tend to end up in the same enclaves.

Backpackers also end up in fashionable destinations, rather than those places where they might expect to find 'real' locals. As one visitor commented, 'some fashionable destinations are great', suggesting that mainstream, fashionable destinations are somehow undesirable, but still something to be experienced by the backpacker. As another said, 'we want to experience it anyway'. But another respondent indicated that more would visit fashionable places if they could: 'those that can afford it choose fashionable destinations' (Figure 2.4).

At least for some, then, the ongoing desire to avoid the masses and inauthentic experiences does imply that there is little evidence of post-tourist irony taking place for these participants in the scene. Others,

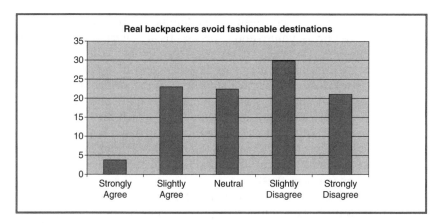

Figure 2.4 Visitor reactions to the statement 'Real backpackers avoid fashionable destinations'

however, revel in the fake and inauthentic, using their imaginations to create their own tourist experience. This tends to problematise the resort cycle in the context of backpacker destinations, which are usually conceived of as 'pioneer' resorts.

The overall picture that emerges from the analysis of visitors' responses is that there is a visible gap between the theory of experiencing difference or being explorers, and the reality of the enclave.

This view is also generally supported by residents and those involved in servicing backpackers in the enclaves of Sydney. There was a significant difference in responses between visitors and residents for very few statements. The visitors were less likely to agree that backpackers exaggerate their stories, that there is a difference between tourists and backpackers, that older backpackers are more sophisticated and that backpackers travel to get away from it all. Otherwise, the patterns recognised by backpackers and other visitors regarding the norms, values and symbols of the scene are also noted by residents and workers in the enclave. The gap between ideology and practice in backpacker travel in the environment of the enclave is therefore reproduced in the social construction of the backpacker concept.

Discussion

Our initial empirical analysis has underlined the gap between ideology and practice that underpins the backpacker experience of the enclave. We would argue that the enclave, in seeking to meet the needs of the backpackers to reconcile desire and attainment, provides them with a space in which norms, values and expectations are effectively suspended between the two. The enclave replaces the 'Other' with 'An Other' constructed by the community of backpackers and maintained with the help of local residents and service suppliers. In the suspended reality of the enclave, the disappointment of unattained experiences is tempered by the new possibilities that are offered, and which are not generally available in other situations; a concentration of new acquaintances, a stage on which to perform, a ready audience (locally and in cyberspace) and a cosmopolitan mix of the local and the global (such as the ubiquitous banana pancakes).

The reassurance of the enclave is therefore provided not just by a rest from the stimuli that are supposed to cause culture confusion, but also through replacing them with new stimuli. In this sense, the enclave is not just a place of rest; it is also a place of active leisure (although some work-orientated enclaves, such as a couple of those in Sydney, may function differently). Although many may wish to leave the leisure of the enclave and get down to some real cultural work outside, the ability to escape an increasingly institutionalised system is limited. Travellers are led by the *Lonely Planet* and other guidebooks and websites to locations where other backpackers congregate. For most people, these are also desirable locations, providing the services needed to support the backpacker lifestyle and a ready supply of new interpersonal encounters to weave the narratives that support backpacker identities. These narratives help to bridge the gap between ideology and practice, because they allow the backpacker to live their adventures vicariously through the exploits of the more outgoing (or exaggerated), and to position themselves as more experienced than the less adventurous or less travelled.

The enclave brings the backpacker into contact with the 'local' in a controlled way, where the locus of control seems to be with the backpacker. However, the ability of the enclave to concentrate the backpackers also turns them into an economic resource and a spectacle for the locals. The issue of control is therefore far from clear, as the backpackers not only become an economic resource to be exploited by locals, but eventually they may also be subject to local consumption, as enclaves become leisure areas for locals and backpackers alike. The enclave therefore becomes a tool for mediating cultures, so that 'culture confusion' is avoided from both sides, while true reversal is also prevented by the constructed familiarity of the enclave.

Therefore, there is a need to look at the function the enclave takes on in different contexts, and the influence of different cultural and social forces on the process of suspension in these different contexts. For example, it would be interesting to know whether there is such a clear difference between work- and leisure-oriented traveller enclaves. Where there is a common language (usually English), there is a far higher tendency for participants to take paid work and this may equate to a longer and very different relationship with the given destination. When do backpackers working in the community become 'local'? Are backpackers in some contexts becoming a model for the modern mobile worker as well as the modern tourist?

Are some traveller enclaves for work and some for play? What it does imply is a need to avoid treating backpacker enclaves as the pioneer destinations in wider tourism spatial and economic development models and start to consider them with more sophistication in terms of their function and also their relationship to their host city, region or country as well as their position in international travel circuits. Do London, Paris and Amsterdam (the gateways to Europe) have a similar function to Bangkok and Singapore (gateways to South East Asia)? To what extent does cultural distance make a difference in the experience of these different places? Certain recent studies have contributed much to the understanding of the work- and learning-oriented, as well as the 'more-than-just-temporary leisure and lifestyle mobility' dimensions of the traveller/backpacker experience (e.g. Clarke, 2004, 2005; Duncan, 2004; Simpson, 2003; Wilson *et al.*, 2004). A continuation of this and other trends outlined in this chapter would constitute a major contribution to research on backpacking and independent travel.

In opening up all of these potential research areas, we need to be aware of the considerable limitations of the current study. In advocating a holistic approach to enclaves, for example, it may also be argued that this obscures the relationship between enclaves and periods of travel. The relationship of experiences gathered in the enclave relative to those on the road is also an important area for future research. The empirical evidence presented here is also preliminary and needs to be followed up with more detailed fieldwork among visitors, service providers and local residents. The enclave spaces could also be mapped through GIS to show spatial inter-relationships. The most important point, however, is to avoid focussing too heavily on the backpackers as individual consumers, and to pay more attention to the actors and systems that support such activities and to their local-specific spatial and temporal contexts.

Chapter 3

The Social Psychological Interface of Tourism and Independent Travel

PETRI HOTTOLA

Introduction

Human behaviour is an issue of fundamental importance for the theoretical and practical understanding of tourism as an individual and collective phenomenon. Tourism is, after all, not built on commerce but on human interaction (MacCannell, 1992: 196–197). The search for interpersonal contacts, or avoidance of them, is present in the social psychology of all types of travel. The most archetypal form of tourism, mass package tourism, is a prime example of the voluntary congregation of people seeking a temporal collective in order to fulfil a common motive; controlled liminoidity in a climatically favourable and reasonably exotic location. At the other end of the scale, independent travellers are also often characterised by their search for in-group membership (e.g. Cohen, 1973; Hottola, 2005).

Five years have passed since the completion of the Intercultural Adaptation in Backpacking in South Asia study, which produced, among other things, the grounded theory of culture confusion (Hottola, 1999, 2004a, 2005; Suvantola, 2002: 195–212; Verhelä, 2003), and introduced the social psychological concept of control with its metaspatial dimension to the discourse of tourism. The term 'metaspatiality' is used to indicate the qualities of spaces that increase both the control of tourists and the dominance of their cultures in relation to the host community (Hottola, 2005: 2). Moreover, metaspatial retreats such as hotel rooms, holiday resorts and other physically or behaviourally segregated places function as important psychophysical safe havens in tourism, much the same way as our home(s) may act as a place of rest and recovery in the everyday. By travelling between tourist metaspaces and public spaces tourists manage the stressful part of their intercultural experience. Similar behaviour has been well documented among immigrants, expatriates and sojourners in a number of studies (e.g. Adler, 1991; Ward & Kennedy, 1993).

A tourist 'metaworld' or 'metaspace' is conceptually close to Henri Lefebvre's (cited in Soja, 1996) idea of 'counterspace', a space of alternative societal rules. Tourists are more in control and less vulnerable in their physical and behavioural 'bubbles' than they are in Other public space, where exposure to cultural difference may easily exceed their adaptive abilities, unless specifically managed. Intercultural *angst* is a real danger, especially in situations where the cultures in contact are significantly dissimilar. On the other hand, problems in intercultural adaptation tend to decrease as similarity between the cultures in contact increases, as often is the case in the globalising world. Tourism itself is an agent of cultural hybridisation; no longer the primary but nevertheless an important ground for the production of new cultural forms on a global scale.

The idea of this chapter is to relate new theoretical innovations, and especially those concerning voluntary segregation in tourism and travel, with discussion in the classical works of Boorstin (1961), Turner and Ash (1975), MacCannell (1992, 1999) and Urry (2002). In their decades old but refreshingly critical approach, these researchers brought out discrepancies between the idealised image of tourism and empirical reality, many of which can also be discovered in backpacking, too. The physically and culturally segregated 'bubbles' of conventional mass tourism have been well described by them and others, but there is no conclusive explanation of the tourist behaviour observed. The respective 'metarealities' of backpacking had also not yet been studied at the time of the above-mentioned analyses.

Package tourists do not usually encounter enough cultural or other contextual problems to develop more than a superficial understanding of the host society (Reisinger & Turner, 2003: 61–62). Backpackers, on the other hand, are less shielded than package tourists and therefore frequently become subjects of the social control characteristic of the society visited (see Hottola, 1999, 2005; and also Riley, 1988; Scheyvens, 2002; Ward *et al.*, 2001). Independent travel and package tourism are, however, located on the same continuum of tourist experience. In addition to disparities and the diversity of site- and time-specific cases, there are features based on universal tendencies in tourist behaviour. As Turner and Ash (1975: 292) pointed out, the pursuit of the exotic and diverse tends to end in uniformity, both among conventional tourists and independent travellers, for reasons revealed in the following discussion.

The seminal works of Boorstin, Turner, Ash, MacCannell and Urry have been later developed and discussed by a number of authors in tourism. The theoretical frameworks emerging in backpacker studies may provide new insights to these debates, and the discourse of tourism in general. In this limited space the focus is, however, on the original ideas of these well known authors, the experience of tourism and the production of tourist space.

Control

The social psychological discourse of control (for example Baum & Singer, 1980; Burns & Buckley, 1976; Friedman & Lackey, 1991; Goffman, 1963; 1974; Hottola, 1999, 2004a, 2005; Langer, 1983; Ward *et al.*, 2001) provides an important contribution to the theoretical understanding of tourist behaviour. In the context of tourism, control indicates the tourist's ability to seek the fulfilment of personal goals and motives, and to predict and regulate the outside interferences that make him or her vulnerable (Hottola, 2005: 2). These abilities are not only vital for our psychological well-being and biological existence in any situation, but they are also the very thing that keeps us going on as travellers. Most of the time, a perception of being in control, being able to make it, is required before an international visitor may relax and enjoy her visit. The level of actual control we have in everyday situations is not necessarily crucial (Hottola, 2004a: 451). According to Langer (1983), it is our control as perceived by us that matters. The perception of being in control may be real or illusory, but it is effective as long as it exists.

Whether in a holiday resort or on the road in South-east Asia, tourists look for pleasure and satisfaction, and engage in problem-solving behaviour in order to master their tourist life. Much of the adaptation process in a tourism destination can be described as search for control, which is achieved by cumulative learning of the Other environment; its societal, geographical and ecological features (Hottola, 2005: 2). In order to be able to adopt new information, we have to be ready to criticise our former knowledge, thereby temporally losing control as we succeed in learning and abandon outdated knowledge, and in best cases eventually gain more knowledge and control than we originally had. Other places are inhabited by Other people, often with different languages, norms and values that together construct an interesting but also difficult-to-interpret mode of interpersonal communication. Even in the best cases, our knowledge of foreign territories tends to be schematic (e.g. Raento & Hottola, 2005).

Exploring other places as a tourist forms a special case of interaction. There is no doubt that both tourists and travellers share an obligation to visit certain places and perform 'rites' such as sightseeing as a modern ritual (MacCannell, 1999: 42–43). For a backpacker, visiting the internationally known shrines of tourism, as defined by the *Lonely Planet* and others, is a significant part of his or her journey. The flesh around the bones in the itinerary is, however, formed by more mundane situations. Not only plans, but interaction with other travellers and hosts, and happenstances on the road, dictate the final outcome. In general, independent travellers expose themselves to more stress and uncertainty than an average package tourist is willing to do, and are also often rewarded by deeper and wider Other cultural encounters.

This voluntary exposure is nevertheless based on a variety of control-enhancing behavioural tactics. In India (Hottola, 2005: 7–10) backpackers travelled between safe havens and preferred to stay longer in locations with a high degree of touristic metaspatiality, instead of places where their hosts were in a dominant position, such as major cities. In addition, independent travellers teamed up with others, especially when on transit between locations, thereby forming travelling 'bubbles' of cultural dominance. In groups they could increase their level of control, decrease their individual burden of learning and regulate potentially harmful outside interference with greater efficiency than a single traveller was able to do. This pattern was discovered to be omnipresent irrespective of the phase of the visit or individual abilities in intercultural adaptation. Backpackers have established their own multipolar and, to some degree, mobile enclave on the Indian subcontinent, and other parts of the world (cf. Westerhausen, 2002: 40–41).

Staged Authenticity and the Tourist Gaze

According to Boorstin (1961), tourists prefer to disregard reality, stay in 'environmental bubbles' rather than in contact with the host society, and enjoy 'pseudo-events' instead of authenticity. Boorstin argued that there was a post-WWII shift from the earlier individual travel to mass society tourism, and the creation of 'pseudo-events' could be seen as a direct consequence of this transition. Turner and Ash (1975), and Urry (2002: 68–70), generally agreed with these viewpoints, with their analysis of a strictly circumscribed tourist world and the oversimplification of culture for tourism consumption; the McDonaldisation of the world (Ritzer, 1996). Urry also made a distinction between the profane mass tourist and noble traveller. According to Urry (2002: 87), the latter is 'on travel rather than tourism, on individual choice, on avoiding the package holiday-maker, on the need to be an educated traveller, and on a global operation that permits individual care and attention'. Furthermore, the traveller is characterised by a romantic tourist gaze; contemplation, solitude, authenticity, private and personal relation to the object of the gaze instead of the collective gaze of mass tourism.

MacCannell (1992, 1999), on the other hand, considered the traveller/tourist dualism to be elitist. He did not see any fundamental difference between tourists and travellers, and was supported by other critics such as Cohen (1972), who pointed out the variety of tourists instead of deterministic generalisations. MacCannell saw tourists as contemporary pilgrims on a quest for authenticity in other places instead of superficial and contrived experiences, somewhat paradoxically away from their everyday life but nevertheless fascinated by Other routines. He also coined the well known concept of 'staged authenticity' and described the ways in which the 'authentic Other' was presented to tourists not only in the megalomaniac theme parks of the USA but also in more commonplace tourism situations all over the world. Earlier, Goffman (1956) had defined the structural division of social establishments into front and back regions, the 'front' acting as a vehicle of standardisation. In tourism, MacCannell (1999: 101–102) established six categories of stages between the front and back, with a variable degree of staged and spontaneous authenticity, places organised to look like back regions or back regions altered to please the occasional tourist.

When 'abroad' in our home country or some international destination, our observations tend to be more detailed than in the everyday, where many objects are noticed in a less analytical manner. Urry (2002: 12–13) describes the objects of a tourist gaze as (1) unique objects to be gazed upon which everyone knows about, (2) particular signs that signify the 'typical Otherness', (3) unfamiliar aspects of what had previously been thought of as familiar, (4) ordinary aspects of social life being undertaken by people in unusual contexts and (5) particular signs that indicate that a certain Other object is indeed extraordinary, even though it did not originally appear to be so, and is marked to be distinctive. From the viewpoint of control: the target of our curiosity is unique and different to everyday experience, or at least perceived to be so, but it ideally also includes a degree of familiarity, which enables us to link the new information into our subjective construction of the world.

The tourist gaze is also about learning the new environment; in other words, building up a satisfactory level of control. The confrontation with new information to learn is enjoyable only to a certain, individually and situationally variable degree. People are inclined to be on guard in the beginning. Searching for reassuring familiarity, the tourist gaze tends to enjoy the expected and avoid the unexpected, as soon as a satisfactory degree of idealised Otherness has been discovered and consumed. Consequently, people have a preference for staged authenticity and common expectations; they distance themselves from the potentially stressful complexity of the world as it is. A sightseeing trip in a bus is a classical example of such behaviour (Weightman, 1987). Contrary to the romantic image of unrestrained globetrotting, independent travellers also share these limitations and for most of the time avoid full exposure to social and cultural disparity. In fact, these self-defensive actions signify most forms of international tourism, enabling people to enjoy and consume the Other from a position of power. Otherwise, the burden of learning and giving up old knowledge would become too much to bear and the liminoidity of travel would be compromised.

In his analysis of back and front stages MacCannell (1999) speaks about participants as performers, those who are performed to and outsiders. Interestingly, the roles were often discovered to be transposed in the South Asian backpacking scene, where the locus of control is predominantly among the hosts instead of the travellers (Hottola, 2002, 2004b). With the arrival of global media, the 'super-real' (MacCannell, 1999: 93) blondes on the screen created unrealistic expectations and Western women travellers experienced the consequences in real life, becoming a tourism attraction on the streets and beaches of India. In a situation such as this, the host gaze may easily adopt the features of tourist gaze, as defined by Urry. Seeing and being seen is interactive. The locus of control is, however, not necessarily altogether on either side, both the subject and object being able to possess power (e.g. Bordo, 1997).

The situation between local men and backpacker women also reflects the idealised side of the Janus-faced Other stereotypes; the common desire for things not available, and the hope that they exist in Other places, beyond the horizon of the everyday. Other similarly constructed expectations, such as all Westerners being rich, make travelling in South Asia a particularly difficult task for a visiting tourist. At the same time, the foreigners visiting the Indian subcontinent tend to see the locals and their environment through a centuries long accumulation of stereotypic images. The Orientalist perception of the East (e.g. Said, 1995) has been imbedded in Western culture and is therefore inevitably reproduced also by backpacker tradition, and confirmed by the accordingly staged representations along the beaten track. MacCannell (1999: 93) speaks about a weakened sense of reality, which could be discovered on both sides of the tourist–host interaction. On the other hand, stereotyping is a necessary psychological tool for control enhancement in a situation of fragmentary and uncertain information (see Adler, 1991; Gannon, 1994).

Metaspatial Retreats

The behavioural aspect of control enhancement is particularly visible in the search for in-group membership, which also serves the need to belong (Maslow, 1970). According to Urry (2002: 44), tourist congregations provide a market for services that tourists desire and create the success of tourism in these locations. The congregations are explained by the fact that the contemporary tourist gaze is increasingly signposted, identifying a relatively small number of tourist nodes, the result being that most tourists concentrate within very limited areas. This explanation is far from exhaustive, and Urry (2002: 52) complements it later: visitors demand to be enclosed in an environmental 'bubble' to provide protection from many of the features of the host society. This aspect may be most marked amongst all-inclusive tour visitors and 'the dependent children', but it is also commonplace among individual travellers such as backpackers (Hottola, 1999, 2004a, 2005).

Tourists are particularly vulnerable to stress in intercultural situations, when they voluntarily expose themselves to a plenitude of new information. A backpacker travelling in South Asia may periodically become overwhelmed by the local people and their customs, and seek temporal refuge from the company of other travellers. Similarly, an 'adventurist' wandering in a foreign city may get tired of the streets – orientation, hit-and-miss communication and the walking itself – and decide to return to the cosy and familiar setting of his resort cafeteria (cf. Verhelä, 2003). In the South Asian backpacker sample (Hottola, 2005: 5–6), five categories of metaspatial retreats were favoured by the Western travellers: (1) private spaces reserved for the travellers such as hotel rooms, (2) semi-private areas with restricted access such as guesthouse dining areas, (3) public spaces of restricted access (e.g. entrance fee) such as museums, (4) spaces of temporary Western domination such as tourist congregations and (5) wilderness areas with no or few local inhabitants such as nature reserves. By travelling between these spatial realms and the public space they were able to manage the potentially stressful process, much the same way a beach enclave tourist may travel between her room, beach and places in the surrounding community.

Nature may also be perceived as the Other. A museum as a collection of natural and cultural objects (cf. MacCannell, 1999: 78–80) provides a place to explore Other realities from a distanced position of control. Parks are places where the complexity of nature is reduced to a level within the grasp of a human being, thereby providing an illusion of understanding and mastery. It is not an accident that the service centres of national parks and nature reserves have often been arranged like parks or gardens, instead of allowing a close approach to the wilderness. In such cropped, savanna-like environments a person is able to observe his or her surroundings more efficiently (cf. Gobster, 1994). Wild beasts will not surprise him or her there, just like touts or other undesirables will not bother him or her behind the gates of a museum or other metaspatial retreats. The traveller arriving in these locations is immediately rewarded by an environment specifically constructed to enhance the desired perception of control.

The MacCannellian (1999: 101–102) sequence of stages can be seen as a succession of increasing and decreasing control, both from the viewpoints of the hosts and the visitors. On the back stage, the locus of control is among the hosts; on the front stage, the tourist has a perception of being in power. With the exception of wilderness areas, as the space available to travellers increases and segregation decreases, the level of perceived and actual control also tends to decrease. A person behind a locked door in his or her hotel room may experience a high degree of control in his or her restricted world but arrives in a slightly more vulnerable situation in the hotel restaurant, not to mention an amusement park open for any paying customer, but is nevertheless not as vulnerable as if visiting a local market. By joining fellow tourists or a guided sightseeing walk he or she can again increase his or her power and control, or he or she could find a more spacious environment with few cultural aspects, such as a national park, where culture confusion is more easily avoided than in urban areas.

On the other hand, the safety and familiarity of metaspatial retreats may soon appear boring, and the 'self-suspended' traveller (see Wilson & Richards, this volume) is once again ready to explore the interesting Other, until the level of stress reaches a saturation point. Resort entrepreneurs have often done their best to diminish the 'metaspatial boredom', by keeping their customers entertained in order to minimise the time spent on private explorations outside the enclave. Unless manipulated, decisions of action are made according to the current psychophysical state, on the borderline zones between the perceived to be controllable but somewhat uninspiring metaspaces and the unpredictable but fascinating Other spaces (Hottola, 2005: 6). Both locals and visitors can enjoy the smorgasbord of high and low culture on an equal level of control (cf. MacCannell, 1999: 169–170) in only a limited number of tourism attractions, such as Copenhagen's adult amusement park Tivoli. This is possible in situations of low cultural disparity between domestic and international visitors, and a universally familiar product range.

Temporal tourist communities may appear superficial and artificial. They are there to serve the imminent, common needs of the participants but lack substance and longevity. As MacCannell (1999: 30) says: 'Modernized peoples, released from primary family and ethnic group responsibilities, organize themselves in groups around world views provided by cultural productions. The group does not produce the world view, the world view produces the group.' The social characteristics of postmodern communities include (1) narcissism (incorporation and domestication of other people and traditions to the point that they disappear), (2) embedding of tradition; totemic exaltation of the past and (3) classlessness (no classes, no political disputes). Furthermore, 'in the postmodern culture the commonality and universality of values is simply assumed. There is no real need for discussion, identification of unmet needs, or other negotiation of the form of communal relations' (MacCannell, 1992: 93–96).

The backpacker communities studied in India and Sri Lanka by this author concur with MacCannell's analysis. In their metaspatial retreats in South Asia, the Western backpackers expressed an instant and unquestioned solidarity based on an assumption of similarity in the presence of the contrasting Other, constructing a boundary of cultural similarity across differences frequently visible in their domestic settings (cf. Goffman, 1963: 124–148; Featherstone, 1995: 92). Being in control, they were open and relaxed, much like package tourists are in their own, specialised playgrounds. As MacCannell (1992: 93–96) says, the postmodern culture is deeply satisfying to those who prefer to live beyond the reach of any corrective or other specification of their behaviour that another person might provide. In their metaspatial retreats, there is both a licence for permissive and 'non-serious' behaviour and the encouragement of a relatively unconstrained 'communitas' (Urry, 2002: 12). All in all, the international and intergender aspects of backpacker gatherings are often so gratifying that the urge to explore outside territories is minimised, especially in cases of strong cultural dissimilarity between the hosts and the visitors.

Conclusions

International tourism has many contradictory features and can only be understood as such. At first sight, the situation may appear almost absurd. Following MacCannell, subjects of corporate capitalism travel at great cost to geographically remote destinations but nevertheless stay in metaspatial 'bubbles' as close to their originating culture as possible. The point MacCannell (1999: 94) and others have made remains valid: 'sightseeings are motivated by a desire to see life as it is really lived, even to get in with the natives, and at the same time, they are deprecated for always failing to achieve these goals'. This is one of the central dilemmas in tourism: people look for something different from the everyday but have limited abilities to deal with the difference. Even though wishing to experience the 'authentic Other', the tourists soon find out that they (1) can only absorb a certain amount of new information and (2) the novelty of difference therefore tends to wear out, (3) producing a desire for familiar things. An American in Thiruvanantha-puram may try the Kerala cuisine and enjoy it, but soon develops a craving for a Coke and a Big Mac (see Hottola, 1999: 161–162).

Also in the case of independent travellers in India and Sri Lanka, the very thing they had been looking for, the authentic South Asia, became a major obstacle to the enjoyment of tourism. The authentic experience of cultural disparity had been expected to have predominantly rewarding outcomes, but had proved to be more complicated than expected, eluding the visitors because of in-born limitations. The backpackers knew when the limits of their individually variable learning capabilities were about to be over-reached and behaved accordingly, by seeking the safety of in-group status, gathering together in mass tourism resorts and backpacker safe havens, and making behavioural and spatial decisions that segregated them from the Other (Hottola, 2005). Nevertheless, the majority of them did not give up their search for intercultural encounters. Continuing the cycle of exploration: (4) the familiar starts to become a bore again, (5) reawakening the curiosity for the different, and a state of suspense which (6) is followed by another process of learning through experience (see Wilson & Richards, this volume). They were successful in their management of stress, with the help of metaspatial retreats, and could both enjoy and learn from their travels.

Much of the survival capabilities in backpacking are socially organised and produced, and therefore less based on individual choice than Urry (2002: 87) anticipated. Also, the backpacker gaze is collective, and guided by influential travel book companies (see Welk, this volume). These collective functions have an important role in supporting the 'independent' traveller, much the same way that the organisation of mass tourism serves its customers, but with alternative representations. A guesthouse on the road and a beach resort answer to the same basic needs of a traveller away from home (see also Cohen, 1989a; Welk, 2004; Westerhausen, 2002). They provide the nutrition, rest and privacy required, the perception of control, and the company to share the experience in a reassuring, rewarding way. The relative 'failure' of not being able to absorb the Other can have 'other' inspirational qualities. According to the Roman philosopher Seneca, people are always seeking something which eludes them and the road is wide open for them. The contradictory nature of the tourist experience also keeps on reproducing one of its main motives.

The prolific presence of standardised, normalised, domesticated and idealised 'authenticity' (cf. Goffman, 1956; MacCannell, 1999) in tourism, including backpacking, and the selective tourist gaze (Urry, 2002) are partly explained by the relative inability of tourists to deal with difference. From a management point of view, the tourism environment should ideally include some aspects of extraordinary, different from the everyday, among the reassuringly aspects of familiarity, and a balance between them. A Chinese person at Helsinki International Airport is relieved to see the familiar signs and designs of the Asian terminal and to hear the flight calls in Standard Mandarin on his or her arrival in a European cultural environment. Cultural hybridity provides features of familiarity and thereby control, supporting the restrained 'adventurism' and learning characteristic to international tourism. Due to the large situational and individual variation, the requirement for a balance is, however, a profoundly case-sensitive one. In mass tourism situations such sensitivity is not always feasible and a number of customers inevitably experience some dissatisfaction.

Discussing this common topic from different viewpoints, all the above-mentioned theorists provide valuable insights into the puzzle of human experience in tourism. Many tourists and travellers are originally looking for authentic experiences and would like to avoid 'staged authenticity'. In the everyday of international tourism, they tend, however, to fail in their search, at least partially. In the wide base of international globetrotting, there have been many individuals with low or average intercultural abilities since the post-war transition (Boorstin, 1961). They may demand authenticity but are in practice not able to face it fully either temporally or spatially. Instead, they turn towards Boorstian 'pseudo-events', the lowest denominator of the touristic encounter with cultural difference, and a practical solution to fulfil their contradictory needs. They also look for the reassurance of touristic environments and the company of fellow travellers in order to feel they are in control. The search for control, with its fundamental socio-psychological implications, provides one collective explanation to tourist behaviour, a conclusive connection across the often superficial disagreements between the classical authors.

Chapter 4

Sustainability Research and Backpacker Studies: Intersections and Mutual Insights

PHILIP PEARCE

Introduction

The potential for sustainability research and backpacker studies to influence one another is explored in this chapter. Each area of analysis is considered with a particular focus on the conceptual development and style of the work and its current directions. The questions about the potential for influencing future studies are asked in both directions viz. how can backpacker research contribute to sustainability discussions and how can sustainability analysis shape research into backpacking? It will be argued that there are a number of easily identified contributions in each direction, in particular more studies of the impacts of backpacker behaviour and more studies of the corporate sustainability status of backpacker businesses. The possibilities for mutual influence extend beyond these direct liaisons. In particular the kinds of insights about non-compliance behaviour undertaken in backpacker health offer insights into non-compliance in the sustainability domain. Importantly this kind of work marries two territories of backpacker studies – sociological and utilitarian or market-oriented routes. Additionally the potential to create global archives of studies for meta-analysis and data mining can also be identified as a consequence of considering the intersection of backpacker studies and sustainability research. Overall the mutual insights that a joint consideration of these two areas generates builds the promise of enlivening and even transforming future backpacker studies.

This chapter thus addresses a large and ambitious agenda. It seeks to identify the potential for sustainability research and backpacker studies to influence one another. Two large-scale questions direct this agenda – how do and can backpacker studies contribute to sustainability discussions? And, conversely, how can issues in sustainability analysis shape new research into backpacking? There are two preliminary discussions that are necessary to prepare for these questions. It is necessary to clarify and contextualise backpacker studies including contemporary directions in this area. A second preliminary discussion requires the style and the diversity of effort in sustainability studies to be established.

Backpacker Studies: A Phenomenon Defined and Deconstructed

In my 1990 social definition of what it means to be a backpacker (Pearce, 1990), a number of key social and behavioural characteristics of budget-based youth travel were identified in an attempt to capture the essence of the emerging backpacker phenomenon. In this socially based definition five criteria are used: the first as a necessary condition and the remaining four as strong indicators of the backpacker phenomenon. The five criteria are

(1) a preference for budget accommodation;
(2) an emphasis on meeting other travellers;
(3) an independently organised and flexible travel schedule;
(4) longer rather than very brief holidays; and
(5) an emphasis on informal and participatory holiday activities (Pearce, 1990).

This social definition and labelling was a point of departure from previous budget traveller analyses. It introduced the new term to the academic literature and in a modest way directed government and policy attention to an emerging specialist market. It was also argued that the newly labelled phenomenon of backpacking had echoes of and roots in the hippie/drifter phenomenon, employment-oriented youth travel, physical health and outdoor adventure seeking behaviours, and travel for personal educational growth and development. This social definition approach to understanding backpackers was subsequently blurred by pragmatic government data collection exercises which used an accommodation-oriented definition. As Slaughter (2004) has argued, the differences in the data and the results they produce are minor rather than substantial in studies using the different approaches.

From a more contemporary perspective there is now a broad consensus among academic researchers that there exist multiple market segments or subgroups of backpackers. This differentiation may reside in the backpackers' nationality, their gender, their independent or group travel style or, yet again, their working, holiday-only or student role (Richards & Wilson, 2004a). Additionally, a variety of motivational and attitudinal segmentations have been emphasised (Richards & Wilson, 2004b; West, 2005). This recognition of diversity in the backpacker market does not negate the value of the original definition but it does draw attention to the purpose and direction of contemporary backpacker studies. Hence, Cohen (2004: 57) argued forcefully that:

> Future research should desist from referring to backpacking as if it were a homogenous phenomenon and should pay much more attention to its diverse manifestations... There is also a need for a reorientation of research on backpackers from the currently prevalent concern with their itineraries, travelling style and interactions to a more emic and reflexive approach concerned with the manner in which they themselves construct, represent and narrate their experiences.

As we plot the present course and the future directions of backpacking research it can certainly be agreed that there has been a restricted geographical and nationality range in much of the published literature. Studies of travellers from the UK, Europe, Israel, Australia and New Zealand travelling to South Asia, South-east Asia and Australasia are indeed dominant. While there are numerous North American backpackers in the relevant destinations, the term backpacker itself remains largely unrecognised in the USA, where it is reserved for specialist hiking and wilderness recreation (Manning, 1999). The backpacker phenomenon in its subtly diverse forms is also present in Southern Africa and throughout South and Central America, as well as in Europe itself. Studies from scholars in these areas and about backpacking in these locations are under-represented in the existing canons of inquiry (cf. Visser, 2004).

There is, however, a little more to the exhortation by Cohen to diversify backpacker studies than simply expanding the nationalities and geographic regions of analysis. In particular he argues for a redirection of effort and emphasises emic and reflexive approaches to the backpackers' social construction and narration of experience. This view is also consistent with emerging trends in the theoretical treatment of backpacker research (Ateljevic & Doorne, 2004). More generally this attention to emic and reflexive studies raises a fundamental issue in tourism research overall and one that is clearly manifested in backpacker studies: it is the issue of the two roads or territories of tourism study (cf. Franklin, 2003; Pearce, 2005; Tribe, 1997).

One road in backpacker studies has emphasised and concentrates on the economic contribution of backpacking, an analysis of markets, product design and operational issues in managing this travel style. It is a part of the territory of tourism fully aligned to Gunn's (1994: 3) definition as follows: 'Tourism research, while no substitute for superior management practices, provides objective, systematic, logical and empirical foundations for such management.'

A second road in backpacker studies leading to the second territory of tourism research lies in emphasising the meaning backpackers attribute to their activities and encounters. This kind of work, and it is the kind of study advocated by Cohen, concentrates on identity and personal growth, on social relationships and their consequences for the visited community and environment. It offers a small link to the territory of sustainability, which will be explored presently.

Each style of backpacker research has its own language. In industry- and government-oriented analyses researchers write about market characteristics, product development, market differentiation, information influences, travel, routes, activity participation and expenditure patterns (Buchanan & Rossetto, 1997; Richards & Wilson, 2004a). For the more sociologically oriented territory, researchers deal with conceptual analyses featuring rites of passage, identity markers, pilgrimage liminality, roles and deviance (Ateljevic & Doorne, 2004; Richards & Wilson, 2004b; West, 2005).

At this point, I will simply note that this demarcation of the two territories is not absolute but a substantial tension and difference in style does exist. In a later section the argument will be developed that an emphasis on long-term sustainability offers the prospect of aligning the joint contributions of these territories of backpacker (and more broadly tourism) studies.

Many of these summary points about backpacker definitions and the deconstruction of the topic are undoubtedly relatively familiar to backpacker researchers and readers. While there is clearly much current activity in the backpacker study area, as manifested by a number of books, conferences and the forthcoming special issue of *Tourism Recreation Research*, the possibility of injecting new dimensions into backpacker research offers further possibilities for developing the area.

Sustainability Studies: Power, Philosophy and Frameworks

The emergence of sustainability as a key political topic and an area of study and research arose at almost the same time as the early backpacker studies. The defining approaches and the foundation agenda were set in the late 1980s but, as was the case with the backpacker studies, there were substantial roots in earlier formulations. As a major point of departure from backpacker studies, which are in essence studies of a specialist market segment in one sector of the economy, albeit an important one, sustainability studies are generalist and cross-sector and reach beyond markets to enterprises and corporations.

An appreciation of the evolution of public and scientific concern about sustainability can be readily gauged from Table 4.1 where the macro-political stage informing sustainability is presented. In Table 4.2 a sample of some better known authors contributing to sustainability concerns is documented.

The influences on sustainability research are indeed diverse but there is much congruence in the definitions of the topic. The major definitions of sustainability mostly exist as a part of definitions of sustainable development. Two key statements summarise much of the emphasis. The document 'World Commission on Environment and Development. Our Common Future', commonly referred to as the Brundtland report, advises: 'Sustainable development is development that meets the needs of the present without compromising the ability of future generations to meet their own needs' (WCEO, 1987: 8).

In a similar style the World Business Council on Sustainable Development (2004: 1) observes: 'Sustainable development involves the simultaneous pursuit of economic prosperity, environmental quality and social equity. Companies aiming for sustainability need to perform not against a single, financial bottom line but against the triple bottom line'. The triple bottom line formulation derives from the work of Elkington (1997) and his imaginatively entitled book *Cannibals with Forks*; a metaphor for civilising the excesses and impacts of big business.

Several points implicit in these definitions are worthy of further emphasis. First, there are fundamental notions of multifaceted outcomes in the sustainability definitions and literature. Second, sustainability can be conceived as a moving target, a desired goal for the striving of human effort rather than a well defined tangible state. Sustainability is therefore linked to a position of learned optimism in that small efforts matter and make progress towards a goal (Seligman, 1998). Third, the focus in the

Table 4.1 Key institutional events guiding the sustainability agenda

1. The reports to the Club of Rome (early 1960s) that stressed a limit to growth approach and quite pessimistic predictions about energy and fossil fuel shortages.
2. The Worldwatch Institute begins publication of annual State of the World reports and Vital Signs report. – In 1981 Brown (the Worldwatch Institute Director and principal author) provided the first definition of sustainability.
3. Reports on international development (such as the 'Brandt' report (Independent Commission on International Development Issues, 1980)) highlighted the growing differentiation between north (affluent) and south (less developed) countries.
4. The International Union for Conservation of Nature (IUCN) in 1980 established sustainable development as a policy consideration.
5. The World Commission on Environment and Development (WCEO, 1987), known as the Brundtland report, focussed on sustainable economic growth. – Brundtland's definition of sustainability is the base for many modified definitions.
6. Business Council on Sustainable Development, 1993, continued the themes of integrating economic and ecological well-being.
7. The Earth Summit in Rio de Janeiro in 1992 with its non-binding resolutions – the Rio Declaration and Agenda 21 provided guidelines for regions and businesses.
8. A follow-up Earth Summit + 5 in New York in 1997.
9. The Kyoto Protocol – a United Nations framework convention on climate change in Japan, 1997.
10. The South African Millennium declaration in Johannesburg 2000 outlining millennium development goals – included sustainability as one of the goals (poverty reduction, education, gender equality, child mortality, maternal health, AIDS/HIV control and business– government partnerships were other goals).

sustainability literature arising from these definitions and roots is on the performance of the organisation, enterprise or corporation. This is in marked contrast to the backpacker literature, where the consumer and the individual, or at least groups of individuals, occupy most research attention. Consumers or customers are not ignored in the sustainability

Table 4.2 Some early key authors identifying sustainability-linked topics

• Rachel Carson (1962) – popularised the need to caretake ecological systems
• Barry Commoner (1966) – advocate for grass roots environmental movements
• Paulo Friere (1966) – demands for social equity, justice, fairness and educational opportunity
• Garret Hardon (1968) – identified the commons dilemma – resources overused with no responsibility
• Ernest Schuhmacher (1973) – popularised small is beautiful – rejected unrestricted growth
• Fritjof Capra (1982) – global crisis of world's resources identified
• Joseph Sax (1980) – argued for the intrinsic value of little altered landscapes
• Ralph Nader (1980) – advocated consumer rights and social responsibility of corporations
• Edward Wilson (1980) – proposed sociobiology – the interdependence of human life and its biological roots
• Stephen Jay Gould (1990) – advocated biological science and humanities as joint paths to understanding human existence
• John Elkington (1997) – developed the triple bottom line approach to sustainability

literature and there is a body of work on 'green' consumers, but the emphasis is modest compared to the corporation or business enterprise focus (Dunphy & Benveniste, 2000; Font, 2001).

The achievements of research and analysis in the sustainability literature can be classified under the themes of establishing frameworks, providing reporting standards, developing indicators, constructing codes of practice and identifying pathways and processes to foster sustainability. Additionally there are some subtle contributions and achievements in understanding the communication of ideas that arise from a consideration of this field. Each of these research outcomes will be summarised succinctly. It is notable that the evidence or style of work that has developed these outcomes is largely a combination of case studies, archival work and inductive reasoning. Much of the contemporary state of sustainability writing could be characterised as descriptive and offering frameworks rather than being theoretically or empirically driven.

The first of the sustainability achievements lies in providing category schemes to define the sustainability behaviours of organisations. The work of Dunphy and Benveniste (2000) is a good example of the approach. Six phases of corporate sustainability are recognised and are summarised in Table 4.3

As well as providing a category scheme to characterise the practices of an organisation at any one point in time, these kinds of schemes can also track the evolution of organisations over time. For example, the International Porter Protection Group and Tourism Concern – a network of people with a social justice agenda in the UK – combined to make the rights of mountain porters a hot topic for Western-based trekking companies. This kind of pressure has arguably moved many of the trekking companies from early positions of rejection and non-responsiveness to compliance/risk reduction and in some instances strategic sustainability and ideological commitment.

A fundamental topic in the sustainability literature is the utilisation and development of a variety of reporting systems; that is systems where organisations communicate achievements to their stakeholders not just in financial terms but in sociocultural and environmental dimensions. Such systems include what McIntosh *et al.* (2003) have labelled the Global Eight: The United Nations' Global Compact, International Labour Organisation conventions, the OECD guidelines for multinational enterprises, the International Standards Organization (ISO) 1400 Series, the Global Reporting Initiatives, the Global Sullivan principles, Social Accountability 8000 and Accountability 1000. All these reporting systems have principles and then specific standards. The former are over-reaching values and the latter are sets of benchmarks to be attained. Several types of benchmarks are possible and embrace processes (such as the development of quality assurance management systems), performance standards (what a company should do, such as pay a living wage), foundation standards (such as identifying and establishing best practices) and certification standards (meet the standards established by the sector's leading body).

The development of indicators of performance has been an important part of the work underpinning the Global Fight and, further, the articulation of sustainability indicators has spread to encompass the activities of smaller businesses as well as global corporations. In the tourism field, for example, the World Tourism Organization (2004) has produced a plethora of potential, if at times imprecise, indicators for assessing the sustainable development of a tourism destination. This kind

Table 4.3 Six phases of corporate sustainability (after Dunphy & Benveniste, 2000)

Phase 1. Rejection
• Environment is regarded as a free good to be exploited
• Hostility to environmental activities
• Production and extraction processes destroy future capacity or damage the ecosystem
• Polluting by-products are discharged
• Employees and subcontractors are regarded as a resource to be used
• 'Lip service' to health and safety issues
• Compliance required of workforce backed up by threats/force
• Little training; few career prospects for employees
• Minimal community concerns
Phase 2. Non-responsiveness
• Ecological environment not considered as a relevant input
• Financial and technological factors dominate business strategy
• Efficiency rules
• Environmental resources wasted and costs not considered
• Training in technical area only
• Wider social responsibility and community concern is ignored
Phase 3. Compliance/risk reduction
• Senior management see the need to comply with environmental laws
• Attempt to limit liability of enterprise
• Obvious environmental abuses eliminated
• Employer seen as a decent employer
• Efforts at safety workplace standards appear
• Organisation practises benevolent paternalism
• Awareness that negative community publicity may be harmful so some community concerns addressed

Table 4.3 (*Continued*)

Phase 4. Efficiency

- Poor environmental practice seen as an avoidable cost

- Review of environmental inputs and waste to minimise expenditure in these areas

- Environmental issues that do not generate avoidable costs tend to be ignored (e.g. aesthetics)

- ISO 14001 procedure may be in place (International Standards Organisation approach for reporting core environmental management practices)

- Coherent HR systems practised

- Team work of staff acknowledged and training begins

- Funding of community projects with a positive return for the company

Phase 5. Strategic sustainability

- Proactive environmental strategies seen as a strategic advantage

- Product redesign to reuse/recycle materials

- Environmental outputs are engineered to be useful

- Competitive leadership sought through spearheading environmentally friendly products and processes

- Workforce diversity sought and used

- Intellectual and social capital seen as a strategic advantage

- Flexible workplace to maximise talent use

- Community-enterprise partnerships to address adverse impacts

Phase 6. Ideological commitment

- Organisation becomes an active promoter of sustainability

- Environmental best practice is espoused

- Organisation thinks about sustainability throughout its entire operation and product range

- Organisation uses its influence with government to promote positive sustainability

Table 4.3 (*Continued*)
• Organisation accepts responsibility for upgrading human knowledge and skill
• Strong promoter of workplace diversity and work/life balance
• Has a corporate ethical position and action plan to pursue human welfare and equitable and socially just practices

of work lies within the ambit of the broader sustainability literature on reporting systems and indicators.

A slightly more sector-focussed approach to sustainability can also be identified in the development of codes of conduct and practice. Typically codes of conduct are self-regulatory rules and advice initiated and sanctioned by a group of businesses or a sector. Codes encourage participating members to both take a leadership role in managing sustainability issues and to build a collective identity of responsibility. The self-regulation works through peer pressure and status determinants, the threat of government regulation and perceptions of business advantages and reduced costs compared to forced compliance or litigation. A criticism of codes of conduct lies in the persistence of some manipulative and promotional claims that are not substantiated by audited assessments of performance. Additionally, self-reports of code implementation may mask practices that are invisible to external stakeholders (Carraro & Leveque, 1999; Lennox & Nash, 2003; Paton, 2000).

A further dimension in the sustainability domain lies in identifying pathways and processes, that is key management mechanisms and ordered steps to promote more viable businesses with more positive environmental and sociocultural outcomes. Examples of such systems include the multiple indicator based system for the chemical industry entitled 'Responsible Care' and the action-oriented but scientifically based systems approach called 'The Natural Step' used particularly in Scandinavian hotels (McIntosh *et al.*, 2003).

On a slightly different level of analysis, sustainability research also directs attention to the sociopolitical dimensions of communication concerning scientific research. Lomberg (2001) notes that in communicating research findings about this whole topic area there is a powerful and all-pervasive litany about the environment and human society. According to Lomberg the litany is that everyone knows the planet is in bad shape and we live in an ever deteriorating environment. Lomberg argues that while many resources and social systems are troubled, much of the pervasive view is not backed up by evidence. He suggests six points of emphasis that amount to a reminder to all researchers in all areas of activity, including backpacker studies, to process information mindfully rather than mindlessly. Lomberg notes the following important distinctions in his myth-busting approach.

(1) Let us really look at what the overall statistics say and not focus on one or two cases.

(2) Let us look at the original examples of the 'evidence' and see how accurate they are, or how limited and circumscribed they were before being endlessly requoted and cited.

(3) Saying that the ecosystems' and man's lot are improved is *not* the same as saying it is good enough – but being able to establish that things are improving (e.g. fewer people starving) is different and more optimistic and more constructive in terms of work to be done than saying it is all getting worse.

(4) We need to look at the scientific evidence, not the media reports, as the media is predisposed to report 'news' and negativity.

   – It is the communication of our environmental knowledge which is one core of the problem.
   – It is not being suggested that the primary research in the environmental field is incompetent or unprofessional.
   – The communication of environmental knowledge taps deeply into 'doomsday', overly dramatic accounts of the state of the world.
   – Environmental organisations, Worldwatch Institute, Greenpeace and the World Wide Fund for Nature, individual commentators and the media do exaggerate and distort the evidence.

(5) The litany, now that it is established, has its own 'life'. It is a social representation, an organised system of shared everyday knowledge, so we 'know' that the environment is not in good shape, making it all the more possible for people to make erroneous claims without evidence. For this reason (our existing social representation) we also tend to be extremely sceptical towards anyone who says the environment is not in such a bad state.

(6) The efficiency of interventions – what we do – to make enterprises more sustainable should be based on a rational critical approach to the factual data, not on presumed, topical, myth-based news items.

In summary, the sustainability literature has a markedly different character to that of backpacker studies. In particular it is built on many disciplinary contributions; it identifies in particular the roles of corporations and businesses but less so consumers; it is replete with organising schemes, systems and frameworks; and it is linked to major sociopolitical and communication processes. It is now the task of this chapter to explore how the two areas of inquiry intersect and could benefit each other.

Backpacking Research: A Contribution to Sustainability Discussions

One way to conceive of the contribution of backpacker studies to sustainability discussions is to view backpackers as an indicator group, reflecting global consumer attitudes to sustainability. In the numerous biophysical analyses pertaining to ecological systems, environmental scientists search for indicator species, effectively those organisms which are a touchstone or pulse for revealing the state of environmental well-being. In the social domain backpackers are a globally interconnected group spanning a well defined age range and can be seen as reflecting international public awareness and the practice of sustainability concerns as they manifestly play out a battle between personal pleasure and more civic responsibilities. As Hampton (1998) and Scheyvens (2002) have argued, backpackers can facilitate local development or generate problems for local communities. In their attitudes and behaviours in such domains as willingness to spend money, use of resources, sensitivity to local customs, sexual behaviour and respect for local regulations, backpackers manifest the values of a global young adult culture. The view that monitoring backpacker attitudes and behaviour in different locations and across time as an indicator of the penetration of a global sustainability ethic represents a large-scale opportunity for backpacker studies to relate to sustainability research.

In addition to backpackers being seen as an indicator group, the study of backpackers highlights the importance of the close analysis of meaning in determining actual on-site behaviour. The emphasis of many researchers in the backpackers studies area places a premium on the meaning of self-esteem and ego protection functions arising from social and environmental encounters amongst backpackers and their hosts and settings. This close analysis as an important area of study in business research in general has been boosted by the writing of Pine and Gilmour (1999), whose work on *The Experience Economy* has effectively stressed the value of the sociological and psychological appraisals for contemporary business and problem-solving concerns. The sustainability literature is limited in its analysis of experience, either of decision makers or consumers. Further, one of the enduring problems in fostering sustainability lies in understanding non-compliance, that is, why people and organisations do not behave sustainably. There are parallel problems in the backpacker literature, notably non-compliance in terms of responsible sexual behaviour and practices. The latter topic has generated a considerable literature driven by the significant medical and public health consequences of sexually transmittable diseases (Clift & Carter, 2000; Clift & Grabowski, 1997; Clift & Page, 1996).

An important achievement of this focus of attention on analysing experience in the backpacker and sexual behaviour arena lies in understanding, through qualitative techniques, the reasons for much non-compliance, especially the lack of condom use, in tourists' sexual encounters. As Black (2000) and Clift and Carter (2000) report, reasons for non-compliant behaviour in this domain are now being clearly articulated, with important implications for changing public communication health campaigns. The predisposing reasons for the non-use of condoms appear to lie in inexperience, disrupting immediate behavioural and emotional sequences, the difficulty of negotiating the use of the product, and reputation and identity concerns (cf. Abdullah *et al.*, 2004; Bellis *et al.*, 2005; Egan, 2001). There is a ready translation of this kind of work, if not in the actual content or findings, to non-compliance in sustainability analyses, raising the prospect of enhancing our close understanding of how to better achieve community and environmental conservation goals. Detailed qualitative appraisals of why people do not comply with desirable sustainable behaviours would appear to be a profitable borrowing from one research domain to the other.

Sustainability Research: Shaping New Research in Backpacking

There is also some reciprocity in the roles sustainability research can play in backpacker studies. It was established in the review of sustainability that there has been a strong focus on organisations in the existing literature. In particular there are clear sustainability reporting systems classifications of organisational performance. There is a ready transfer of this kind of emphasis for backpacker researchers who can develop the somewhat neglected task of assessing how backpacker-linked businesses fit sustainability guidelines. The range and number of backpacker activities and the organisations that provide these settings and experience is extensive and offers considerable scope for regional studies, benchmarking of performance across subsectors and international comparisons (Becken *et al.*, 2001; Thyne *et al.*, 2006; Visser, 2004). This emphasis reaches beyond backpacker accommodation establishments, which has been one starting point of concern (Firth & Hing, 1999).

A larger implication of the sustainability research for backpacker studies derives from the availability of data informing global reporting and assessment systems (cf. Lomberg, 2001). A particular feature of the sustainability literature, which is being developed, lies in the construction of standards and assessment systems for benchmarking and comparing data. This emphasis was described in the previous review under the discussion of the Group of Eight reporting systems. An implication of this emphasis for backpacking studies lies in the topic of data warehousing and data mining. More specifically, the potential can be seen to create a substantial global archive of data and information about backpackers. This kind of facility would assist scholars and analysts to more readily compare studies, to conduct secondary analyses and to do meta-analytic work. It remains a feature of backpacker studies, compared to sustainability research and even some broader tourism market topics, that the existing resources for researchers are limited to their own primary data sets or qualitative immersion experiences buttressed by occasional forays into national data banks. The concept of a backpacker data warehouse is worthy of more extensive consideration.

A third influence that sustainability studies can bring to backpacker research lies in contemplating the rhetoric of public communication about research. It has already been suggested, following the work of Lomberg (2001), that areas of study can develop a litany of the correct or standard way of summarising findings. Typically these kinds of myth-building assertions take place when researchers justify their interest to others, such as in the context of seeking grants and emphasising the economic importance of their work. This communication dimension, the rhetoric of topic justification, permeates the introductions and summaries of many research papers. It is possible to suggest a line of research concerning this justificatory rhetoric in backpacker studies, as demystification of what is said and supposedly agreed on in backpacker research. This challenge could be enacted upon in a number of ways, one of which might be to sample the levels of researcher agreement with up to 10 statements summarising the achievements and findings of all previous work. As with the sustainability literature, the body of knowledge that we think we share and know is always worthy of mindful re-examination.

Conclusions

The generative power of juxtaposing areas of study and seeking to benefit from their mutual intersection has been the guiding style of this analysis. It can be concluded that aligning backpacker studies and sustainability research has consequences and implications for both areas of activity. More specifically, backpacker research can contribute some special insights for the sustainability domain by viewing backpackers as an indicator group for assessing the sustainability agenda. Additionally, the close analysis of experience and non-compliance existing in the backpacker literature could also be used as a style of research for non-compliance in sustainability analyses. Backpacker research itself might be refreshed by a greater focus on the organisational and business level of analysis. Additionally the prospect of constructing a data warehouse for backpacker studies can be identified by analogy with similar macro-level archival reporting efforts at work in the sustainability field. It is also possible to view an analysis of the public rhetoric and the justificatory communication about backpacker research as a topic of study as in the sustainability field this kind of questioning of the accepted litany has been a stimulating force.

The interplay of these concerns also addresses a further issue – the two territories of tourism and backpacker research. It can be suggested here that the continued existence of both of these styles of work is demanded by the new directions outlined above – both the detailed qualitative emic understanding of the phenomenon and the utilitarian etic assessment of its distribution and consequences are important for the expanded future of backpacker studies considered in this chapter.

Chapter 5

Are Backpackers Ethical Tourists?

CLARE SPEED[1]

Introduction

The aim of this chapter is to discover the extent to which backpacker tourist behaviour exemplifies that of an ethical tourist. Backpacker tourism has sometimes been characterised as 'good' tourism, in comparison with mass-market packaged tourism, often characterised as 'bad'. However, backpackers are not universally lauded as good tourists, with some destinations attempting to distance themselves from travellers they consider to be low-budget drifters.

In order to explore this concept of the 'good' tourist, some kind of understanding of the concept of good should be explored. Many destinations consider good tourists (or those they wish to attract) to be those who spend more and cause the least harmful impact. However, tourism impact studies suggest that the underlying behaviour, motivations and spending patterns of tourists will significantly influence the positive effects of tourism on a destination. Consideration must be given to the behaviour and motivations of individual tourists, rather than to the tourism industry as a whole, particularly as it has been acknowledged that backpackers should not be considered as a homogeneous group (Richards & Wilson, 2004a).

An investigation of ethical tourism is considered an appropriate means of distinguishing 'good' or 'bad' tourists as 'ethics characterise behaviour, in the context of a relationship as right or wrong, and this involves social responsibility in decision-making' (Wheeller, 1994a). Therefore this paper proposes to consider the meaning of ethical tourism and investigate the extent to which backpackers consider themselves to be ethical tourists in the choices they make whilst travelling.

The Origins of Ethical Tourism

'Ethics is concerned with human behaviour and is a phenomenon of choice' (Wheeller, 1994a). 'The contemplation of ethical behaviour has taken place during all of human civilisation' (Krohn & Ahmed, 1991), and 'academics have long been involved in philosophical debate over the ethical nature of human kind' (Fennell, 1999). The huge literature base focusing on the subject reflects this. Early writings took a purely theoretical approach, but the first conference on business ethics in 1974 (Bowie, 1986) instigated an applied approach. Although theoretical writings helped to shape such application, applied ethic studies now shape theory (Fennell, 1999) and as such, form the basis of this study.

Until the early 1990s, only limited attention was given to the application of ethics to tourism, despite a rapid increase in the quantity of both tourism and applied ethic studies (Fennell, 1999; Lea, 1993). The study of applied ethics focused on industries other than tourism, whilst the study of tourism focused on various social, ecological and economic impacts, successfully ignoring evident ethical issues (Fennell, 1999). Consequently, there was a very weak foundation of research into tourism ethic studies (D'Amore, 1993; Fennell, 1999; Lea, 1993; Payne & Dimanche, 1996).

The majority of ethical tourism studies focused on the hospitality management sector (Hall, 1992; Hegarty, 1992; Whitney, 1989, 1990); principally owing to hospitality's relationship with service and business (Wheeller, 1994b). Industry studies, meanwhile, focused on codes of conduct (for example: the Tourism Industry Association of Canada, 1991, cited in D'Amore, 1992; The Ecotourism Society, 1993, cited in Fennell, 1999; High Places, 1994, cited in Wheeller, 1994b); Malloy & Fennell, 1998), the inauguration of which, coupled with pressure group action and subsequent media and consumer attention (Weeden, 2001), can be linked to the origins of ethical tourism (Lea, 1993).

The introduction of sustainable tourism development studies in the late 1980s also led to a growing recognition of the importance of ethical practices (Fennell, 1999). This recognition, which Hughes (1995) states was responsible for the drive towards sustainable development in the first place, has only recently been acknowledged in the tourism literature, where ethics have subsequently received increased attention (D'Sa, 1999; Fennell, 1999; Fleckenstein & Huebsch, 1999; Holden, 2003; Mintel, 2001; Ryan, 2002; World Tourism Organization, 1999). This increasing body of literature questions the ethical nature of tourism's growth, and analyses the ethicality of 'alternative' types of tourism (Cleverdon, 2001; Cleverdon & Kalisch, 2000; Curtin & Busby, 1999; Karwacki & Boyd, 1995; Mowforth & Munt, 1998).

Ethical Tourism and Ethical Tourists

According to Mintel (2001), there are various forms of tourism that come under the ethical umbrella: sustainable, community, green, responsible and eco are just a few represented in the literature. The tourists consuming such products, however, are rarely the objects of consideration (Crick, 1989; Swarbrooke, 1999). Swarbrooke (1999) states that 'often the only mention of the tourist... is as the cause of the "problem" in terms of the environmental, economic and social impacts of their activities.'

The ethical tourism literature reinforces this, by revealing four research agendas, none of which focus on the tourist specifically. The largest interprets business ethics (Dunfee & Black, 1996; Fennell & Malloy, 1999; Fleckenstein & Huebsch, 1999; Raiborn & Payne, 1990; Walle, 1995), including substantial writings on tourism marketing ethics (Krohn & Ahmed, 1991; Weeden, 2001; Wheeller, 1994a; Wight, 1993a, 1994). Emanating from this study's focus on *tourist* behaviour rather than that of *business*, such literature is left largely redundant. Papers from the remaining three research agendas: environmental ethics (D'Amore, 1993; Fennell & Malloy, 1999; Holden, 2003; Karwacki & Boyd, 1995), social concern ethics (Botterill, 1991; Hughes, 1995; Ryan, 2002; Tearfund, 2001) and development ethics (Cleverdon, 2001; Cleverdon & Kalisch, 2000; Curtin & Busby, 1999; D'Sa, 1999; Lea, 1993), therefore form the literary foundation of this study. It is proposed that these three research agendas represent the issues affecting the ethicality of tourist behaviour.

'Ethical behaviour is not easily understood in theory or application, with each person holding their own perception of what is "good" or "bad"' (Beck, 1992: ix). Defining the ethics of tourism is also 'fraught with difficulties in such a complex and fragmented industry that covers a wide diversity of cultural and business practices' (Weeden, 2001). This review, therefore, presents a multifaceted approach to the subject, drawing from the literature to develop a definition of an ethical tourist.

Environmental Ethics

Tourism literature deliberating environmental impacts created the foundation for the popular environmental ethical discussions of today (Fennell & Malloy, 1999). 'The changes in nature induced by human action have led to a questioning and re-evaluating of ethical positions towards it' (Holden, 2003). Given tourism's dependence upon the natural environment, an understanding of tourists' ethics towards nature is essential. Holden (2003: 106) concluded that, 'the rationale of the

environment ethic remains anthropocentric, compared with the economic and social well-being of communities, rather than recognising the
rights of nature.' The question of whether this was the correct environmental ethic for tourism however, was left unanswered.

A number of papers dealing with environmental ethics specifically
focus on the ethics of ecotourism (Fennell, 1999; Fennell & Malloy, 1999;
Karwacki & Boyd, 1995; Wight, 1993a,b, 1994). Ecotourism offers one
approach to ethical tourism (Wight, 1993a,b), whereby ecotourists exhibit,
'moral and ethical responsibilities and behaviours towards the natural
and cultural environment' (Wight, 1993a: 3). Ethical successes of ecotourism are presented (Fennell & Malloy, 1999; Karwacki & Boyd, 1995; Wight,
1993b), as are other forms of apparently environmentally ethical tourism
including 'nature tourism' (Olindo, 1991) and 'green tourism' (Yenckel,
1995), but the long-term merits are left untested. There is, therefore, a
growing body of researchers who take issue with such alternative forms
of tourism (Butler, 1990; Cohen, 1989a; Wheeller, 1991, 1992, 1993).

Codes of conduct, including suggested environmentally ethical tourist
behaviour, also remain empirically unproven. High Places (1994, cited in
Wheeller, 1994a) request tourists to limit deforestation by discouraging
fires, using kerosene and encouraging locals to do likewise. Paradoxically, the brochure also advises tourists to respect local customs, of which
fires are surely a part. Yenckel (1995), meanwhile, advises tourists to stay
in environmentally sensitive lodgings, yet disregards the widely debated
nature of what such a statement implies. Despite such contradictions, the
literature generally supports the need for tourists to tread softly on the
environment of their hosts, by conserving scarce resources, and only
supporting those companies implementing environmentally friendly
practices (High Places, 1994, cited in Wheeller, 1994a; Lea, 1993;
Mowforth & Munt, 1998; Schwepker & Cornwall, 1991; Tourism Industry
Association of Canada, 1991, cited in D'Amore, 1992; Yenckel, 1995).

Swarbrooke (1999: 27) subsequently rejects this by stating the 'green-
est' i.e. the most environmentally ethical tourist, is one who do 'not take
holidays away from home at all so as not to harm the environment in any
way, as a tourist'. However the ethicality of this statement can be debated
too, by depriving people of the opportunities that tourism can present,
especially in the developing world (Butler, 1990; Lea, 1993).

Social Concern Ethics

Ethical tourism links the environmental concerns of ecotourism with
the social consciousness of aid organisations (Lea, 1993). Environmental

progress has been acknowledged (Schwepker & Cornwall, 1991; Tear-fund, 2001), but a dearth of social commitment to host communities is criticised (Tearfund, 2001). Despite explicit evidence that tourism is leading to the destruction of social structure and cultural values (Butler, 1990; Lea, 1993; Mathieson & Wall, 1982; Smith, 1989), the literature has left the ethicality of the issue largely untouched. Indeed, a higher premium seems to have been placed on nature issues at home than on human welfare elsewhere (D'Sa, 1999; Lea, 1993).

Ethics characterise behaviour, 'in the context of a relationship as right or wrong, and this involves social responsibility in decision-making' (Wheeller, 1994a). Tourism is dependent upon interactions between its stakeholders, specifically between host and guest, and as such, social responsibility is pivotal to ethical tourism (Hultsman, 1995; Wheeller, 1994a). Though concern about the lack of such social responsibility and the ethicality of tourism's interactions has been reported (Botterill, 1991; D'Sa, 1999; Hughes, 1995), problems have been left unanswered. An ethical concern towards the local population has been conveyed simply as being educated about the local culture, speaking the local language and respecting local traditions (Mintel, 2001; Tearfund, 2001), therefore, exhibiting 'intelligent tourism' characteristics, by desiring to learn something from one's holiday (Swarbrooke & Horner, 1999).

Ethical tourists are also described as being concerned about social issues such as human resource policies, therefore avoiding destinations where human rights have been violated (Mowforth & Munt, 1998; Swarbrooke & Horner, 1999). An example provided by the literature is Burma, where 'whole communities have been forcibly relocated... and forced to work without pay' in the name of tourism (Mowforth & Munt, 1998). Further practices such as dressing appropriately and only photographing with permission are other common guidelines for ethical tourists (D'Amore, 1992; Ecumenical Coalition on Third World Tourism, 1988, cited in Harron & Weiler, 1992; Tearfund, 2001).

The lack of a more comprehensive literary analysis in the ethicality of tourism's social and cultural interactions may be explained by the fact that, 'ethics is indigenous to a society' (Raiborn & Payne, 1990), and a 'critical problem in developing standards of ethics is that ethical standards are, for the most part, culture specific and may vary from one country to another' (Payne & Dimanche, 1996). Comprehensive analysis of the ethics of social and cultural interactions has therefore been fairly limited in scope and often lacks host community research. As Crick (1989) observed, 'we need to know the local perceptions and under-standings of tourism'. Instead, there is concern that those writing about what is 'good' in tourism reflect personal travel preferences, as if in self-justification (Swarbrooke, 1999), rather than as a realistic assessment of what is 'good' for the people on which tourism impacts (Butler, 1990; Swarbrooke, 1999).

Development Ethics

'Development ethics is a well-established field within the sociology of development literature and ... international tourism is viewed here as a major component of world-trade between rich and poor countries' (Lea, 1993). Much of the literature deals with industry or government transactions, thus being of little relevance to this study. However, the underlying importance of tourism development ethics relates to tourists' economic power and how they can influence such transactions (Cleverdon, 2001; Cleverdon & Kalisch, 2000; Curtin & Busby, 1999). The rise of green consumerism (Schwepker & Cornwall, 1991) forced the adoption of eco-friendly industry practices. Therefore, the rise of ethical consumerism represents a potentially powerful force (Malloy & Fennell, 1998). Thus, by questioning companies' ethics, ethical tourists can potentially change industry conduct.

D'Sa (1999) meanwhile posits that tourism is manifestly unethical, underpinned by global capitalism, and simply a product of the prevailing unjust economic and social order. He states that 'respect for autonomy and concern for justices are regarded as core ethical principles in the West' (D'Sa, 1999), yet third-world development sacrifices these principles, with the profit-seeking elite taking precedence (Cohen, 1989b; D'Sa, 1999).

Ethical tourism addresses this issue by channelling tourists' money away from global travel operators, and towards the local community, to enable community-controlled tourism (Cleverdon, 2001; Cleverdon & Kalisch, 2000; D'Sa, 1999; Lea, 1993; Mintel, 2001; Tearfund, 2001). This tourism is increasingly referred to as 'fair trade tourism' (Cleverdon, 2001; Cleverdon & Kalisch, 2000; Tearfund, 2001), where tourists are advised to purchase locally produced goods and services, and pay a fair price for them.

Defining Ethical Tourism

The literature suggests that approaches to ethical tourism include eco, community and fair trade, amongst others, whilst simultaneously labelling them as approaches to sustainable tourism too (Weeden, 2001). The principles of sustainable and ethical tourism are very similar. With ethics characterising human behaviour 'in the context of a relationship as right or

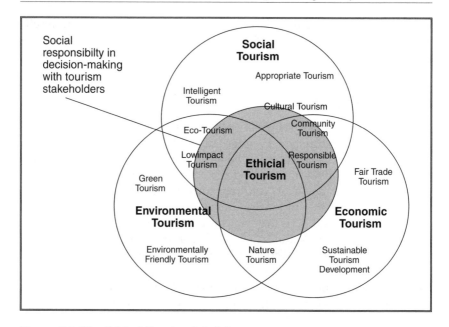

Figure 5.1 The Ethical Tourism Model
Source: based on Wight (1993b), Mowforth & Munt (1998), Swarbrooke &
      Horner (1999), Swarbrooke (1999), Weeden (2001), Wheeller (1994a)

wrong...involving social responsibility in decision-making' (Wheeller, 1994a), ethical tourism should be defined placing an overriding importance on socially responsible decision-making amongst tourism stakeholders, thus distinguishing ethical tourism from sustainable tourism.

Emanating from this understanding, the Ethical Tourism Model has been developed (Figure 5.1). It is evident that ethical tourism is characteristic of many 'alternative' types of tourism, but only by adopting the different values of such tourism types and ensuring that all decision-making with all stakeholders, regarding environmental, social and economic issues, is socially responsible is it ethical tourism. In this way, although ethical tourism adopts other tourism type characteristics, these tourism types are not necessarily ethical.

Defining the Ethical Tourist

Increasingly, market researchers have been attempting to define the alternative segments of the marketplace (Hall & Lew, 1998). Research has revealed that environmentally or ethically concerned consumers are better educated and older than mass-tourism consumers, financially secure and more likely to be female (Mintel, 2001; Roberts, 1996).

To demonstrate the behaviour of the ethical tourist, the Ethical Tourism Model (Figure 5.1) was adapted to form the Ethical Tourist Paradigm (Figure 5.2). It is evident that ethical tourist behaviour takes three fundamental forms: environmental, social and economic, whilst incorporating social responsibility into decision-making with tourism's stakeholders. The model reflects the ethical tourist's predominant interactions with the host community and tourism employees within this community, rather than other tourism stakeholders. From this a definition of ethical tourists can be proposed.

Ethical tourists respect their hosts: by treading softly on the environment; by being educated about the culture; by ensuring their stay returns fair, economic benefits, and by ensuring all decision-making with all tourism's stakeholders is socially responsible.

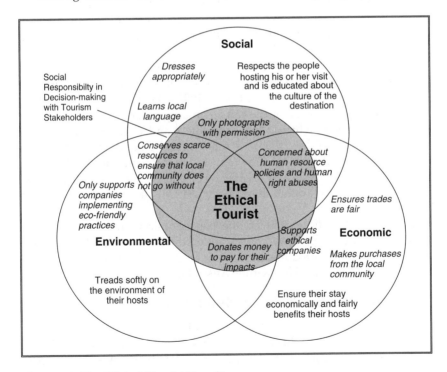

Figure 5.2 The Ethical Tourist Paradigm
Source: Author

Investigating the Ethical Characteristics of Backpackers in the Backpacker Literature

If the model of ethical tourist behaviour has three fundamental forms: environmental, social and economic, whilst incorporating social responsibility into decision-making with tourism's stakeholders, then it would be appropriate to investigate the extent the literature characterises backpackers in these three areas.

Literature examining the backpacker phenomenon has historically been contradictory, with backpackers being defined in both positive and negative terms (Riley, 1988). Early backpacker studies focused on conceptualising the backpacker phenomenon, utilising mass tourism as their comparison (Cohen, 1973; Teas, 1974; Ten Have, 1974; Vogt, 1976). Cohen's (1973) sociological discussion of the phenomenon refers to it as a counterculture, with the abandonment of accepted standards and conventional ways of life. The stereotypical presentation of the backpacker as an unkempt, immoral individual has gained much credence by official tourism planners who wish to discourage the development of backpacking tourism (Hampton, 1998; Noronha, 1999; Scheyvens, 2002; Wheeler, 1999; Wilson, 1997).

The last decade has witnessed the recognition, within the literature at least, that the backpacker culture constitutes an important market segment (Hampton, 1996, 1998; Loker, 1993b; Pearce, 1990; Riley, 1988; Scheyvens, 2002). This literature can be broadly described as containing a marketing concept, which often contradicts and challenges the earlier conceptual works. Riley (1988), by defending the backpacking phenomenon, introduced the change. She reported that the pursuit of adventure, satisfaction of curiosity and escape from one of 'life's junctures' were motivation for travel, rather than Cohen's (1973) alienation from Western society.

Riley's (1988) study changed the conceptualisation of backpacking, moving it from being viewed as a counterculture to a subculture. Pearce (1990) further supported this move by identifying the growing economic significance of backpackers within Australia.

Environmental Backpacker Behaviour

Ethically environmental behaviour involves tourists treading softly on the environment of their hosts (High Places, 1994, cited in Wheeller, 1994b; Lea, 1993; Swarbrooke, 1999; Wight, 1993a, 1993b; Yenckel, 1995). Backpackers 'self-identify their traveller status as distinct from the more traditional "tourist", primarily focusing on what they perceive to be values embracing environmental integrity' (Doorne, 1994, cited in Ateljevic & Doorne, 2000a), enjoying pristine, uncrowded destinations (Cohen, 1982). The ethicality of such behaviour is widely debated in the literature.

'For the simple reason that backpackers want to spend less and thus generally consume fewer resources, they can be more environmentally friendly' (Scheyvens, 2002). Content with swimming in the sea, and taking cold showers, the backpacker market has been quite kind to the environment, especially, '... compared to the resource-guzzling five-star tourists' (Noronha, 1999). Loker (1993b) suggests, however, that backpackers place greater strains on community services because of their extended length of stay.

Bradt (1995) critiques backpackers further, stating that just by getting away from the crowds, finding new places 'off the beaten track' and searching for 'authentic experiences' they do the most harm. Elsrud (2001) illustrates that such behaviour is a form of risk taking, increasing status among backpackers. She also observes how fellow travellers pose a risk to such status enhancement, '...by pushing the *avant garde* of backpacking even further' (Elsrud, 2001), therefore, furthering detrimental, unethical impacts. Backpackers are subsequently blamed for tourism's global problems:

> In their rush to escape the mass tourist, the so-called aware, educated, 'I'm going ethnic' individual traveller is forever seeking the new, the exotic, the unspoilt – the vulnerable. Inevitably, however, they are inexorably paving the way for the package tour. The sensitive traveller is the perpetrator of the global spread ... Who, in the long-term is responsible for the most damage ...? (Wheeller, 1991: 92)

Hutnyk (1996) even blames the problems of the world's economic inequality on backpackers, stating:

> Budget or 'alternative' travel, like the alternative trade promoted by many organised aid groups, can be criticised as an illusion of 'nice' cottage capitalism, soothing ideological anxieties while extending commercialisation and the tourism industry. Rather than working towards social transformation, alternative travel and charity work seems often to tinker at the edges of capitalist expansion into new market niches.

It is widely accepted within the literature that backpackers pave the way for mass tourism (Barnett, 1999; Butler, 1980, 1990; Cohen, 1972, 1973; Spreitzhofer, 1998; Wheeller, 1991). However, unless *not* travelling, as suggested by Swarbrooke (1999), there seems little the individual backpacker can do. Instead, it is proposed that backpackers undertaking eco-friendly practices exhibit ethical behaviour. Firth and Hing (1999) sought to determine whether eco-friendly practices influenced back-packer hostel choice, but only a small, convenience sample of back-packers were surveyed, making the research fairly inconclusive. Only 2% of backpackers ranked the implementation of eco-friendly practices as most important to them, thus suggesting a lack of ethical environmental behaviour amongst the backpacker population.

Social Backpacker Behaviour

Tourists exhibit ethical social behaviour when they are educated about the culture of their destination and respect the people hosting their visit (Mintel, 2001; Tearfund, 2001). According to Loker (1993b), backpackers are keen to share the local lifestyle, and Riley (1988) states their prime motivation to be 'to meet the people', with many learning some of the local language to facilitate such interaction. The contact between back-packers and local people is said to be more intensive than between other tourists and local people (Aramberri, 1991). Participants themselves also 'believe that as backpackers, they are automatically rendered "low-impact", benign and responsible' (McMinn, 1999), and, therefore, ethical.

An increasing body of literature challenges this belief, observing the invasive and unethical nature of such tourism (Bradt, 1995; Butler, 1990; Lee, 1999; Mandalia, 1999; McMinn, 1999; Mintel 2001; Smith, 1992; Spreitzhofer, 1998).

Backpackers, by seeking out new destinations, but by failing to understand cultural norms, can have a long-lasting influence on the host community (Aziz, 1999; Bradt, 1995; Noronha, 1999; Spreitzhofer, 1998). Mandalia (1999) quotes an agitated guesthouse manager in holy Pushkar, '... the foreigners just treat the place as a fun theme park. They drink and smoke in the temples and show no respect'. Wheeler (1999: 16, italics added), founder of the *Lonely Planet* guidebooks, explains, 'that for some reason *when travelling*, they *(the backpackers)* seem to feel that the rules don't apply any more. People forget that many locations they visit can be very ... conservative.' Acting out this perceived freedom from social commitments thus leads to inappropriate behaviour (Lee, 1999; Noronha, 1999).

Scanty or excessively casual dress, drug and alcohol abuse, and casual sexual encounters can all cause insult to local residents (Aziz, 1999; Hutnyk, 1996; Mandalia, 1999), 'whose reliance on income from tourism often leads them to tolerate what they feel is outright denigration of their customs' (Scheyvens, 2002). Far from expressing an interest in local culture, backpackers seem to place primary emphasis upon social activities within their group, excluding locals and conventional tourists (Aziz, 1999).

Novelists have also picked up on this trend, with recent books including Sutcliffe's (1997) *Are You Experienced?* And Garland's (1997) *The Beach*, which critique elements of backpacker culture. Sutcliffe (1997) tells the story of Dave who goes backpacking because everyone else is. Dave's enthusiasm for meeting a fellow Briton whilst travelling in India is tested when he receives a biting analysis of backpacker travel from him:

> University of Life ... got to the Third World and survived. No revision, interest or sensitivity required ... it's not hippies on a spiritual mission who come here any more, just morons on a poverty-tourism adventure holiday ... Your kind of travel is all about low horizons dressed up as open-mindedness. You have no interest in India, ... and treat Indians with a mixture of contempt and suspicion which is reminiscent of the Victorian colonials. (Sutcliffe, 1997).

Based on such characteristics of backpackers, some authors have questioned the right of backpackers to take the moral high ground when comparing their tourism behaviour to that of conventional tourists (Hutnyk, 1996; Lee, 1999; Mowforth & Munt, 1998; Spreitzhofer, 1998). Spreitzhofer (1998) asked, 'Does the low-budget tourism of the 90s meet the requirements of a "better" socially responsible third-world tourism?', though did not supply an answer to this question.

Mowforth and Munt (1998: 135) suggest that rather than ethically concerned tourists, backpackers can be included in the category of self-centred tourists they call 'ego-tourists' or 'curriculum-vitae builders'. However 'while self-gratification and indulgence may be the primary motivation for one category of backpackers, others may be driven by a genuine interest in learning about other people and environments, and many may fall somewhere between these extremes' (Scheyvens, 2002: 150). The literature is clearly divided as to whether backpackers exhibit socially ethical behaviour, or whether they are just 'ego-tourists' in search of 'self-gratification'.

Economic Backpacker Behaviour

Economically ethical behaviour ensures that all economic transactions are a fair trade and that the host community benefits from such transactions (Cleverdon, 2001; Cleverdon & Kalisch, 2000). Economic issues ranging from backpackers' budgeting to economic development have been widely debated in the literature, viewing backpacker behaviour as both ethical and unethical. Scheyvens' (2002) research is particularly applicable, with both the pros and cons of backpacker economics being comprehensively reviewed.

One common criticism of backpackers is that, in ensuring that their funds will last for the duration of their travels, they become obsessively focused on budgets and bargain-hunting (Bradt, 1995; Goodwin, 1999; Goodwin *et al.*, 1998, cited in Scheyvens, 2002; Teas, 1974). According to Riley (1988), 'status among travellers is closely tied to living cheaply and obtaining the best bargains which serve as indicators that one is an experienced traveller'.

Backpackers have been described as exploiting their powerful market position: they 'use guidebooks, sometimes seriously dated editions, to establish prices and then try to secure accommodation at a lower price' (Goodwin, 1999). A Balinese tour guide criticises such behaviour (cited in Wheat, 1995): 'now tourists are going to Indonesia not to see the culture or the people, but to compete with other travellers about how cheaply they can travel. They all want to be the winner and don't realise how rude they are to local people'. Bradt (1995) further questions the ethicality of such behaviour:

> It is a matter of pride for all 'real travellers' to walk away from the market having bargained the vendor down to half the asking price. We tell ourselves this is the way of the country, that the people will not respect us if we don't bargain. Is it really fair to pay five or ten pounds for an article which will have taken a day to produce? Is it reasonable to shout abuse at a taxi driver because he is hoping to get a 'tourist' fare out of you?

Examples of such behaviour abound within the literature (Aitkenhead, 2001; Sutcliffe, 1997). Sutcliffe (1997) narrates an argument over Liz's excessive haggling whilst securing a ride in India. Liz justifies the ethicality of her behaviour, whilst Dave queries it:

Dave: Well done Liz...You saved us at least 15p there...

Liz: Will you stop acting like such a spoilt Westerner? We're in India, now. ... you have to haggle. It's part of life.

Dave: You don't have to. Stump up a few extra pennies, and you don't need to stand in the midday sun screaming your head off like some demented memsahib.

Liz: It's not about that, and you know it... if you just take the first price they offer, you look stupid,... And if Westerners go around paying

> double for everything, it gives us a bad reputation... It makes us look spoilt, and far richer than we really are.
>
> **Dave:** But we are rich. Ten rupees is nothing...
>
> **Liz:** That's not the point. If we did that, it would completely upset the local economy.

A further critique evolved from governments of less developed countries wishing to discourage backpacker travel in their countries. This negativity grew from the perception that backpackers' budgeting meant little revenue for destinations (Scheyvens, 2002). Research in Australasia, however, has challenged this, finding that due to longer trip duration, backpackers actually spend more than other tourist categories (Haigh, 1995, cited in Scheyvens, 2002). Furthermore, 'backpackers spread their spending over a wider geographic area, bringing benefits to remote and otherwise economically depressed regions' (Scheyvens, 2002).

Through purchasing locally produced goods and services, backpackers also contribute significantly to local economic development (Hampton, 1998; Mintel, 2001; Riley, 1988; Scheyvens, 2002; Wheeler, 1999; Wilson, 1997). Wilson (1997) argues that in Goa backpackers are welcomed because their needs are easily serviced, resulting in an industry characterised by '... wide local ownership of resources and the broad distribution of benefits throughout the local community'.

Both Hutnyk (1996) and Noronha (1999), however, identify backpacking as just one small facet of the large, unethical global tourism industry, reinforcing inequitable links between the north and south. With local government support, however, to halt multinational control of tourism, and with backpackers only choosing locally produced products and services, backpacker tourism can become one way of increasing local participation within a sustainable and ethical development strategy (Hampton, 1996).

In summary, then, it appears that there are conflicting views about the ethics of backpacking in the literature, for each of the three areas identified: environmental, social and economic. It appears that the backpackers describe themselves as ethical tourists, but much of the backpacker literature contests this. It can be concluded that the literature describes the backpackers' social behaviour as being the least ethical, with inappropriate behaviour, scanty dress and rude and aggressive haggling causing offence to the host community. Backpacker economic behaviour is more ethical, with their purchasing of locally produced goods and long length of stay contributing economically to the local community. However, they are criticised for exploiting their powerful market position

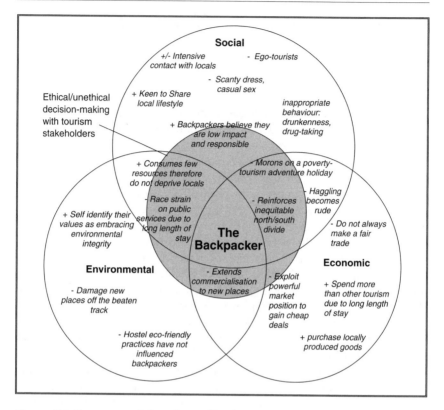

Figure 5.3 Summary of the ethics of backpacking derived from the literature
Source: Author

to drive down prices and not making 'fair trades'. By consuming fewer resources in comparison to conventional tourists, backpackers exhibit environmentally ethical behaviour, though the effect of visiting places 'off the beaten track' has been questioned, as has their lack of commitment to companies exhibiting environmentally ethical behaviour.

These conclusions are presented in Figure 5.3, which attempts to summarise the positive and negative aspects of backpacking identified in the literature.

Web-based Survey of Backpackers

Figure 5.3 is used as the basis for a primary research investigation. Rather than relying on the literature to answer the question of whether backpackers are ethical tourists, this paper goes on to test whether

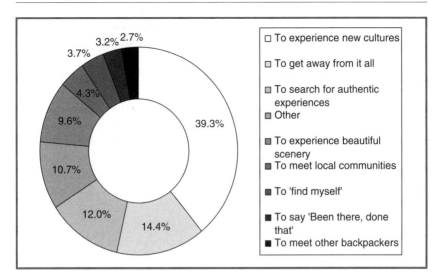

Figure 5.4 Respondents' main reason to go backpacking (*n* = 374)

backpacker behaviour in practice conforms to either the model of ethical tourists presented in Figure 5.2, or indeed corresponds to the conclusions derived from the literature on backpacking, presented in Figure 5.3.

A questionnaire survey was carried out with the aim of targeting international backpackers. Difficulties in intercepting backpackers, which have been identified in other studies (Speed, 2004), led to the selection of a web-based survey, with a self-completion questionnaire being distributed on backpacker websites, using the logic that backpacker websites are predominantly visited by backpackers, in the same way that Pearce (1990) argued that backpacker magazines are predominantly read by backpackers. The recognition of the 'odd wishful thinker' (Pearce, 1990) responding was controlled with a question posed regarding the respondent's backpacking experience.

The sample frame (backpackers using backpacker websites) was anticipated to be representative of backpackers worldwide, due to the proliferation of Internet cafes along popular backpacker routes and the evident importance of the Internet within the backpacker community (Aitkenhead, 2001; Scheyvens, 2002).

Mohsin and Ryan (2003) support this, finding that the 'two major sources of information used by backpackers are word of mouth recommendations and the Internet'.

Websites were utilised to distribute the questionnaire and locate the sample for undertaking primary research. The websites were selected by searching via popular Internet search engines for the term 'backpacker'. Each selected website had a message board, which was more commonly referred to as a forum. On each forum, a short message was placed, inviting backpackers to connect to the questionnaire webpage. Several forums separated the messages into different subject categories. Where this was the case, a neutral category was chosen to avoid bias.

Three hundred and eighty responses were received in a 28-day period, giving a sample size of 374 who had taken at least one backpacking trip. The six excluded from the analysis were respondents who had not taken a backpacking trip.

Survey Results

Respondent profile

Sixty percent of respondents had undertaken several backpacking trips (more than two trips), while a further 19.0% had taken two trips and 13.0% had taken only one trip. The remainder (7.0%) spent the majority of their time 'on the road'.

There was an almost exact 50:50 split between male (49.9%) and female (50.1%) respondents while, by age, more than two thirds (68.7%) were under 30 years of age. The average age was 28.6 years and median age 27 years. Of further interest is that 9.1% of respondents were aged over 40 years. With the exception of Mohsin and Ryan (2003), who identified 12.7% of respondents over 40, the older backpacker appears not to have been sufficiently recognised. This emerging market has been infrequently acknowledged (Ross, 1997; Ryan & Mohsin, 2001), but these older backpackers demand further attention. In this respect, some attention is given in this paper to the different responses made by the under and over 30s.

Thirty-two different countries are represented in the sample, although the great majority of respondents are from English-speaking countries – UK/Ireland (29.0%), USA/Canada (33.2%) and Australia/New Zealand (15.8%). The large proportion of North Americans is likely to be attributable to the use of the Internet to distribute the questionnaire. The only other study (Helbert, 2002) experiencing such a high North American representation also used an online questionnaire methodology. Respondents from Europe made up a further 17.7% of the sample, so that the main developed nations accounted for 95.7% of the sample.

The main motivation cited for backpacking by far was to experience new cultures. The other main reasons received a relatively similar proportion of responses.

Environmental ethicality

Respondents were asked several questions regarding their tourist behaviour from an environmental perspective. As shown in Figure 5.5, only around 1% rated eco-friendly practices of accommodation providers as the most important aspect when choosing a place to stay.

In terms of their own eco-friendly practices, the majority of respondents (60.7%) showed a strong a commitment (those indicating 'Always' or 'Most of the time') (Figure 5.6). A further 25% undertook environmentally friendly practices 'Sometimes' while travelling, showing that overall 86% of respondents had an awareness of environmental responsibility. The views of those who 'Rarely' or 'Never' undertook such practices, and which corresponds to some of the literature (Firth & Hing, 1999; Wheeler, 1999), were best articulated by the respondent who noted that:

> In environmental matters I think it is the local people who influence me the most, e.g. in India I thought, what's the point in carrying around rubbish looking for a non-existent bin, when 1 billion locals are throwing it on the ground. (23-year-old female from Ireland)

A much larger proportion of over 30 year olds (33.6%) indicated 'Always' compared to 18.3% of those under 30 years of age, suggesting

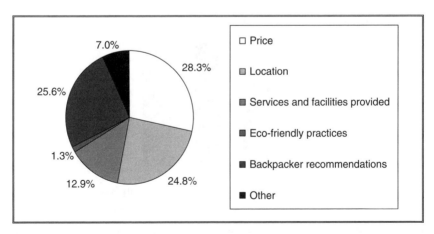

Figure 5.5 Most important aspects for backpackers when choosing a place to stay ($n = 371$)

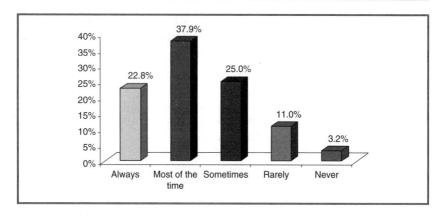

Figure 5.6 When backpacking I carry out environmentally friendly practices, such as recycling and conserving water supplies (*n* = 372)

greater environmental ethicality among the older age group. Additionally, respondents who had indicated being motivated by beautiful scenery were significantly more likely (41.7%) to carry out environmentally friendly practices than other backpackers (20.8%).

A third scenario regarding environmental issues was put to respondents, asking them whether they would take part in a tour that was potentially damaging to a destination (Figure 5.7). Almost one quarter (23.6%) agreed that they would participate even if the tour had

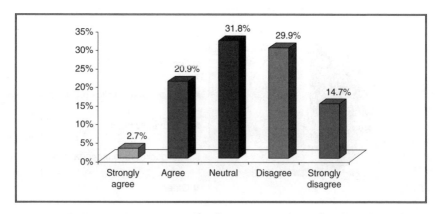

Figure 5.7 Responses to the question: 'Some untouched wilderness can only be experienced with tours. I would take such a tour despite the tour having questionable environmental practices' (*n* = 374)

questionable environmental practices. Less than half (44.6%) would not take part, while almost one third remained neutral on the question. This response from the sample would suggest a lack of ethicality regarding the environment.

Respondents over 30 years old appear to exhibit more ethical behaviour, with over half (52.2%) indicating 'Strongly disagree' or 'Agree', compared to 41.4% of under 30 year olds. There was no significant correlation between backpackers motivated by seeing beautiful scenery and them taking a questionable tour, suggesting that for some a desire to see beautiful scenery overrides environmental activity.

Social ethicality

Ethical tourists were described earlier as taking time to talk and interact with the host community. Responses from the survey would suggest that backpackers do not exhibit this characteristic strongly (Figure 5.8). Nearly half of the respondents (45.6%) spent 40% or less of their time with locals in comparison with fellow backpackers. Aziz's (1999) observations of inward group behaviour are supported in this respect. One 26-year-old female from New Zealand even challenged the practicality of talking to locals:

> Depends on the country! Language difficulties, talkativeness of the people. Not going to spend too long having a conversation in rural China are you!...If I'm going to be in a place for a few weeks, I'm not

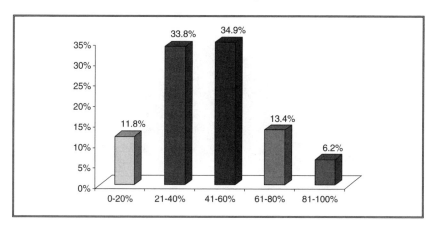

Figure 5.8 The amount of time spent talking to locals compared to fellow backpackers ($n = 373$)

going to night classes, but if I'm travelling around South America for months, then I would do Spanish classes beforehand. Learning a bit of every language you are going to encounter on a South East Asian trip before you went though would be silly. Plus show me a night class that teaches Khmer!

The one-fifth of respondents spending over 60% of their time interacting with locals represents a small group of more socially ethical backpackers, perhaps exhibiting drifter-like characteristics (Cohen, 1973). Such intensive contact, however, has also been criticised (Bradt, 1995; Noronha, 1999; Spreitzhofer, 1998), suggesting that the most equitably ethical group is that which spends its time equally between locals and fellow backpackers.

Although many backpackers did not spend much time conversing with locals, the majority (69.4%) did attempt to learn some phrases of the language and found out about the countries prior to visiting (89.1%).

As shown Figure 5.9, there is a social awareness among most respondents with regard to appropriate clothing. Over three quarters (77%) indicated having deliberately worn clothing at some point in recognition of local customs. Nevertheless, this leaves almost one quarter of backpackers who do not see this as an important issue.

Females were almost twice as likely as males (54.8% compared to 29.8%) to 'Always' dress appropriately. This is perhaps a function of the countries visited by backpackers, where women are expected to cover up and cause most offence by not doing so. Or, it may indicate reluctance

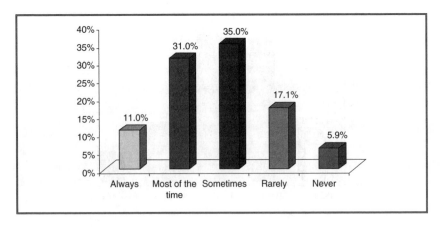

Figure 5.9 Behaviour of backpackers in wearing appropriate clothing in respect of local customs (*n* = 374)

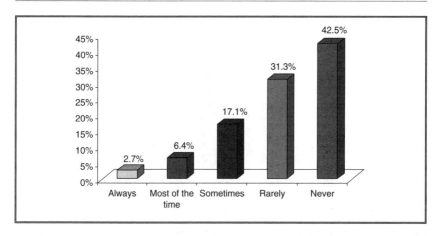

Figure 5.10 Behaviour of backpackers in taking part in drug and alcohol consumption where it is *not* approved by the local community (*n* = 374)

among Western males to wear skirts or robes in countries where such dress is common.

Less than half of the respondents (42.5%) indicated never taking part in drug or alcohol consumption that was disapproved of by the local community (Figure 5.10). As such, more than half have done so at one time or another. Many respondents perhaps use their own cultural background as a guide to what is acceptable behaviour and apply this wherever they go. As shown in Figure 5.10, most respondents would not participate in behaviour that is unacceptable in their home country, however herein lies the problem. Many backpackers may take with them the idea that what is acceptable in their own country is acceptable anywhere else. This may particularly be the case among Western people, who wrongly feel that they are visiting socially undeveloped cultures just because these countries have not advanced economically in a similar way to that of their home country.

This fault in perception is perhaps the most difficult obstacle to overcome in managing the impact of backpacking, especially in untouched cultures and physical environments.

There are also a significant proportion of respondents (16.3%, Figure 5.11) who see backpacking as 'releasing' them from the strictures of their own culture, or indeed being given carte blanche to act however they wish regardless of the social environment. There is also a high level of 'Neutrals' who necessarily may be persuaded to participate in activities unacceptable to both the host and home cultures.

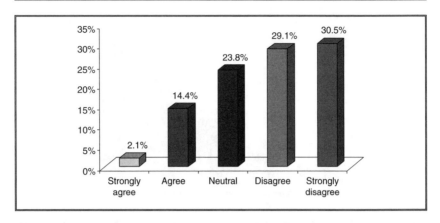

Figure 5.11 I participate in activities which would be considered unacceptable at home ($n = 374$)

The question provoking the most divided response among backpackers regarded human rights abuse. The literature suggested that ethical tourists would not visit destinations where human rights are violated, but almost half of the respondents (44.5%) indicated that they would. However, open-ended responses to this question argued that this was not necessarily a bad thing:

> The question about Burma is difficult. I would normally agree, you shouldn't go, but having heard from people who have been and have said that the local people want you to go and report home has made me reconsider that view to some extent. Isolation changes little it is true. (36-year-old male from the UK)

This highlights the complexities of ethics and how difficult it is to decide what is and what is not ethical. Perhaps the fact that respondents had thought through the situation is indicative itself of some scale of ethical concern.

Economic ethicality

As shown in Figure 5.12, only a small proportion of respondents (4.6%) indicated 'Always' ensuring that they purchased goods produced by the local community. This may be a function of a trade-off between economic practicality and economic ethicality, as most backpackers are travelling on a tight budget and need to balance what they want to buy against what they can afford to buy. As shown earlier, price was the key

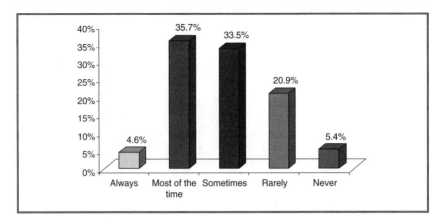

Figure 5.12 Backpacker behaviour regarding purchasing locally produced goods ($n = 373$)

determinant in deciding where to stay and this behaviour is likely to be transferred to other touristic purchases.

The subject of haggling produced significant debate among respondents and one-fifth (20.4%) participated in this practice on a regular basis. A further 41% indicated that they haggled 'Sometimes'. Pro-haggling backpackers justified the practice typically as:

> I haggle because it's almost rude not to in lots of cultures. It's part of the deal. It's like a social conversation. So it's not JUST to keep my costs down! 'Fair deal' is relative. If you don't haggle, they will laugh at you behind your back, or think you're a snob, trying to show off how rich you are. Also, you will drive up prices for future tourists. (29-year-old female from the Netherlands)

The over 30 age group was less likely to haggle than the under 30s, 51.4% compared to 33.3%. Whether this illustrates age influencing different levels of ethical behaviour or different levels of comfort with such transactions is difficult to ascertain from this exploratory survey. Nevertheless, other behaviour that appears to show an age correlation would suggest that it does affect how people weigh up such situations. Backpackers also appear to reject checking for an ethical code of conduct among tourism providers such as accommodation operators or airlines. As shown in Figure 5.13, over 70% of respondents rarely or never look for such a guarantee. It could be argued that most backpackers therefore, by using unethical companies either through

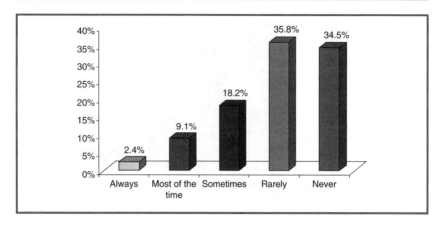

Figure 5.13 Checking the ethical code of conduct of tourism providers before purchase ($n = 374$)

choice or ignorance, are displaying unethical behaviour driven mainly by economic motivations.

Backpacker perceptions of their own ethical behaviour

Respondents were divided about whether backpacking is a more ethical form of tourism than packaged tourism (Figure 5.14). Males (47.3%) were more likely than females (31.9%) to identify backpacking as

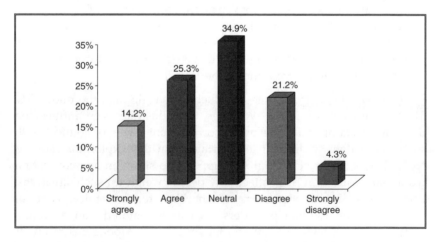

Figure 5.14 Backpacking is a more responsible and ethical form of tourism than packaged tourism ($n = 372$)

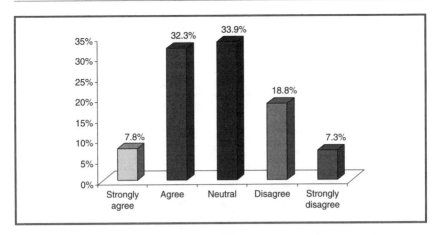

Figure 5.15 Backpacker behaviour would be more responsible if tourism providers were more responsible ($n = 372$)

the more ethical tourism form. This difference in perception was also apparent between graduates and non-graduates, with the former disagreeing significantly that backpacking was more ethical than packaged tourism. The results contradict the literature in the sense that the majority of respondents did not self-identify with the proposition that their travelling status was ethically superior to packaged tourists, as suggested.

Most respondents also placed significant responsibility for their behaviour on the conduct of tourism providers, such as hostel owners and tour organisers (Figure 5.15). Over 40% agreed that their behaviour would change for the better if such organisations were more responsible. This sends a strong message to industry. The under 30s were more likely to agree with this proposition (43.2%) than those 30 years or over (33.3%), which probably reflects greater experience and self-reliance.

Conclusions

Both existing backpacker literature and the web-based survey undertaken for this chapter have shown that backpackers do not exhibit particularly ethical tourist behaviour as propounded by ethical tourism models. However, this does not suggest that backpackers are unethical tourists, only that they do not fully conform to theoretical models of ethical behaviour. Indeed, the results may bring into question existing models of ethicality and their founding assumptions.

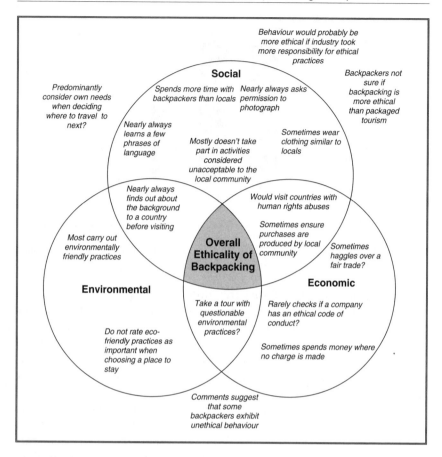

Figure 5.16 Key findings

A small proportion of respondents to the survey do, nevertheless, apparently come close to model ethical behaviour, whereas another small group would appear to exist at the other end of the continuum. In between, there is a range of other backpacker groups that to one extent or another reflect some model ethical characteristics. It is argued therefore that the term ethical behaviour is relative, as argued cogently by some backpackers in the survey.

This has significant consequences for tourism providers who service the backpacker market. It is easy to categorise and provide for backpackers via marketing, demographic or motivational groupings, however it is much more difficult to service their different needs while ensuring appropriate behaviour that optimises positive impacts. A significant proportion of respondents to the survey indicated that they would change their behaviour if tourism providers were more responsible. This raises the issue of an international industry standard code of conduct that is recognisable to the range of backpackers and helps influence individual behaviour. To some extent, this may occur in originating countries and some developed host countries through industry itself or legislature, but it is likely to be less regulated in many host destinations. However, this may go against the spirit of backpacking.

Results showed that positive and negative behaviour was exhibited across social, environmental and economic spectrums, allowing us to maybe identify specific types of interaction that can be managed to the betterment of both host and visitor outcomes. This could be developed at source, or information source to be more exact. Existing on-line and hard copy sources such as the *Lonely Planet* could be persuaded to be more proactive in highlighting particular issues related to identifiable and changeable behaviour.

These conclusions are based on a survey research methodology that, although providing initial insights, is inevitably limited in ascertaining the actual behavioural characteristics of backpackers. Richer data may be gathered through qualitative methods such as observational research, which might highlight the difference between stated and actual behaviour.

Note

1. The Author acknowledges the help of Annabel Hartnell in the writing of this chapter.

Chapter 6

The Lonely Planet Myth: 'Backpacker Bible' and 'Travel Survival Kit'

PETER WELK

Introduction

'The growth of backpacker tourism and the alternative guidebook publishing success share a common history. The importance of the latter for the growth of the former can hardly be exaggerated' (Sørensen, 2003: 859). Sørensen's analysis, though insightful, tells only half the story, as the growth of alternative publishing – and of Lonely Planet Publications in particular – would hardly have been possible without the growth and mainstreaming of backpacker tourism. It is hard to estimate whether processes in the history of backpacking had greater influence on the development of *Lonely Planet* or vice versa, but without doubt the impact both had on each other is so significant that their interdependencies as well as the peculiarities of *Lonely Planet*'s history are worth studying in order to understand the whole phenomenon.

The history of the largest guidebook publisher and backpacker-focused company in the world starts with a misunderstanding. Some time in the early 1970s, Tony Wheeler, a young Englishman, was listening to the Joe Cocker song 'Space Captain', understanding 'lonely planet' instead of 'lovely planet', and liked it – the name of the first backpacker-oriented company was born (*Lonely Planet*, 2005).

Two decades later, when Bill Gates, founder of the Microsoft Empire, visited Australia, he met two people: the Prime Minister, and Tony Wheeler, meanwhile founder and owner of Lonely Planet Publications, based in Melbourne, Australia. Apparently Gates offered $50 million to buy the guidebook publishing company, but Wheeler declined (Cummings, 2005a). The travel veteran could though in fact be called the 'Bill Gates of backpacking'. Parallels between the two self-made millionaires (and billionaires respectively) are strikingly obvious: both started their careers in their roaring twenties as ambitious, devoted pioneers of their respective businesses without external support and became icons of a whole generation, striving to monopolise their market segments: Gates by interconnecting all the world via his 'Windows' operating systems – and Wheeler by interconnecting all backpackers via his 'travel survival kits'.

And both cultivate their immodest 'myths of origin'. Every *Lonely Planet* issue recounts Tony's and his wife Maureen's honeymoon trip of 1972 – overland from England to Australia by motorbike – in the style of a 'classic travel adventure' (Finlay, 1999: 20), which was 'handstapled' into their first guidebook, *Across Asia on the Cheap* – followed by what was to become the 'yellow bible', *South-East Asia on a Shoestring*, just as humbly 'put together in a backstreet Chinese hotel in Singapore in 1975' (e.g. Hämäläinen, 1991: 224). This is the stuff backpacker myths are made of, and today these two trips, subconsciously morphed into one, are widely perceived as the prototypes of backpacking.

With respect to Cohen's observations in the early 1970s and Tomory's (1998) collection of hippie anecdotes in India, what the Wheeler's call a 'pioneering trip' (Finlay, 1999: 16) into a region where 'visitors were few and far between and facilities distinctly limited' (p. 17) was already taking place on a beaten (drifter) track; otherwise there would hardly have been a market for a guidebook that sold 8500 copies in Australia alone (Friend, 2005). But in public, the Wheelers avoid mentioning this contradiction – even in their quite detailed account of the trip in the jubilee edition of *South-East Asia on a Shoestring* (Finlay, 1999: 16–19), featuring photos in which no other Westerners can be seen. On the contrary: they put much emphasis on the remoteness and sleepiness of their destinations as well as on the hardships of travelling back in the 1970s. Thus, many backpackers, oblivious to the extent of the hippie trail, do perceive the Wheelers as *the* pioneers of backpacking.

But Wheeler's success is in his favour: nobody else has proven such empathy for the motivations and dynamics, ideals and realities of the backpacker scene, and for their need for someone to guide them around the snares of independent travel. He utilises his expertise to further promote his legacy, thus establishing his place in backpacker mythology as *the* progenitor of the scene, 'one of the people who changed the way the world travels' (*Lonely Planet*, 2005). He has always made sure that his and his company's names are interlinked inseparably in the minds of his customers. And with a successful marketing strategy, he has made generations of backpackers believe that without *Lonely Planet* (and thus without Tony Wheeler), their travelling lifestyle would not have come into being, and that he is their role model. Every backpacker must dwindle away in awe and envy alike when reading remarks like the following:

> This year, for example, I've done a scuba diving trip to the Truk Lagoon in Micronesia. I've driven around the island of Tasmania, to the South of Australia, in an Alpha Romeo sports car. I've stayed in some very luxurious hotels in Bali. I've driven across the Western Desert of Western Australia in a 4 × 4. I've walked for a week out to the west of Alice Springs in Australia, and I've been to the Opera Festival in Verona in Italy. And lucky me, that's all work!' (Wheeler in Fortune Small Business, 2000)

Backpackers have thanked him by turning him into an icon, a mystic father figure guiding them around his lonely planet. Countless tales wind about him, nearly everybody claims to have met him or at least someone else who has met him or other legendary *Lonely Planet* veteran writers such as Joe Cummings, but hardly any travellers have ever come across him themselves. Wheeler may be absent physically, but he is always with us when we go backpacking, his spirit looming in the guidebook in our backpack. And should he nevertheless pop up in traveller circles, they will rally around him like a guru. Naturally, the scene is full of gossip and mythmaking:

> I have heard various different versions of the weird death of . . . Tony Wheeler: a sports car accident in Africa, a bus over a cliff in Nepal, under the foot of an elephant in Thailand and pierced by the tusks of a wild pig in Highland New Guinea. (Hutnyk, 1996: 63–64)

> There were hundreds of variations of the tale, but all had Wheeler running out of luck at the end of the trail somewhere: in a train, bus, or motorcycle accident; from malaria; at a bullfight; at the hands of the mujahideen. (Friend, 2005)

These are 'heroic deaths' to the very taste of backpackers, featuring the early stages of a personality cult.

Joe Cummings, who has covered Thailand and other South-east Asian destinations since the early 1980s and may be second to Wheeler in terms of *Lonely Planet* celebrity status, recounts how the American embassy in Mexico launched a major search operation for him after traveller circles falsely rumoured that he went missing (Cummings, 2005a).

Biblical references blossom in the scene, but also in the media. In 1996, The *New York Times* described Wheeler as the 'trailblazing Patron saint of the world's backpackers and adventure travellers' (cited in *Lonely Planet*, 2005). The 'Thorn Tree', *Lonely Planet*'s online forum, features contributions discussing whether *Lonely Planet* 'was not written, but revealed' (Friend, 2005) to Wheeler on Mount Sinai.

Who is in Control?

The self-mythologisation is only the most subtle step of the *Lonely Planet* empire in its efforts to acquire complete control of the backpacker travel guide market. With its easy-to-use guidebooks, which are tailor-made for the backpacker market by simulating the casual conversation tone among backpackers with their colloquial, anecdotal style, *Lonely Planet* has determined in the last 30 years the 'places to go' and 'things to see' for the backpacker movement, channelling traveller streams to ever-new, yet 'undiscovered' destinations, simultaneously reflecting and further fuelling backpacker cravings: 'when you spend months with a guidebook that speaks to you in an intimate, conversational style, it becomes a bosom companion' (Friend, 2005). Today, a clear majority of backpackers are travelling with the company's guidebooks, ranging from over 60% (Newlands, 2004: 227) to 84% (Hottola, 1999: 67), depending on the area of research, often by far outstripping word-of-mouth and local people as the main source of information (cf. also Richards & Wilson, 2004b: 23; Spreitzhofer, 1997: 166). Since it established itself as the 'backpacker bible', *Lonely Planet* has thus had a firm grip on its customers' needs and self-consciousness.

With the economic power 'the company that understands travel better than anyone else' (*Lonely Planet* about *Lonely Planet* in Tomory, 2000: 245) has on the market as a quasi-monopolist, it can determine whether 'hotels close, good places go bad and bad places go bankrupt' (e.g. Wayne, 1990: 4) – as was innocently announced in every issue's foreword for years. With only a few lines, *Lonely Planet* can make a place boom or let it fall into disgrace. This is why many hostels, bars and restaurants promote themselves with *Lonely Planet* (even false) recommendations (cf. Bhattacharyya, 1997: 376).

The market power of the guidebooks has also caused some bizarre phenomena among service providers. Friend (2005) asserts that 'If they recommend the Resthouse Bangalore, then half the guesthouses there rename themselves Resthouse Bangalore'. In Penang, Malaysia, I found two interesting variations of the 'recommended in *Lonely Planet*' phrase: a recently opened guesthouse featured a banner pronouncing 'To be recommended in *Lonely Planet*'; and a restaurant that had obviously chosen anti-backpackers as its target group proudly proclaimed on a board: '*Not* recommended in the *Lonely Planet*'. Some anti-backpackers (cf. Welk, 2004, 2006) systematically avoid places recommended by *Lonely Planet*. While they consider themselves to be particularly independent, it should be obvious that *Lonely Planet* is still in control of the choices they make. Ridout notes that experienced touts can tell your guidebook by which guesthouse you choose (Reader & Ridout, 2003).

With its specialisation in remote destinations, the company has even become 'pretty much the authority on the spelling of place names' in many parts of Asia (Gluckman, 1999: 54). And – involuntarily – it has even played a role in the latest Gulf War:

> The series' authority is such that the team accompanying Jay Garner, the first American administrator of occupied Iraq, used *Lonely Planet Iraq* to draw up a list of historical sites that should not be bombed or looted. (Friend, 2005)

A Tale of Three Guidebooks

But *Lonely Planet* is not alone on the market, and has never been. In the mid-1970s, the Wheelers not only came across a long established 'Banana Pancake Trail', but also across already existing budget guidebooks. In India, 'the first guidebooks were personal notebooks' distributed and copied around the hippie scene (Hottola, 1999: 64). In 1972, Wilcock and Aaron published *India on $5 to $10 a day* (Hottola, 1999: 66), which has never been mentioned in any *Lonely Planet* publication or quoted by any *Lonely Planet* author. *Let's Go* had been ruling the market on Europe and North America since the early 1960s (*Let's Go*, 2001), but they had neglected covering Asia. The Wheelers targeted this gap in their early years, and so no reciprocal harm was done. What happened then is shrouded by competitive propaganda. According to a now expired *Let's Go* homepage (*Let's Go*, 1999), it was not until *Lonely Planet* penetrated into the *Let's Go* domain of Europe in the late 1980s and *Let's Go* started issuing several Asia guidebooks in the counter-move that a trade rivalry broke out between the two. Wheeler, on the other hand, saw competition coming from the *Rough Guides*, which were founded in 1981:

> After *Penguin* bought a majority stake in *Rough Guides*, in 1996, Wheeler noticed that *Rough Guides* were undercutting *Lonely Planet*'s

prices. 'So we thought, How can we hit back?' he told me, with a steely grin. 'We targeted their twelve or so top-selling guides and produced competitive titles for every one. They stopped being so aggressive on pricing.' (Friend, 2005)

But the competition was not only about shares on the budget travel market, but also about the intellectual and ideological predominance in the scene. While *Let's Go* has a policy of exclusively recruiting students from the conservative Harvard University in Massachusetts (*Let's Go*, 2005), a significant number of *Lonely Planet* authors, especially in its early years, graduated from the left-wing, alternative Berkeley University in California – thus, there was also a regional twist to the contest between the North American East and West coasts. The ideological component seems to have decreased, though, and cannot be retraced in the guidebooks, but competitive promotion is still rampant (cf. *Rough Guides*, 2005).

Today, *Lonely Planet* clearly dominates the market for the Australia–Pacific region, in Asia, Africa and Latin America, while *Let's Go* apparently has been able to maintain a slight dominance for Europe and North America, which reflects the fact that the latter is traditionally more in use by North American travellers. An ad hoc survey among bookstall owners in Bangkok's backpacker enclave Khao San Road revealed that *Let's Go* and *The Rough Guides* are catching up, though, even in *Lonely Planet*'s traditional domains in Asia.

Authors, Readers and Service Providers

The vast impact of *Lonely Planet* guidebook recommendations and critique puts the company's authors into responsible positions. Joe Cummings acknowledges that *Lonely Planet* recommendations help channel traveller streams into recently established destinations. For example, he says Khao San Road may not have developed at the speed and to the extent it has had he not included it in the first Thailand edition in the early 1980s (Cummings, 2005a). On the other hand, he rejects claims *Lonely Planet* helped places such as Koh Phangan or Boracay to be 'loved to death' (Richard Bangs of Mountain Travel Sobek, quoted by Friend, 2005) due to having encouraged a massive influx of backpackers.

[The Wheeler's claim] that change is inevitable, that guidebooks don't inspire travel so much as channel it, and that it's better to have educated travellers than clucks on tour buses. (Friend, 2005)

Lonely Planet has also always emphasised their authors' principle of not revealing their identities to accommodation hosts and other service providers. The guidebooks also claim that:

> *Lonely Planet* does not accept advertising in guidebooks, nor do we accept payment in exchange for listing or endorsing any place or business. *Lonely Planet* writers do not accept discounts or payments in exchange for positive coverage of any sort. (e.g. Cummings, 2005b: 13)

However, this policy has been much contested by attentive travellers around the world who claim they have met *Lonely Planet* authors who made no effort whatsoever to hide who they were. Whatever the case, the fact that every *Lonely Planet* guidebook features not only a biography but also a picture of contributing authors makes it rather easy for anyone to recognise them, no matter how hard they may or may not try to keep a low profile. Cummings does not deny that there may be some black sheep among his *Lonely Planet*-contracted colleagues, however the temptation to let oneself be bribed into favourable recommendations is high in times of tightening research schedules and declining royalties amidst frequent efforts by service providers to bribe authors into positive coverage (Cummings, 2005a).

Empirical evidence, though, suggests that while some veteran authors' names are well known among travellers, their faces are not. This enables fraud on the part of the more cheeky backpackers: quite frequent are cases in which travellers swindle themselves into freebies from service providers by pretending to be *Lonely Planet* authors. One traveller, for example, systematically posed as Joe Cummings for months while touring Malaysia, living off freebies and extorted bribes (Cummings 2005a) – despite the fact that Malaysia is not even Cummings' territory.

Not only do some travellers pose as authors to exploit *Lonely Planet*'s market power for their purposes, service providers sometimes pose as travellers for the same reason, misusing the high degree of traveller contributions going into the guidebooks' content (see below). Says Cummings (2005a): 'I've been burned before. The way I've been handling reader suggestions for the last 15 years or so is never to believe anything they say until I check it out for myself. No exceptions.'

Market Power and Responsibility

Still, it is not *Lonely Planet* but the travellers who 'discover' a new destination and make it accessible to others through word-of-mouth. But this means of communication can reach only a relatively exclusive circle of fellow travellers within a short time. Only *Lonely Planet* can open the place up to a large audience, and thus with its inclusion in the guidebook the 'golden hordes' are bound to follow the 'explorers'.

Tony Wheeler is somewhat at a loss over the idea of the 'better tourist' he once ventured out to create. He acknowledges today the role his company has played in promoting the backpacker way of travel and in opening up a widening range of destinations to the at times excessive spin-offs of backpacking (Friend, 2005). Says a protagonist in the cult novel *The Beach*: 'There's no way you can keep it out of the *Lonely Planet*, and once that happens it's countdown to doomsday' (Garland, 1997: 139).

For too long, it seems, the authors only served their customers' needs without observing the interests of the promoted destinations. Joe Cummings admits that on the bottom line, he is more committed to his clientele than to local communities. He does not ask whether a new place or a single service provider wants to be included in a new edition but makes this decision himself – and in the past has done so even against a provider's expressed opposition (Cummings, 2005a). However, *Lonely Planet* authors are very aware of the responsibilities they have to convey:

> I think our books have always been very conscious of fitting in when you travel, and the fact that you have a responsibility towards the places you travel to, whether it's the environment, or the culture of the people who live there. (Wheeler in Fortune Small Business, 2000)

> Although inclusion in a guidebook usually implies a recommendation, we cannot list every good place. Exclusion does not necessarily imply criticism. In fact there are a number of reasons why we might exclude a place – sometimes it is simply inappropriate to encourage an influx of travellers. (Cummings, 2003: 10)

The question is: after having covered even the most peripheral areas, how many 'unspoilt' places are left that have not been 'discovered' by *Lonely Planet* and thus turned into backpacker destinations? Perhaps *Lonely Planet* has woken up a bit too late for this self-critical stance to be entirely plausible.

With their tagline 'a travel survival kit', introduced in the early 1980s and dropped in 1997, *Lonely Planet* guidebooks suggested indispensability and adventure. In a publicity brochure, the company presented itself as 'the most important item of luggage next to toilet paper ...' (1993; quoted in Hutnyk, 1996: 63). To newcomers in particular, the guidebook opens up a destination, telling them about price levels, offering a choice of hostel recommendations, providing orientation with detailed maps in the apparent chaos of Third World cities, and helping them to survive culturally with tips on appropriate behaviour and language sections. *Lonely Planet* guidebooks 'taught a whole generation how to move through the world alone and with confidence' (Friend, 2005) – guidance, literally. An anonymous traveller marvels:

> Tony, I lived, breathed, and followed everything written in your *Lonely Planet* guide for New Zealand. Thank you for making my first solo travel experience so special! ('Miss Issabella–guest' in Fortune Small Business, 2000).

> I think one of the dangers is that some people use books like blueprints. They feel they have to follow the guidebook as if it is a recipe for making a cake. (Wheeler, responding in Fortune Small Business, 2000)

The guidebook provides a sense of security and structure, and in contrast to the constantly transient nature of the backpacker scene, it is the only reliably loyal companion. Like a medical kit, it may in fact rarely be used but always has to be at hand in case of need. Losing one's guidebook in remote places comes close to losing one's orientation. Dave, the main character in the backpacker novel *Are you Experienced?*, is shocked when a fellow traveller throws his 'BOOK' out of a window (an act – see above – that constitutes the facts of blasphemy): 'If you don't have The Book, then you don't know where all the other travellers are. How do you expect to meet up with other travellers?' (Sutcliffe, 1997: 181–182). Without *Lonely Planet*, it can be concluded, many would not have had the courage to go travelling in the first place. Consequently, the use and even possession of a guidebook, which is 'seen as a symbol of the lesser [i.e. inexperienced] traveler' (Sørensen, 2003: 860) by the more 'sophisticated' shoestring travellers, decreases with improving travelling experience.

In her analysis of *Lonely Planet India*, Bhattacharyya advances the thesis that a causal nexus existed between the self-perception of the guidebook as a 'travel survival kit' and the image of India it conveys – a country full of hazards, imponderabilities and bad surprises (Bhattacharyya, 1997: 378). Anderskov (2002) confirms: '. . . in films made by *Lonely Planet* the narrator is almost constantly alone, managing difficult border crossings and being hassled by strange, exotic locals all on his own.' *Lonely Planet*, Bhattacharyya (1997: 376) asserts, fails to disclose that this image is based on constructions:

> The India described to the reader of *LP India* is presented as *the* only India, as a straightforward, self-evident description of reality rather

than as a socially constructed representation. The language of the book never acknowledges that it is moulding and presenting a certain image of India...

A Serbian traveller also criticises this 'wiser than thou' attitude of the guidebooks such as 'Why is our travel information the best in the world? It's simple: our authors are independent, dedicated travellers. ... They personally visit thousands of hotels, restaurants, cafés, bars, galleries, palaces, museums and more – and they take pride in getting all the details right, and telling it how it is.' (e.g. Cummings, 2005b: 18). She says other guidebooks such as *The Rough Guide* present themselves in a more transparent way to the readers, revealing their own subjectivity and thus leaving more room for the travellers to make up their own mind.

The lucky ones in the scene make it into the 'Acknowledgements' section of a *Lonely Planet* guidebook (e.g. Hämäläinen, 1991: 3), which poses as an ersatz 'Walk of Fame' for backpackers. Everybody who has contributed to updating a new edition is granted this honour – a prestige lifter to strengthen their faith in the 'bible'. And the company also benefits from it directly: 'What we publish comes from people who've been there and found out for themselves. Not from glossy travel brochures' (e.g. Wheeler, 1981: 4). This way, *Lonely Planet* presents itself as the prolonged, institutionalised arm of the informal backpacker communication network. Such an advance of credibility is invaluable in a scene that lives in constant distrust of its commercialisation by the tourism industry.

Lonely Planet's monopolisation of the backpacker market is far from settled, and its range of products has increased sharply in recent years: in addition to over 20 different book series covering every corner of the globe and catering to all kinds of special interest travellers (trekkers, divers, cyclists, city enthusiasts, gourmets, wildlife watchers, etc.), Wheeler has started to translate the guidebooks into Spanish, Italian, French, Hebrew and Japanese, in direct competition with non-English publishers such as the *Guide Routard* or *Stefan Loose* off the market. *Lonely Planet* airs its own TV channel as well as a photo-trading agency and has conducted the as yet largest market survey among backpackers. Its homepage counts more than a million hits per day (Gluckman, 1999: 56). In the course of the 1990s, turnover rose by 24% per year to AUS$82 million in 2001 and reached US$72 million in 2004, 'with annual sales of more than six million guidebooks' (Friend, 2005). *Southeast Asia on a Shoestring* is the third-most shoplifted book in Australia

(Cummings, 2005c) – which seems to be a reason for pride rather than embarrassment.

Since more and more backpackers have started taking a taste from the tourist apple and demanding higher-quality goods and services, *Lonely Planet* has been struggling with a redefinition of its target group:

> The books' iconoclastic tone has been muted to cater to richer, fussier sorts of travellers, many of whom, like the Wheelers themselves, fly business class. (Friend, 2005)

Thus, with the takeover of 30% of Lonely Planet Publications by Australian advertising tycoon John Singleton, who brought in his own editors, lawyers and accountants (Friend, 2005) and considers *Lonely Planet* to have 'more potential than any other Australian brand' (at Inside Business, 2005), the guidebooks are now covering more mid-range services than ever and feature a new style rather appealing to conventional tourists, with more colour pages and professional art-house photography; only the 'Shoestring' series still targets mainly budget travellers (Power, 2003). A 'Highlights' section as well as a whole 'Best of' guidebook series have been added, route recommendations, authors' favourites and advertisements. The 'travel survival kit' tagline had already been abolished in 1997; it was decided that its implication of Third World countries being hazardous travel destinations was outdated, Cummings (2005a) says. While this is true, it looks like the measure was rather aimed at *Lonely Planet* shifting its focus to target groups that seek more comfortable and less adventurous travel in the first place. To downsize the books from brick-thick backpack to palm-pleasing handbag dimensions, authors had to slash particularly the sections with background information on country and people. Thus, *Lonely Planet* seems to have given in to mere commercial interests the educational objective that was once one of the outstanding cornerstones of their guidebooks' quality. And although Wheeler forces new members of staff to join authors on update missions so as to appreciate the hard work they are doing (Power, 2003), the impression seems to be of short duration.

Not much has been left from the personal, at times intimate, original style of the early books; the language has been scaled down to the interchangeable, unimaginative drivel of travel writing:

> And so 'palm-fringed beaches' and 'lush rain forests' and other 'sleepy backwaters' are invariably counterpoised against 'teeming cities' with their 'bustling souks.' Every region has a 'colorful history' and a 'rich cultural tapestry.' And every place on earth is a 'land of

contrasts.' As the Arabian Peninsula guide observes, 'Bedouin tribesmen park 4WDs alongside goat hair tents; veiled women chat on mobile phones while awaiting laser hair removal,' and so on. (Friend, 2005)

Friend's *Lonely Planet* doesn't seem to speak to him any more but only indulges in listening to itself. At times, even experienced *Lonely Planet* authors slip into the stereotypical 'primitive-turned-noble savage' rift, such as Joe Cummings (2005b: 4) in the most recent *Thailand* edition: 'Lose yourself in the cool mist of a mountain-top trail trod by post-Stone Age cultures ...'. Thus *Lonely Planet* guidebooks are losing their distinctive, colloquial character. They have lost their ability to serve as a 'travel survival kit' or a 'bosom companion' (Friend, 2005) to the traveller. Wheeler bemoans:

> Those vivid colors of the early books, ... once they get blended with so many other authors and editors and concerns about what the customer wants, they inevitably become gray and bland. (quoted by Friend, 2005)

It has come a long way from the 'small organisation' (Wheeler, 1977: 4) of the 1970s to become 'the world's most successful independent travel information company' (*Lonely Planet*, 2005) with 650 titles in its catalogue (Friend, 2005). Even Joe Cummings, *Lonely Planet* veteran since the early 1980s, is lost for an answer to where expansion might come to an end (Cummings, 2005a). The young editors in Melbourne seem to be eyeing new services: *Lonely Planet* has already ventured beyond just publishing guidebooks, travelogues, pictorials and merchandise; most recently, a hostel booking service has been established on the homepage (Cummings, 2005a). Whether or not these developments call into question the company's much-relished independence and incorruptibility, will have to be answered by Wheeler's heirs, who nowadays seem to be more in control than the founder himself.

Conclusions

And the Wheelers? Where is their place in a glamorous corporation publishing glossy mainstream guidebooks? Tony is *Lonely Planet*'s main stakeholder and icon, the company is unimaginable without him, just as much as Microsoft is unthinkable without Bill Gates. According to Maureen, he is a great visionary and 'wheeler-dealer', but not a good manager; that has rather been her role: '... he was travelling a lot, because he didn't want to deal with [the business]. ... Without Tony,

Lonely Planet wouldn't exist; without me, it wouldn't have held together' (Friend, 2005). Wheeler does not hide that he has always been more interested in travelling than in running his business: 'We are able to let people do the things they want to do, and we are able to do the things we really like to do. And to a large extent, that's travel' (Fortune Small Business, 2000). As a mere icon, he has detached himself from many decisions in Melbourne (Power, 2003). To a certain degree, Wheeler has gone the way of much of his clientele: he flies business class, recommends five-star hotels on his homepage and owns three fancy cars, but moans about the fleet of Mercedes in *Lonely Planet*'s parking garage (Friend, 2005). The countercultural, ideological traveller of the 1970s is still present in his rhetoric, but much of his travelling is contradictory to that, as it is with many modern travellers. He doesn't mingle much with locals any more. He is interested and observative wherever he goes, but he does not talk to anyone, always keeping a distance (Friend, 2005). Nor does he mingle much with modern travellers. They are not what they used to be, and consequently the Wheelers titled their autobiographic *Lonely Planet Story* nostalgically *Once While Travelling* (Wheeler & Wheeler, 2005). 'It's his obsession. He has to go farther than the tourists. And, if there's someone else around that bend, he'll keep going until he's past them, until he's the farthest out' (Maureen, quoted by Friend, 2005).

Note

1.   Wheeler is living in Melbourne and in the best of health.

Chapter 7

Challenging the 'Tourist–Other' Dualism: Gender, Backpackers and the Embodiment of Tourism Research

ERICA WILSON and IRENA ATELJEVIC

Introduction

In an attempt to critically question the structures, power bases and historical stories associated with tourism, some academics are increasingly embracing the deconstructionist discourses offered by postmodernism, poststructuralism and postcolonialism. As it has in leisure studies (Aitchison, 2001), poststructuralism has led to a crisis of sorts in tourism research, though this has happened gradually and with some resistance, and has usually been led by those working outside of tourism theory (such as sociologists, anthropologists, feminists and geographers). Essentially, the poststructuralist project does away with grand theorisations about society and culture, and questions the all-imposing nature of societal and cultural structures on our everyday lives (Coalter, 1997). Examined through a poststructuralist lens, tourism and the tourist experience are unravelled as diverse, complex and pluralistic phenomena. The poststructuralist approach insists that we try to understand social life through a perspective that encompasses 'both–and' rather than 'either–or' (Denzin, 1991), and that we always connect the tourist experience with the wider social, cultural and power structures at play in everyday life (Ateljevic & Doorne, 2005). Uriely (2005) explains that postmodernist and poststructuralist forms of theorising 'are associated with a variety of characteristics, including deconstruction, subjectivity, skepticism, anti-empiricism, intertextuality, and relativity' (Uriely, 2005: 200–201).

Reflecting this wider postmodern shift, and underpinned by the broader 'crisis of representation' within the social sciences (Denzin &

Lincoln, 2003; Marcus & Fisher, 1986), tourism academics are building a new body of knowledge that provides space for more interpretative and critical modes of inquiry (Phillimore & Goodson, 2004). As Tribe (2005: 5) points out, 'the totality of tourism studies has now developed beyond the narrow boundaries of an applied business field and has the characteristics of a fledgling postmodern field of research' creating the wave of 'new' tourism research. This shift in thought has been labelled as a 'critical turn' in tourism studies (Ateljevic *et al.*, 2005), and represents a notable move towards deconstructing the cultural politics of research and knowledge-making in tourism academia. It is within this emerging critical school of tourism studies that this chapter is positioned.

Within this new poststructuralist configuration of the tourist experience, fixed typologies, segmentations and grand theorisations about backpacker travel do not hold as much power as they once did (Ateljevic & Doorne, 2004; Hottola, 1999; Uriely, 2005). The backpacker phenomenon has not escaped the critical eyes of poststructuralism, in addition to other deconstructionist forms of inquiry such as feminism, race studies and new cultural studies. In an attempt to understand tourist and backpacker experience, researchers have focussed to a large extent on either classifying tourists or understanding their motivations (Ateljevic & Doorne, 2004). A noticeable shift can be detected over the last two decades with regard to the way backpacker tourism has been investigated. Ateljevic and Doorne (2004) demonstrate that backpacker inquiry has moved from being purely viewed as a demarketing concept through to an emphasis on market segmentation and motivation, and then again to those studies that explore associated issues of cultural and economic development. This proliferation of research interests 'has in recent years produced new discourses of hybridity, informed by broader theoretical perspectives outside of the now "traditional" focus of tourism studies literature' (Ateljevic & Doorne, 2004: 61). Indeed, we would argue that our understanding of backpacker tourism has been broadened and deepened with these emerging critical reinterpretations, and welcome a more hybrid, postmodern and qualitative arena in which to study the complexities of backpacker travel.

Taking a poststructuralist approach, this chapter focuses on backpacker travel as an embodied, gendered experience and aims more widely to challenge a number of assumed dualisms surrounding the tourist experience. We begin with an overview of the core theoretical trajectories that have developed in analyses of the 'body' in tourism, followed by a history of women's independent travel and a review of backpacker studies with relation to gender. Finally, and more central to the key thrust of this chapter, we present a poststructural discussion (rather than empirical results) of our field experiences with female backpackers. It should be noted that the discussion in this chapter is not drawn from results of one empirical study, but rather employs a feminist collaborative methodology of two female authors who conducted a number of research projects with female backpackers and independent travellers in Australia, New Zealand, China and Fiji, over the course of six years (1998–2004). Examples from the female backpackers' stories demonstrate that their travel experiences cannot be separated from the realm of the body, or from the arena of their everyday lives and social–cultural structures. Their stories show individual resistance against forms of power that pervade their everyday and tourist lives, challenging traditional dichotomous conceptions of the tourism experience, particularly the dualism of 'tourist' and 'Other'. The poststructural focus on the self as being subjected to control whilst allowing for self-knowledge (Foucault, 1980) reveals the perpetual process of human becoming (Grosz, 1995) – that is the self is 'a work in progress'. A step beyond dualisms offers the conceptual advancement of 'third space thinking' to capture the complexity of plural meanings, multiple subjectivities and lived experiences.

Embodying Tourism Research

The relationships among tourists, their bodies and the places they visit have recently forged a more coherent path in poststructural analyses of tourism. As part of this deconstruction of tourism, the use of tourist space and the tourist experience, the complexities of gender, race, class and ethnicity can no longer remain invisible on the tourism research agenda. Those writing under the banners of 'new' tourism, feminist human geography and cultural studies have argued that spaces and places are social as well as physical constructions, shaped by the complexities of gender, race, culture and history. Work by cultural and feminist geographers suggests that travel destinations are not empty stages or places on which people merely perform and act out tourist behaviours (Crouch, 2000). If travel destinations are viewed as embodied 'spaces', imbued with time, sensuous, feeling bodies and emotion, then no longer are destinations static places to which people travel and then return from (Crouch, 2000). Essentially, the embodiment of tourism moves us beyond the fixation with the tourist 'gaze' and the objective sightseeing of the flaneur (Urry, 1990), and insists that we reflect on the 'being, doing, touch *and* seeing' of tourism (Crouch & Desforges, 2003: 7, emphasis in original).

The recognition of 'the body' – beyond the passive nature of the tourist gaze (Urry, 1990) – has created three main theoretical concerns in tourism studies. Firstly, the realisation of 'the body' has introduced sensitivities and a sensuous awareness in the context of experiencing places and 'the doing' of tourism. Secondly, 'the body' also has been discussed in the context of representation in which culture is inscribed and with it power and ideology are given spatial reference. Here the body defines the limits of subjectivities, identities and practices of encountering the world as discursive experience. Lastly, we can observe the interiority of authoring in the reflexive situating of critical perspectives, which seek to encounter the very essence of subjectivity itself.

It was, of course, Veijola and Jokinen (1994) who, more than a decade ago, brought the body firmly to the research agenda by accusing tourism studies as having 'no body'. By this, they meant a lack of the subjective and personal voice in tourism research, and a reliance on essentialist and unchanging characteristics of the tourist experience. In an innovative and inventive shift, which fully embraced a feminist preference for challenging traditional academic writing styles, these two female researchers took an imagined vacation and held conversations with a number of eminent male tourism researchers. They made the claim that early tourism researchers, such as MacCannell (1976), Urry (1990) and Krippendorf (1987), had ignored the 'body' of the tourist in their studies, focusing on the host as the objectified 'other'. Veijola and Jokinen also noted the lack of the body in methodology, where researchers were positioned as objective, nameless and genderless writers. The authors further concluded that only through a feminised, gendered approach to the entire tourism research process can the body be fully integrated and acknowledged.

These dimensions of embodiment have been discussed through metaphorical mobilisations of performance and encounter. For example, Edensor (1998, 2000) introduced an extensive account of the tourist performance metaphor, examining the diverse enactments that centre upon the Taj Mahal stage. He contends that 'tourism is a process which involves the ongoing (re)construction of praxis ... [whereby] the whole of social life can be considered as performative' (Edensor, 2000: 322). Similarly, Franklin and Crang (2001: 17–18) claim that 'the cultural competencies and required skills that make up tourist cultures themselves suggest a "Goffmanesque" where all of the world is indeed a stage'. Coleman and Crang's (2002) edited volume represents an extensive collection of seeing tourism as embodied and performed engagement with places, and demonstrates the mutual entanglement of practices, images, conventions and creativity.

Crouch (1999) and Crouch *et al*. (2001) use the idea of embodied practice through the metaphor of the encounter, a process whereby:

> The subject actively plays an imaginative, reflexive role, not detached but semi-attached, socialised, crowded with contexts ... [as] the subject bends, turns, lifts and moves in often awkward ways that do not participate in a framing of space, but in complexity of multi-sensual surfaces that the embodied subject reaches or finds in proximity and makes sense of imaginatively. (Crouch, 1999: 12)

The process mixes the elements of spatiality, subjectivities, gender, race, class with emotional dimensions of humans as poetic beings. Rather than these aspects of encounters informing a process of framing place as per the tourist gaze, the process of negotiating 'the sense of the world' takes place through refractions in which '[t]he subject mixes this with recalled spaces of different temporality' (Crouch, 1999: 12). The argument is that this discussion of embodiment and creation of the knowledge of the world cannot be separated from notions of power/ideology and the micropolitics of cultural negotiation.

Gender, Backpacker Travel and Problems with 'Othering'

The above overview has demonstrated the pressing need to challenge the perceived neutrality of disembodied constructions of tourism knowledge (Aitchison, 2001, 2003; Johnston, 2001; Veijola & Jokinen, 1994). Margaret Swain (2004) links the dual project of embodiment to its feminist influences. In doing so, she raises questions about the 'perceived neutrality' of what has been predominantly Western, masculinised knowledge about the tourist experience. From a feminist/gendered perspective, Wearing (1996: 80) refers to embodiment as:

> the values, perceptions and gestures that are inscribed in and through the body and how we live these experiences through our bodies as men and women. Thus the body is engendered – inscribed with gender specific meanings that reflect the social, cultural, economic and political milieu of its experience.

Gendered studies of tourism and backpacker travel tend to remain focused on sociostructural aspects as they apply to 'women', such as constraints faced during the travel experience (Westerhausen, 1997;

Wilson & Little, 2005), or their motivations and benefits (Elsrud, 1998; McGehee *et al.*, 1996). Whilst these contributions are not in dispute, and the structures that constrain women are still acknowledged, we take discussions further to use the backpacker travel of women as an ideal context in which to tease out broader issues of the current academic/ political agenda in tourism studies. Specifically, we are interested in raising awareness of the fact that feminist approaches are not primarily about inequities and inequalities between men and women, where the focus is on issues of 'women'. A significant advance of the poststructuralist argument is the potential of moving beyond the view of underrepresentation, victimisation or marginalisation of women (e.g. Davies & Bradbery, 1999; Marshment, 1997), which, while acknowledged, often merely perpetuates the unhelpful dualistic process of 'Othering'. Othering is a postmodern, poststructural concept that recognises the positioning of people in terms of their opposition to others, and relies largely on binary social and cultural divisions; for example, man/woman, black/ white, us/them, host/guest, powerful/powerless. Rose (1995: 16) defines Othering as 'defining where you belong through a contrast with other places, or who you are through a contrast with other people', which inexorably entails the power relations of domination and subordination, centre and periphery, etc. In other words, the structuralist argument of marginalisation and/or victimisation of women, or the commodification of the 'Other', give power to seemingly neutral phallocentric practices and bodily discourses in which there is always a centre against which others (women, 'natives', etc.) are positioned and evaluated.

Pritchard and Morgan (2000a; 2000b) take a poststructural approach to introduce the concept of a male tourism landscape, which implies a historical perpetuation of the heterosexual, white, male gaze that is sustained by the construction of the 'Other'. In doing so, they challenge the universality of 'Western subject and experience' and reveal the human characteristics and cultural values of the powerful structural forces that continue to be reproduced by deeply embedded stereotypes and social norms. Aitchison (2001) and Ateljevic and Harris (2005) have accused critical tourism studies (of which they themselves are a part) as being an 'Otherness machine'. In doing so, these authors have challenged both the authority of white feminist theorising as well as the masculinity of postcolonial theory. Indeed, tourism studies seem to have been affected with a preoccupation with representing the exotic Other, as well as offering authoritarian theories on 'other' landscapes, destinations and sights (Aitchison, 2001). Conceptualisations of the mass tourist experience have traditionally relied upon on a separation between 'host' and 'guest'. Tourists were fashioned as the wealthy elite, in search of 'authentic' cultures, peoples and artefacts that they could claim as a form of cultural capital upon returning home. In this scenario, 'hosts' (normally depicted as those from less developed countries) existed only as an authentic backdrop to a 'destination', placed there for the tourists' convenience, and interactions were limited between the two groups. In the tourist–Other dichotomy, power rests with the tourist, while the 'Others' are constructed as powerless or disenfranchised.

'New' forms of tourism, such as ecotourism, cultural tourism and backpacker travel claim to forge a bridge over the tourist–Other chasm. In these forms of alternative travel, there is a recognition that tourists may actually desire a closer interaction with 'hosts', and may even wish to learn something from the cultures they visit. At the same time, backpackers have also been discussed in pessimistic terms due to their potential for penetrating too deeply into culture of the 'primitive Other', and have been blamed for closing out higher-end, more lucrative tourism development and income in developing countries (Cohen, 1989b; Smith, 1990). Maoz (2004) discusses how Israeli backpackers demonstrate an attitude of patriotism and disrespect toward the 'Other' in India, who are positioned as 'inferior' by the Israeli travellers. No matter how they are studied, backpackers still seem to remain essentialised into a position of power over the 'Other', and rarely are the hosts' voices and experiences heard. Still there exists a sense of distance and separation from local people, rather than a focus on the ways in which local people and tourists may negotiate to realise their sameness, rather than always emphasise their difference. The structuralist argument of having and exercising the power *over* someone or something is challenged by opening a space for the recognition of individual resistance and subjects' self-knowledge and agency (Foucault, 1980).

Therefore, it is argued in this chapter that a combination of a feminised, embodied and poststructural approach to tourism and back-packer studies is crucial as it forces us to look beyond essentialised categories, binaries and dualisms. It allows us to look at the ever-changing friction and relationship between 'host' and 'guest' (and even to move beyond such divisive terms), as well as the circulatory power shifts that can happen within the tourist–Other dichotomy. According to Aitchison (2005: 31), a poststructuralist perspective, despite its faults, can help us move beyond the 'unhelpful rigidity' of such dualisms:

> Tourist destinations and tourism hosts are represented as pure and authentic rather than being viewed as constantly evolving places and

people with changing characteristics resulting from the mutually informing process of productive consumption derived that that in-betweenness of global and local, tourist and host.

The tourist–Other dualism is questioned and deconstructed in the following section, using female backpackers'/independent travellers' experiences as an example. We aim to locate these women travellers as active and embodied participants in, and consumers of, the travel experience. We glean our insights on the female backpacker experience from years of conversations, interviews, observations and from our own experiences as 'solo' female tourists. The informed insights and 'find-ings' are integrated into an analytical discussion and only a few quotes are presented to illustrate key points. As such, we clearly position ourselves as embodied authors of this chapter, to which we bring our own experiences and travels as women. Furthermore, during our various research projects and interviews, our position as women (and women who have travelled) allowed us access to the women's lives, where we were able to establish trust, rapport and some level of a 'shared experience'.

Two themes of the female backpacker/tourist experience are analysed to demonstrate the problems with simple and disembodied divisions between 'tourist' and 'Other'. Firstly, the concept of cultural capital is critiqued in terms of its relevance for the women backpackers with whom we spoke. Secondly, the tourist–Other division is minimised through a demonstration of the meaningful, equal and long-lasting relationships that many of the women had with their so-called 'hosts', enabling them to feel a sense of universal sameness with the people they met, rather than only a sense of difference.

Challenging the 'Tourist–Other' Binary

Over the last decade, backpacker travel has appeared in the literature as representative of a travel lifestyle, an expression of consumer identity, as well as a coherent cultural form and industrial complex (Ateljevic & Doorne, 2001; Richards & Wilson, 2004a). Backpacker travel research has drawn on the binaries of core and periphery, alternative traveller and mainstream tourist, authentic and inauthentic. The obsession with the periphery in backpacker travel is often bound to the collection and appropriation of identities of the 'exotic Other', through touristic commodities, experiences and stories that collectively lead to the reconstitution of embodied identity. Desforges (1998), for example, explores the notion of consumer identity through the practice of 'collecting places', as a way in which travellers relate to the 'Other'. With respect to perceived 'authenticity', he identifies its markers as the absence of the travel industry and other tourists. Drawing on Bourdieu (1984), Desforges discusses travel as a form of cultural capital, which serves as a sign of distinction and enables the traveller to gain access to elevated social classes both during and following the travel experience. In these ways, cultural capital is viewed almost as a negative, or something that further separates the power/class differential between tourist and 'Other'.

Ateljevic and Doorne (2004) argue that production and consumption often become blurred as producers consume their own cultural contexts and take a role in reproducing and performing their roles as 'exotic other'. Through their case study of Dali in China, Ateljevic and Doorne (2005) revealed a common ground in the production–consumption dialectic, by demonstrating the power that entrepreneurs had in commodifying aspects of their lives for backpacker tourists' consumption. In this way, power happens more on a fluid, negotiated and changing spectrum, rather than on a simple binary that elevates the power of the tourists and disempowers the host. The resistance to the globalised tourism complex and discourses of difference is reflected in the internal transformation of self and the mutual constitution of human relations. This perpetual process of becoming is affected by either the creation of meaningful relationships between 'tourists' and 'host' or casual but very memorable encounters, hence blurring the distinction between the two groups.

While the search for 'exotic other' and 'authentic self' were indeed motivations for many of the women backpackers with whom we spoke, their collective stories did not seem to fit neatly with the acquisition of cultural capital. Upon returning home from their overseas travels, rather than feel they could impress and regale others with stories of their trips, many women found those at home were uninterested in their newfound sense of identity or increased cultural awareness:

> Nobody was even taking the slightest bit of attention, like, other than saying a disinterested, 'oh, so how was your trip? Good, now, I've got new curtains and let me tell you about my new curtains'. (Dee, 40)

> Often your friends don't really want to hear about your travels when you come back. (Karen, 62)

> When I said to people at work that I had been to Vietnam they were
> kind of horrified, like 'why on earth would you want to go there?'
> They just couldn't understand it. (Sarah, 32)

While a 'consumption' of other cultures and countries did lead to
increased confidence and a renewed sense of self and identity for many
of the female backpackers, they were also forced to rethink their own
values and assumptions about the world. Chris, a 45-year-old solo
woman traveller who had spent time living and working in Ethiopia and
Kenya during the hunger crises of the 1980s, wrote the following in one
of her travel reflections:

> I don't think you always like the things you find out through travel
> ... I was really conscious of feeling like I was eating too much ...
> like I was surrounded by people in famine and refugee camps and I
> mean, I think I was eating more than I normally would because –
> probably because of the stress, and it kind of was all focused around
> food ... the scarcity of it and how difficult it was to get it ... and I
> was really conscious of something in me that sort of seemed
> incredibly greedy and mean. That sort of surprised me ... I think
> you learn as many good things about yourself as bad things, though.
> I think the trip that I did in Africa was life-changing, but it was also
> quite devastating in its way, because of some of the things that I saw
> and had to deal with ... growing up in Australia I don't think
> anything prepares you for what a famine is like, and the ... one of
> things about that kind of travel and work ... I think is that you're in
> and out of it, it's not like it's an experience you go through – it's like
> you're sort of dropped in it and then pulled out of it again, and that's
> sort of very difficult to reconcile.

This excerpt was from an interview with Chris almost 20 years after
her travels in Africa, yet the experience still haunts her as she struggles
today to reconcile what she saw and felt. For Chris, her experiences in
Africa were bodily reactions, as much as they were mental ones, as the
act of eating and consuming food became an increasingly socially and
politically uncomfortable behaviour. She became aware of her Western
lifestyle, overconsumption of food, and staying in hotels that seemed
strangely removed from the realities of what she witnessed outside.
Hardly a story of acquiring cultural capital or searching out the 'exotic
other', Chris's story demonstrates the deep unsettling that can come
through travel and through a building of identity. Her story also reveals
the physical and mental reaction that people can have to their travel, and

how this can spark a lifelong process of questioning and criticism of dominant discourse and Western systems of power and inequality. Chris was extremely aware of her cultural and political role as a Western tourist, and of the situations that had led to the starvation of these people, and this extended into her desire to work with disadvantaged people upon returning home to Australia. Essentially, this story serves to demonstrate the long-lasting physical and mental impacts of travel, and renders the tourist–other binary unworkable in that it questions the mere consumption of 'Other'; the travel experience becomes a huma-nised, embodied process.

Construed as a way of acquiring status and identity (Desforges, 1998), cultural capital becomes much too simplistic a notion when viewed from an embodied, gendered perspective. As a concept, it does not seem to address the difficulties women and other travellers face when confronted with the 'Other' and with different ways of life. Rather than merely lead to a renewed sense of identity and self-esteem, much of what these women saw and experienced was challenging and forced them to question themselves and their material lifestyles; transition was not easy, and cultural capital from the 'exotic Other' was not so easily gained. Individual agency was exercised through social interactions and perfor-mative life in which 'a work in progress' on themselves and others was recognised. The continuous uncertainty of 'who am I?' and 'what have I come to see?' is expressed in the simultaneous and paradoxical interplay of ethical discomfort and romanticisation of the 'exotic Other'.

The female backpackers were aware of their difference and were sensitive to cultural mores for women in other countries. Most were conscious of their difference as white, Western women travellers, and were very aware of their bodies and the cultural representations their bodies might effect. For the most part, it was apparent that these women were concerned about the people they were visiting, aware of their impacts as tourists and sensitive to the complex power and gendered relations in the countries through which they travelled. They were also cognisant of the social, cultural and spatial limitations placed on them as solo female travellers. At the same time, however, they needed to find ways to negotiate so as to make the most of their travel experiences. So, while the social and cultural constraints of the destinations inhibited the women's travel behaviour in terms of preventing the freedom of movement or creating fear for personal safety, these power boundaries were continuously recognised and negotiated.

With a constant shifting in positions of power between the women and the people they met, there evolves a mutually informed process of learning from one another. Often feeling pessimistic about the economics and lifestyle of the West and overwhelmed by 'corporate' culture and alienation of their own society, the social encounters were used as a form of nostalgia, seeking the reassurance of traditional lifestyles, the personal human touch and a 'direct contact with nature and the Universe'. Addressing the conflicting ethical questions of sense of guilt for luxury of their comfortable lives back home whilst simultaneously feeling oppressed by an intrinsically dehumanised lifestyle, the boundaries became arbitrary and thus learning was reciprocal. As one female backpacker expressed:

> I didn't know it's such a great variety of people and races here and then I always kind of admire that I can feel the happy attitude towards life where you don't worry too much or you just enjoy what you have and you know, your family and all that, that connects especially with these villages where it's a really strong bond ... I thought that's something that more people should kind of learn about, because I think when we're living in the city, we kind of lose reality in a way that we are not in touch with our surroundings and neighbours and people who we encounter everyday. (Rae, 32)

When moving beyond the gaze of viewing locals as primarily culturally different, the power networks of stereotypes were reconfigured for these women and the connections of a sense of universal humanity at the individual level were sought and often found. Once the social and cultural boundaries of norms and traditions are deconstructed against this individual humanity, the universal communication of understanding the nature of human existence could be achieved:

> I've travelled in all these different countries on my own, and I've met all these different people from different nationalities, and what I realised at the end of the day was every human being has the same issues to deal with. No matter where they come from, no matter what their upbringing, no matter what the structure of society is, their culture ... every single human being ends up with the same issues. (Dianne, 49)

> Not uncomfortable in a bad way ... only slightly uncomfortable because the experience is new ... the situation you were in ... like the church service ... we didn't really know when to stand up or sit down ... you know ... you were uncomfortable in that sense but you didn't know what to do and you didn't know what their customs

were and that … but not made uncomfortable by people … locals. (Michelle, 28)

One thing I learned about is that human beings-it's not that we are so different, it's interesting that we are so alike – especially women. I'd almost say that the cultural differences are superficial. … I think sometimes the cultural differences are sort of like the accessories of life, but the heart is that we are all human – it's just those accessories that make us look a little different. … We're more alike than we are different. (Tara, 55)

It just took me on just a huge growth curve. It just expanded my horizons, changed my belief systems and made me be more flexible toward, and more tolerant I think, towards other races and understand for what it is like for people, for strangers, to come into a land. I would have much more sympathy, empathy and hospitality. (Alison, 45)

To summarise the above discussion, backpacker travel for these women is an embodied interaction, in which both parties (hosts and guests) can be equally powerful and share the meanings of their lives with each other on an equal basis. In stating this, we do not mean to suggest that economic, social and political differences do not exist between Western tourists and locals in less developed countries, nor that 'host' and 'guest' are always on an equal footing. Like the female backpackers we interviewed, we do indeed recognise the disadvantages that many in the less developed world face in terms of accessing equal rights to power and basic human needs. What we *are* saying is that the 'difference' is often far too heavily emphasised in the backpacker travel experience, and that the relationship between 'tourist' and 'Other' should be discussed in terms of its dynamism, fluidity and shifting power relations. We present a picture whereby both tourists and local people walk away from their interactions learning something new about each other, or about the way their (not so opposite) worlds operate. For many of the women to whom we spoke, often these interactions produce friendships that lasted a long time. Mementos were swapped and letters were written that both host and guest would keep and attach an emotional connection to for the rest of their lives. Their interactions with the so-called 'Other' were not easily forgotten, and were brought into women's everyday lives to become part of their future selves. Physical travel to visit other places and cultures becomes part of their perpetual journeys of becoming, empowering their corporeal sense of being to resist the dominant power discourses on how to perceive self and other.

Conclusions

While the Othering of women and marginalised groups has been a central platform of poststructuralist studies (de Beauvoir, 1989) and has helped to delineate male/white/heterosexual power and control over others, as a concept it has come under debate from feminists and poststructuralists alike for its over-reliance on binary divisions and all-imposing societal structures. White Western feminists have been accused of focussing too much on speaking for and about others, rather than letting others speak for themselves (hooks, 1990). At the same time, there are also those who worry that an over-focus on poststructuralism means that we run the risk of ignoring structures and women's oppression altogether, which in effect further cements men's power to reproduce a malestream account of society (Harstock, 1990). Therefore, some balance needs to be struck between recognising the constraints of Othering and marginalisation and an acknowledgement of individual power to resist and negotiate. Responding to these critiques, Aitchison (2001) offers the useful conceptualisation of the 'social–cultural nexus' in studies of leisure and tourism. The social–cultural nexus merges the common concerns of feminism and poststructuralism, ensuring that we engage with collective cultural theories of leisure and tourist behaviour without neglecting the power of societal structures on the individual. The social–cultural nexus remains particularly important for feminist and gendered analyses of tourism and backpacker travel, in that it recognises the limitations and constraints associated with women's travel at the same time as demonstrating their power and ability for resistance within the dominant culture(s) both at home and away. As Aitchison (2001: 134) argues:

> Post-structuralism's emphasis on social criticism as contextually, temporally, and locally specific negates theories of power as system phenomena. With no systemic power relations there can be no overall system of domination and oppression, only specific contexts of subordination, resistance and transformation.

Through this statement, Aitchison (2001: 44) highlights that post-structural and postcolonial feminist critiques will move us forward from essentialising discourses 'in acknowledging both the structural and cultural power relationships (re)created and/or (re)negotiated through tourism'.

Leading on from this, then, tourism research should not only be concerned with the physical movement and economic impact of people travelling from home to destination and back again, as it is also a sociopsychological phenomenon through which people find meaning, change and self-expression (Bruner, 1991; Leiper, 2003; Noy, 2004a; Pearce, 1993). Squire (1994: 198) noted that 'tourism is a subjective experience linked to special moments in people's lives but it is also tied to wider social and cultural trends'. We argue here that it is no longer possible or accurate to differentiate between tourism life and everyday life, or to construct tourism as something that happens only when a person leaves home and lands in another country. Uriely (2005) refers to this as the 'de-differentiating' of the tourist experience. In true post-modern style, Lash and Urry (1994) called this turning point in thought the 'end of tourism'.

Through its examination of the women's narratives, bringing 'the body' into tourism discourse lead us towards a more complex, integrative and less restrictive understanding of the backpacker travel phenomenon. Mobilising the body does not suggest that it simply becomes an elementary adjunct to understanding what the tourist does; rather, the body 'emerges as a central feature in developing the larger cultural questions in tourist studies concerning identity and power, and in the larger world of contemporary cultures and their geographies' (Crouch & Desforges, 2003: 19). Critical work on embodi-ment focuses not only on the tourist, but also on us as tourism researchers and authors who have been traditionally 'concealed' by claims of scientific objectivity. Veijola and Jokinen (1994: 149, emphasis added) have led the way in this reflexive debate, claiming that 'the tourist has lacked a body because the analyses have tended to concentrate on the gaze and/or structures and dynamics of waged labor societies ... Furthermore ... the analyst *himself* has, likewise, lacked a body'. Through our analysis in this chapter, we rapidly realised that the focus of our attentions and relationship with research participants was driven by the fact that their interpretation resonates with our own understanding. Our analysis in this sense represents a reflexive relation-ship with research participants and thus the use of pronouns 'them and their' becomes also 'us and ours'.

In conclusion, we argue that the prevailing political, economic and sociocultural environment remains a core context for both the manifesta-tion of backpacker tourism and the continued evolution of research perspectives. We argue that while research on women's travel is much overdue, the results in and of themselves cannot be divorced from the broader social, cultural and gendered landscapes of both home and abroad. Researchers working in this gender-aware age (Kinnaird & Hall, 2000) must continue to argue the point that studies about women are never *only* studies about women, nor are they only relevant to women (Deem, 1999; Henderson, 1994). Explorations of women's experiences must always be related back to the broader sociocultural milieu, and the potential of the work to better understanding social complexities *as a whole* must be emphasised. Embodied accounts of tourism move us one step closer to this wider understanding of tourism and the backpacker experience, and the relevance of an embodied approach is that it 'may inform all qualitative tourism research in useful ways, not just feminist research' (Swain, 2004: 115).

The poststructural/postfeminist perspective gives us the opportunity to engage with subtle norms and values shaping our cultures in the process of which the normalised discourse of dehumanisation and 'un-bridging cultural differences' can be revealed. The traditional dualistic conceptions of mind/body, home/away, work/leisure, self/other need to be deconstructed in order to reveal that they lead to limiting and suffering of *both* men and women under the global discourses of fear, stereotyping and alienation.

Part 2

Profiling Backpacker Tourism

Chapter 8

'Van Tour' and 'Doing a Contiki': Grand 'Backpacker' Tours of Europe

JUDE WILSON, DAVID FISHER and KEVIN MOORE

Introduction

It is commonly accepted that the 'drifters' of 30 years ago described by Cohen (1973) have become 'backpackers' as they have moved from the periphery to become an important component of mainstream tourism. A corresponding change occurred in the way this group was understood in the tourism literature as the focus switched from discussions of marginal behaviours to a need for researchers to understand more about what has become an attractive market for the tourism industry (Ateljevic & Doorne, 2004). For the backpackers themselves there appears to be an increasing gap between the ideology and practice of backpacking (Cohen, 2004). The ideology of the backpacker might still be epitomised by notions of freedom and mobility and yet the reality often describes travellers collected together in the enclaves of Khao San Rd in Bangkok or King's Cross in Sydney (Cohen, 2004; Loker, 1994; Loker-Murphy & Pearce, 1995; Richards & Wilson, 2004a; Scheyvens, 2002), or those travelling on organised backpacker travel networks such as the *Kiwi Experience* in New Zealand (Moran, 1999; Vance, 2004). Indeed, one could be forgiven for thinking that the only destinations attracting backpackers are either the 'exotic' locations in Asia, South America and occasionally Africa (Sørensen, 2003) or those countries found 'down under' such as Australia and New Zealand (Loker, 1994; Loker-Murphy & Pearce, 1995; Newlands, 2004; Riley, 1988).

The need to research a wider geographic diversity of destinations and backpacker contexts has been recognised as an area of concern in backpacker studies (Richards & Wilson, 2004b). While a range of studies and market reports have variously addressed the 'youth' or the 'student'

113

travel market, most have considered Europe as a *source* of outbound backpacker travellers and not as a destination *per se*. The 'global' nomad survey reported some European travel by European backpackers; this travel was seen as a precursor to gaining travel experience before moving up a travel career ladder (Pearce, 1993) to visit more exotic locations (Richards & Wilson, 2003). Another large body of work looks at the experiences of Israeli backpackers but, again, few of these involve travel in Europe (see, for example, Maoz, 2004; Noy, 2004a; Uriely *et al.*, 2002). With the exception of a study of the future travel intentions of New Zealand students by Chadee and Cutler (1996), one group of travellers that has, thus far, been mostly ignored in youth, student and backpacker studies is 'outbound' Australasian backpackers. This chapter addresses backpacker tourism in Europe, an important destination for several reasons: first, Europe is where backpacker tourism originated; and second, European destinations continue to attract many thousands of backpackers.

For decades there has been a tradition of young New Zealanders and Australians going to Britain and Europe on extended travel trips. In New Zealand such an experience is called the 'OE' (sometimes the 'Big OE'), a trip of extended duration that usually involves living, working and travelling outside New Zealand for a number of years. Investigation of the OE offers a unique opportunity to trace some of the changes in backpacker travel over time as practised and experienced by a specific group (or nationality) of travellers. With its focus on Europe, an exploration of OE travel also adds to the geographic diversity of destinations studied. Also, while the numbers of New Zealand back-packers might be small on a global scale, this belies their significance to backpacker tourism research. The OE has been directly responsible for the establishment of some of today's 'global' travel companies; many others owe their continuing operation to the OE for the regular source of clientele it provides. Also, as one of the first examples of a 'working holiday', the New Zealand OE remains a forerunner of trends in backpacker travel. OE travel is an integral – and therefore difficult to isolate – part of the broader experiences of the working holiday, a phenomenon that is increasing on a worldwide scale.

This raises the question of whether the 'working holidaymaker', the 'backpacker' and the 'OE participant' are one and the same. While it is beyond the scope of this chapter to engage in an extended conceptual debate, we suggest that just as there are differences between 'types' of backpackers, so too do working holidaymakers vary. OE participants can only be 'categorically' described as backpackers whilst they are engaged in travel episodes; they are *sometimes* a working holidaymaker and *sometimes* a backpacker. This differs from the position taken by other studies. Clarke (2004; 2005), for example, appears to have considered working holidaymakers in Australia to be backpackers throughout their entire trip. The difference may be that, compared to New Zealanders on OE, working holidaymakers in Australia are on shorter trips and remain much more within the 'structured' backpacker industry.

To understand the travel behaviour of any group, the contexts within which it occurs – historical, temporal, global, social, cultural, institutional, spatial – are important. In spite of political, social and institutional changes in tourism over time, OE travellers still follow the same routes and travel patterns they have for decades; yet in many ways their experiences *have* changed over time. This chapter explores these travel patterns and the changes within them, focusing on two iconic travel experiences of the OE, the 'van tour' and 'doing a Contiki'. To begin, in order to 'situate' OE travel, two contexts are necessary; first an OE 'background', then a brief review of backpacker tourism.

The 'OE'

As with 'backpacker', there is no definitive understanding of what an 'OE' is. The acronym 'OE' has been in use since the mid-1970s and stands for 'overseas experience'. Interestingly, while young Australians engage in very similar travel experiences they do not 'name' theirs in the same way. Over time the OE has become a part of New Zealand culture and is seen as an iconic New Zealand experience (albeit one that occurs outside New Zealand). Bell (2002: 143), for example, described the OE as a 'young adult's rite of passage or a "coming of age" ritual'. The OE began in the 1960s and really 'took off' (in terms of the numbers going) in the 1970s as a result of social and technological changes. The 1970s was a decade characterised by a large volume of emigration from New Zealand as the birth cohort produced by the 'baby boom' were passing through the most migratory-prone phase of the life span (Heenan, 1979). Social changes, along with delayed marriage and childbearing, also brought increasing freedom for women (McGill, 1989). New Zealand at this time had a high standard of living and this, coupled with the advent of more frequent air services, made overseas travel more affordable (McCarter, 2001).

Geographical isolation is cited as a determinant of travel for most young New Zealanders going on an OE. New Zealand's remoteness has, for many years, engendered a need in its population to see the 'rest of the world' (see, for example, Mulgan, 1984; Sinclair, 1961; Stead, 1961). This remoteness also makes travel more difficult; the distance that needs to be travelled to 'get away' from New Zealand is much further than for the majority of the world's population, making it more expensive. This, when coupled with a traditionally weak currency (by Western standards), makes long-term travel viable only if one can live and work overseas. The availability of working holiday visas facilitates this, and New Zealand's historical and ancestral links to Britain are important. Over time a tradition of travel to London became established. While in the 1960s London was the 'swinging capital of the world', for much of the world's youth it had also become 'the centre of the Pakeha[1] world' (Easthope, 1993: 20). The Earls Court area of London became the gathering place for young Australians and New Zealanders as working sojourns interspersed with continental travel became popular.

Today, with easily affordable and more convenient travel options available, many more New Zealanders travel, although it is difficult to estimate how many go on an OE, as migration figures are inconsistent and the OE itself is poorly defined. Investigation of governmental migration statistics and working holiday visa issues (along with anecdotal evidence) suggests that there has been a regularly departing OE population of around 15,000–20,000/year since the 1970s. Not all of these return permanently to New Zealand and in 2004 the number of New Zealanders 'living' in London was estimated to be between 100,000 and 200,000.[2] This expatriate population has spread well beyond the boundaries of Earls Court and is supported by its own infrastructure. For OE travellers there are specialised travel agencies, companies offering travel insurance and visa services, numerous travel-focused media publications, along with websites that advertise tours, 'match' travel companions and offer travel forums and advice.

From 'Drifters' in Europe to 'Backpackers' in Asia

The development of the OE coincided with the growth in travel of all types of tourists and facets of the tourism industry. Because of their age and the length of time they are away, those on OE can be likened to Cohen's (1973) 'drifters', Riley's (1988) 'long-term budget travellers' and Pearce's (1990) 'backpackers'. The characteristics of these types of tourists are well documented in the tourism literature (see, for example, Adler, 1985; Ateljevic & Doorne, 2004; Cohen, 1973; Desforges, 1998, 2000; Elsrud, 2001; Loker, 1994; Loker-Murphy & Pearce, 1995; Murphy, 2001; Pearce, 1990; Richards & King, 2003; Richards & Wilson, 2004b;

Riley, 1988). Most accounts suggest a temporal progression as each of these 'types' has, to some extent, replaced its predecessor. There also appears to have been a geographical succession, at least in tourism research and literature (if not in reality), as the 'drifter' centres of Europe have been replaced with 'backpacker' enclaves in many other parts of the world.

According to Cohen (1973) it was the introduction of cheaper airfares, along with cheap accommodation and surface travel, that had the most impact on the expansion of drifter tourism during the 1960s and 1970s. Drifter or youth travel has become more institutionalised over time, albeit in tourism systems that paralleled mainstream tourism development. Youth travel, however, did not grow merely as a result of developing institutional facilities. Cultural, economic and political motivating factors all encouraged participation in what Cohen (1973) termed the 'drifter subculture'. These are neatly summed up in Michener's (1971) novel *The Drifters* which, through the stories of a group of young travellers, illustrated the attractions of the exotic and various modes of escape available through travel. Travel was used as a means of evading societal pressures and of avoiding routine work. The associated growth of the drug culture offered escape on a more personal level. The current generation of 'backpackers' epitomised by the characters in Garland's (1997) novel *The Beach* are similar to the characters in *The Drifters*; having found a paradise on earth and a ready supply of drugs, they live communally in a state of escapism. Only the geographical location has changed as the beach in Thailand offers today's backpackers what Torremolinos and Pamplona in Spain, Portugal's Algarve, or Marrakech did in the 1970s. For OE travellers, however, Pamplona, the Algarve and Marrakech are still sought-after destinations.

Structurally, Europe has been geared for backpacker tourism for at least 30 years and yet little attention has been paid in the research to those travelling in Europe. This may be a result of the difficulty of separating the backpacker from mainstream tourism and tourists identified by some researchers (Scheyvens, 2002; Welk, 2004). Also, identifying backpackers is a challenge when they do not 'look' different to the locals (as in the case of New Zealanders in Europe). The current trend in research to go out 'on the road', or to research backpackers in their enclaves, is perhaps a function of this; focusing attention on those places where backpackers are easier to identify. This not only results in researchers missing many backpacker locations; it also presents a risk of ignoring many varieties of backpacker travel as it predetermines which 'type' of backpackers are being researched.

According to Pearce (1990), backpacker tourism is characterised by a preference for budget accommodation, an independently and flexibly organised travel schedule and longer rather than shorter holidays. In many cases such a broad categorisation is not overly useful as it allows for most types of travel and yet fits few travellers (Sørensen, 2003). This appears to be the case with the OE. While an OE is long-term, the travel episodes within this may be relatively short because a substantial proportion of time is taken up with work. The role of work within the OE is quite different to that undertaken by the travellers for whom work on the road 'allowed them to continue their travels' (Riley, 1988: 319), or the varieties of 'travelling workers and working tourists' outlined by Uriely (2001). Riley (1988) suggested that the necessity to 'travel on a budget' is a natural result of extending travels beyond that of a cyclical holiday. Budget travellers '... are escaping from the dullness and monotony of their everyday routine, from their jobs, from making decisions about careers, and desire to delay or postpone work, marriage, and other responsibilities' (Riley, 1988: 317). The entire OE experience is encompassed by such a description, not only the travel episodes within it. An OE experience is a combination of *both* of Graburn's (1983) kinds of modern tourism as it incorporates the modal type (annual vacations or holiday breaks) into the longer-term and self-testing 'rite of passage' tourism.

Insights into OE travel can be found in a piecemeal fashion from a wide range of backpacker studies. While some recent studies have adopted more ethnographic perspectives and concepts to help describe travel behaviour, they miss the cultural contexts of the backpackers they are studying. Desforges (2000), for example, described ways in which tourism consumption was mobilised for self-identity, while Sørensen (2003) described the development of a culture of international back-packers; neither of these allowed for culturally specific travel as found in the OE experience. The OE appears similar to the 'journeys' of young Israeli backpackers, whose travel is sanctioned by the home society and has developed into distinct patterns and cultural expressions that have more to do with the travellers in question than the destinations visited. Such culturally distinct travel has implications that have only recently attracted the attention of researchers. As Urry (2002: 157) pointed out in the updated edition of *The Tourist Gaze*, 'The importance of travel to culture and how cultures themselves travel, can be seen from the nature of nationality. Central is the nation's narrative of itself'. What follows is the New Zealand OE participants' narrative of travel; it describes travel patterns and behaviours that have been followed for over 50 years to become part of a New Zealand cultural icon.

OE Travel

While this chapter specifically addresses the travel component of the OE experience, it is part of a much broader inquiry that explored the OE from a variety of perspectives. The primary data collection was through qualitative interviews with 100 New Zealanders who had been, or were still on, their OEs. Archive and Web searches of travel advertising and literature provided supporting data to the interview findings. These combined data sources described travel experiences and patterns that have spanned five decades, from the 1960s up until the 2000s. Analysis of the data took an emic approach, drawing on the terminology used by the participants to describe their travel. The researchers of the global nomad survey also purported to use an emic approach although they 'offered' their subjects a choice of titles (tourist, traveller or backpacker) to identify with (Richards & Wilson, 2003). Similarly, Riley (1988) reported 'asking' respondents if they were travellers or tourists.

Those interviewed for this research closely resembled the backpackers described in other literature yet they did not call themselves 'backpackers', or even 'travellers'; rather they talked of going on 'trips' and 'holidays'. The language used by tourists to describe their own behaviour can impart information on that travel. Some of the past traditions of the OE, for example, are embedded in the language used by participants, even when the activity they describe no longer exists. The term 'fresh off the boat', once a literal description of the means of arrival in Europe – a transport option not available for almost 30 years – is still used by today's OE participants to describe a new (innocent) arrival from New Zealand.

The simplest differentiation made by respondents was between 'travelling' and going on 'holiday'. One 1996 OE participant described his OE travel: 'We went travelling through Europe – hired a car and just camped. After that we went back to London to work and did loads of holidays – skiing in Europe, to the States, long weekends in Paris – even did a British-type holiday when we went to the Canaries for Christmas'. Travelling usually involved multidestination trips of longer, rather than shorter duration. These, however, were not necessarily undertaken independently of the travel industry. Organised tours also counted as travelling. How travel is judged by others is an important consideration, and is a common theme in tourism literature. Doing it 'right' can endow participants with what Munt (1994) and Desforges (1998) termed 'cultural capital', Elsrud (2001) entitled 'hierarchical positioning', and others referred to more generally as 'status' (see, for example, Riley, 1988; Sørensen, 2003). With OE, travel status could be gained through 'independent' travel, with the degree of independence determined by the mode of transport used. This is an interesting finding in light of Vance's (2004) assertion that backpackers' choices of transport modes have scarcely been considered in backpacker literature. Other studies have reported that status accrues from cheapness of travel or from visiting unique, or previously undiscovered, destinations (Riley, 1988). The 'iconic' travel experience of the OE is a Grand Tour of Europe, a 'tour' that visits some of the most expensive and popular tourist cities and sites in the world.

The attraction of Europe, for OE travellers, can be explained in several ways. It may be a result of what Graburn (1983) described as 'ritual inversion' whereby modernity (New Zealand) is replaced with history (Europe). Desforges (2000) suggested that for young Europeans increasing familiarity with their neighbours no longer makes them the 'Other'; for New Zealanders Europe is still the 'Other', the exotic or something worthy of Urry's (1990) 'gaze'. In a practical sense moving 'home' from New Zealand to Britain offered those on OE a range of new tourism experiences. As one OE participant said, 'Once you get to London the options are huge. I mean we can't [in New Zealand] hop on a plane and go across to Paris for the weekend'. Also, over time a tradition of OE travel has become established with its own set of destinations, travel styles and behaviours. Bell (2002: 143) likened the OE to secular pilgrimage, and described it as '... a quest or pilgrimage from one of the world's most remote countries, to the places familiar in national and family histories, popular media, and in tales from previous OE travellers'.

The Grand Tour of Europe

A core component of an OE is to go on at least one extended trip around Europe, much like the early 'Grand Tour' (Hibbert, 1969; Towner, 1985). According to a London newspaper article, 'spring heralds the arrival of Aussies and Kiwis in London' as, 'Every year they come to our cultured continent to do what has become known as the Grand Combi Tour. But they are not in search of culture. Armed with Vegemite and enough alcohol to float every navy in Europe, they're out to drink, drive and inject drugs' (Ferns, 1995). An OE tour is usually of three or four months' duration and takes place in the European summer, following a circuit that begins in Pamplona, Spain in July at the *Running of the Bulls* (colloquially referred to as *'Pamps'*) and finishes in Germany in October at the Munich *Oktoberfest* (the *'Beerfest'*). Between these markers the tour winds its way through Europe, to Portugal, with a side trip to Morocco, then the coastal route from Barcelona to Rome. The vans are 'parked' in Athens while their occupants visit the Greek Islands. After Greece, the 'ultimate' destination is Munich and the *Beerfest*. The speed of travel and routes taken are dependent on how much time and money the travellers have left.

All of those interviewed were familiar with this tour although few followed it exactly. Some did sections of the tour or shorter trips to the 'markers' at either end, 'did *Pamps* one year and the *Beerfest* a couple of times, but not the tour'; others recognised that they had their timing slightly wrong, 'we did a combi trip and did the circuit but left a month later than usual... but we did end up at the *Beerfest*'. *New Zealand News UK*, a London publication for expatriate New Zealanders, featured travel articles on the *Beerfest* and Pamplona (although this did not mention the *Running of the Bulls* festival) as long ago as 1965. *LAM*, another London publication for Australasians, advertised specific trips to *Pamps* and the *Beerfest* in 1978. A travel article in the same magazine the following year suggested that the popularity of *Pamps* was a direct result of Michener's (1971) book *The Drifters*.

There are many ways to 'tour' Europe and transport options fall on a continuum from independent (hitchhiking, cycling, hiring a vehicle or purchasing one's own vehicle – such as the 'combi' van mentioned in the above quotations) through public transport options (purchasing independent tickets or travel passes), the use of hop-on hop-off bus services (in more recent years) to going on organised tours (such as Contiki or Top Deck). Again, the majority of those interviewed were familiar with all the options possible and some types of travel were seen as 'better' than others, as issues of travelling 'properly' came through in many interviews. The two most talked about means of travel were the 'iconic' touring options: 'van tour' and 'doing a Contiki'.

'Van Tour'

The purchase of a van in which to 'independently' travel around Europe, and the route this tour takes, has become so established over time that it is commonly referred to as 'van tour'. Van travel became popular in the 1960s and 1970s; an early example of young people travelling in a 'pop-top' is described in *The Drifters* (Michener, 1971). By the late 1970s a specialist guidebook was available for 'van' tourists. This guide described different models of vans,[3] gave details of the van street market in London, explained which routes to take and how to budget for van travel and so on (Odin & Odin, 1979). In the early 1980s van tour was the subject of the 'hit' Men at Work song *Down Under*: 'Travelling in a fried-out combie, On a hippy trail, head full of zombie' (Hay & Strykert, 1982). More recently van tour has been immortalised in the New Zealand movie *Kombi Nation* (Lahood, 2003).

Outwardly, van tour appears to have changed little over time; the vans have not changed at all and the reference to 'fried-out' in the song lyrics above is indicative of the number of years each van had done the tour. They are often marked as 'van tour' vans, with the years they 'toured' recorded on their bodywork. Today, instead of 'parking' in an informal street market in London, vans for sale are 'posted' on the Internet and, in 2005, the vans selling were 1970, 1973, 1986 and 1986 model vehicles (Gumtree, 2005). For participants, recognition by others that that they are on 'van tour' is important. A group of 2003 van travellers, for example, when asked if they had a New Zealand flag on their van said, 'Yeah we painted it on – we actually did it about half way through the trip – until then it didn't really stand out as a van tour van – it was just a blue van'. This supports Desforges' (1998: 189) notion that 'the audience is central to the transformation of travel into cultural capital' although there 'might be tensions when the audience contests the value of travel'.

The value of such travel *is* contested by some today, associated with the perceptions of many that the tour has changed. Two participants, who did van tour in the late 1980s (early in their OEs) and were still involved with OE travel in 2004 (as travel agents), talked about some of these changes: 'Van tour has become pretty feral. In its heyday in the 1970s and 1980s there were upwards of 200 vans collected in various European cities; [in 2004] there were probably less than a 100. Today's travellers are not as adventurous – I know that when we went out we were going on an adventure – just the fact that you weren't going to be able to contact people – we were going out to sample European culture – possibly not as much as a cultural student – we were going out to drink but we were going to visit as much as possible as well.' Another participant did 'van tour' in 2003, 30 years after her mother and said, 'My Mum did van tour in the early 1970s and it was different – they stayed in places for three weeks at a time and took drugs and that – back then they had no money and all they did was travel in vans and eat nothing – they had the best time. Maybe it was easier to travel like that then because the facilities weren't there like today – it is hard to turn down what is there.'

Some of this change was seen as beyond the control of participants (the world and the contexts in which they were travelling had changed) and some was attributed to participants themselves (and the way they travelled or behaved while travelling). Increasing facilities and better communications have made 'van tour' less of a challenge and the van tour of the past was seen as 'better' for a variety of reasons – the participants had less money, travel was slower, time was spent sightseeing as well as having 'fun' and there was greater interaction with local cultures. While van tour always involved a degree of hedonism, over time the hedonistic aspect of the tour appears to have become much more significant. This, coupled with the development of the informally 'prescribed' tour route, has reduced the 'value' of this type of travel (Desforges, 1998). The modern van tour resembles the 'trip' described in a review of *Kombi Nation*, 'A lack of interaction with the locals makes Kombi Nation more a transplanting of Kiwi culture than a compelling overseas experience' (Croot, 2003: E4).

'Doing a Contiki'

In the past 'van tour' was usually lauded (for its independence), while 'doing a Contiki',[4] the other 'iconic' OE travel experience, was denigrated (for being 'organised' travel and for the hedonistic behaviour associated with it). Yet ironically, these two perceived 'extremes' of travel not only display many similar characteristics but had the same beginnings. The early tours began as rough camping tours, using vans much like those travelling on the independent combi tours. The Contiki company, for example, was started in the 1960s by John Anderson, a New Zealander who, after presenting himself as a travel guide, took bookings and deposits for a tour of Europe; with the money he collected he then bought the van to be used for the tour (White, 2005). The other major tour company to have survived since the early days of the OE – Top Deck – was launched in a similar fashion by a young Australian. In Earls Court, in the late 1960s and 1970s, 'you only had to leave the back doors of a transit van open for five minutes and you'd return to find half a dozen people in the back waiting to leave for Europe' (Top Deck, 2004b).

Doing a tour was generally looked down on although it was an (almost) acceptable option if one had just 'arrived'; it could serve as an introduction to both the destinations and the mechanics of travelling. For most there was a degree of self-awareness of their naivety and inexperience as travellers; a tour was a sensible option for someone who was 'fresh off the boat'. As one 1984 participant explained, 'We did a Contiki trip around Europe – I remember at the time thinking it was a kind of tacky thing to do – but it was our first proper big adventure and we thought it would give us an idea of which countries we wanted to go back and visit'. Also, some destinations were acceptable by tour: Scandinavia–Russia tours were very popular before the Berlin Wall came down, as were overland tours across Europe to Asia (on the hippie trail) until political trouble closed this route. For some, however, an organised tour was never an option, as one 1988 participant commented, 'I don't like package tours personally – having never done one in my life. It is probably an identity thing – because I don't want the social stigma of being a bus tripper'. Again, the opinion of one's audience was important (Desforges, 1998).

A major issue was the 'party' reputation some tours had; as one participant said about her tour, 'it was just one big long party – we spent most of it drunk – I missed things entirely – like the Sistine Chapel – I was so hung-over – I have felt ashamed of that for years'. Despite this party aspect of the tours, most found them good introductions to travel and enjoyed them immensely. Many of today's OE participants do the same trips their parents did a generation ago although it is questionable how 'similar' these tours would have been. Tours have changed considerably over time as, 'Gradually more luxury was added – 54-seat Mercedes coaches with TV, reclining seats and toilets replaced Ford Transit vans ... and castles and comfort replaced camping' (White, 2005: 55). Contiki still offers camping tours but also runs hotel and 'concept' tours that stay in luxury, or unusual accommodations; in a shift further into mainstream tourism the company opened a resort on the Greek Island of Mykonos in 2004 (Contiki, 2005). Camping tours are advertised 'nostalgically' as, 'the original Contiki classic. Traditional touring combined with a can-do team spirit' (Contiki.com, 2003: 80).

There have also been changes to this type of travel. Some tour options have become less structured and are more like independent travel. In 2002, for example, the Contiki company began offering European Getaways, which, according to their brochure, are 'different city combinations designed to give you flexibility and freedom but still all the advantages of group travel' (Contiki.com, 2003: 43). These trips are also shorter than the 'traditional' Contiki tours, a trend across most types of OE travel. For many of more recent OE participants work commitments restricted their travel episodes to these quick trips or weekend breaks to European capitals, rather than month-long odysseys 'doing a

Contiki' or 'van tour'. Top Deck also offers a range of 'festival tours' that are only of a few days' duration. The focus, however, is still on the markers of the Grand Tour: *Pamps* or the *Beerfest*.

Conclusions

While those on OE went on many different trips and holidays in the years they were away, engaging in a myriad of types or styles of travel, this chapter has focused on the Grand Tour of Europe as experienced on 'van tour' or through 'doing a Contiki'. In these travel experiences there is evidence to support tourism changes found in other research and literature. Most evident are the institutionalisation and commodification of the tourism product as travel experiences have become increasingly organised and packaged for quick consumption. Technological changes have also affected the way travel is organised and planned. Yet despite such changes the core experience has remained the same – the destinations, the routes followed and the way travel is practised are so well established in the OE as to constitute the experience, rather than merely describing its characteristics. A core component of this is the hedonistic nature of these travel experiences. These OE participants appear to more closely resemble Cohen's (1973) drifters than they do the backpackers travelling in Australia or New Zealand in search of outdoor adventure experiences, or in a quest for self-identity (Desforges, 2000; Loker, 1994; Loker-Murphy & Pearce, 1995).

This chapter highlights the need to consider the contexts in which travel is practised. The focus of travel in Europe by OE participants, for example, can be attributed to colonial history, to the availability of working holiday visas, to geographic remoteness and to longstanding OE 'traditions'. The OE is a cultural expression of New Zealand, not of Britain, where these OE travellers live and from where they travel. This has implications for research on both practical and theoretical levels. OE participants' relatively long-term residence in Britain means that tourism statistics record them as domestic British tourists and yet they travel to different destinations and in different ways than do most British tourists (including British backpackers). One participant, for example, was called 'backpacker girl' by her British workmates, because she took her backpack into work every Friday to go away for weekends. Some of those interviewed had enjoyed 'British-type' holidays; the unusual or different 'type' of holiday experience recognised as much as an attraction as the destination of the holiday itself. The working holiday experience, with its blurred boundaries between work and travel, adds to the challenge of understanding these travel experiences. While Top Deck is primarily a travel company, for example, it also recognises the extended nature of the OE experience of its clientele; the company hosts 'reunion' parties in London bars post-tour for its clients and runs a London 'Deckers Club' that offers members advice on living in London, holds mail for them, and runs day tours and other social events (Top Deck, 2004a).

There is a degree of self-awareness found in these OE tourists, something that has been overlooked in backpacker and other tourism studies. These OE participants had not only considered what type of tourists they were but also understood where, and how, their own travel traditions fitted with other types of tourism experiences. By interviewing a group who had engaged in the same travel experiences over many decades, very rich data could be collected. Those who had travelled in the earlier years, for example, were familiar with current travel options; recent OE participants were familiar with the way 'it used to be'. The data collected combined narratives of personal experience and opinions on OE travel. Some of those interviewed also offered 'professional' information and opinions on OE travel as a result of their involvement in the travel industry. Supporting data from various media sources and guides, along with advertising and popular literature, added the context in which this travel occurred. The final point this chapter makes is that the 'voices' and language of those being researched needs to be listened to more carefully. Those on OE have been following the same travel patterns around Europe for over 50 years despite numerous changes in tourism infrastructure, in technology and in travel fashion. Over time the terminology used by OE participants to describe their travel experiences had not changed and yet the experiences themselves were very different. The 'backpackers' described in this chapter travel around what the literature regards as non-backpacker destinations and, over time, OE travel has become institutionalised to the point where 'organised back-packing' has emerged. However, most OE travellers do not fully 'do' this organised form.

This chapter clearly illustrates that Europe is a major backpacker destination for non-Europeans. This is an area of research that deserves much more attention and should include travel from other non-European generating regions such as North America, South Africa and perhaps even South America. Backpacker tourism is *not* just travel to third world countries and Australasia. Given the long history of OE travel, the numbers involved and the impact these OE travellers have had on the development of tourism in Europe, it could also be argued that the facilities for backpacker tourism in Australasia are a direct consequence of OE experiences. Again, this needs further investigation.

Notes

1. 'Pakeha' is a Maori word commonly used to describe a New Zealander of European ancestry.
2. These figures are based on market research done by Sky TV to determine the potential audience for a 'domestic' Australian and New Zealand news programme to be broadcast in Europe (personal communication, Nick Samitz, August 5, 2004).
3. The Volkswagen Combi was one of the more popular makes of van used. While there were many other makes of van, the term 'combi' was used by many participants to describe *any* van. There was a range of internal conversions that could be made to these vans and the relative merit of each type was a frequent topic of conversation.
4. While Contiki was only one tour company among many, it is one of the 'survivors' from the early days of the OE. Perhaps because of this, the term 'doing a Contiki' was used generically by most to describe *any* organised tour.

Chapter 9

Uncovering the International Backpackers to Malaysia

LEE TZE IAN and GHAZALI MUSA

Introduction

According to Tourism Malaysia statistics, tourist arrivals to Malaysia were 15.7 million in 2004 and tourism receipts were RM29.6 billion (US$7.8 billion), representing 6.6% of Malaysia's Gross Domestic Product (GDP). Given the significance of this industry, it is not surprising that the Government of Malaysia placed much emphasis on this sector in its Eighth Malaysia Plan (2001–2005). The thrust of Malaysia's tourism plan was to achieve sustainable tourism growth so that the full potential of employment- and income-generating effects can be realised at the national, state and local levels. Among the key strategies adopted during this period include developing new tourism products and the branding of Malaysia through the *Malaysia Truly Asia* tagline (EPU 2001).

In terms of developing new markets, the focus has been on international mass tourists, particularly those from 'non-traditional' markets like the Middle East and China. However, while tourist arrivals and tourism receipts from the new markets saw strong growth, there was a decline in tourists from the 'traditional' developed economies. What this suggests is that the tourism authorities in Malaysia need to find new ways to segment its 'traditional' markets and identify niche segments so that the needs of these tourists can be better satisfied.

A segment that has been largely ignored or even discouraged by tourism planners, not only in Malaysia but also in a number of South-east Asian countries, is the backpacker segment. In some less developed countries, the government planners were keener to promote upmarket tourism. Indeed, Richter (1993: 185) has noted that:

> Not generally welcome in Southeast Asia as they are in Europe, North America or East Asia are budget travelers. Malaysia contends they are welcome but the facilities promoted do not confirm that.

Golf courses, not camp grounds, Hyatts not budget motels, man-made amusements not national parks are in the expectations of most planners and policy-makers.

The scenario is vastly different for Australia, where backpackers spend a total of AUS$2.5 billion (RM6.5 billion) a year. They spend more than twice per visitor than the average for all visitors (ATC, 2004). In 2003, backpackers accounted for 10% of all international visitors to Australia (BTR, 2004). If estimates from the Australian case can be postulated here, then approximately 300,000[1] foreign backpackers would visit Malaysia each year. Hence, this segment of tourists holds potential for Malaysia and deserves a closer look.

Research Purpose and Significance

Although Malaysia is a key stopover in the backpackers' South-east Asia circuit, there is a dearth of locally published work on the characteristics of this group of tourists. On the other hand, there has been considerable interest in tourism research into the backpacker phenomenon outside of Malaysia. Ironically, backpacker tourism is not a new phenomenon in Malaysia. If anything, South-east Asia is widely regarded as the birthplace of mass backpacking, with the publication of Lonely Planet's *Southeast Asia on a Shoestring*, the so-called 'Yellow Bible' (Spreitzhofer, 2002). Malaysia, along with Thailand, Singapore and Indonesia, are long-established destinations for many backpackers. Thus, a quantitative study of Malaysia is timely.

This study is exploratory in nature and is aimed at uncovering certain characteristics of international backpackers to Malaysia that could serve as a basis for segmenting the tourist market here. There are five objectives in this study:

(1) to obtain a demographic profile of foreign backpackers to Malaysia;
(2) to ascertain backpackers' identities;
(3) to understand backpackers' transportation and travel characteristics;
(4) to determine backpackers' sources of information used in planning; and
(5) to understand backpackers' consumption patterns.

Backpacker Typologies

One of the earliest typological references to backpackers in the contemporary sense is the 'drifter' (Cohen, 1972). In this widely cited literature, Cohen differentiated between the institutionalised (organised mass tourist/individual mass tourist) and non-institutionalised tourists (explorer/drifter). The institutionalised tourists comply with the conventional features of mass tourism: 'familiarity, prior planning, safety, dependence and minimal choices' (Vogt, 1976). On the other hand, the non-institutionalised tourist, such as the 'drifter', comes into less contact with the tourist industry and attempts to share the lifestyle of those in the culture with whom he or she comes into contact.

Non-institutionalised tourists have also been referred to in the literature by various terms: *nomads* (Cohen, 1973), *wanderers* (Vogt, 1976), *trampling youth* (Adler 1985) and *long-term budget traveller* (Riley, 1988). What this literature suggests is that while the non-institutionalised tourists share certain characteristics that are distinct from the institutionalised mass tourists, they are not a homogeneous group. In fact, the characteristics of this group of tourists have also evolved over time to reflect the changing values of Western society. Riley (1988) noted that the differences between the 'budget traveller' and the 'drifter' of the 1960s and 1970s described by Cohen were considerable. There was greater emphasis in the 1960s and 1970s on the use of drugs and stronger expressions of alienation compared with the 1980s.

Since then studies tend to refer to them as 'backpackers', a term that is well known and accepted by the tourism industry in Australia, Southeast Asia and New Zealand (Loker-Murphy & Pearce, 1995). Loker-Murphy and Pearce defined backpackers as young and budget-minded tourists who exhibit a preference for inexpensive accommodation, an emphasis on meeting other people, an independently organised flexible itinerary, longer than brief vacations and an emphasis on informal and participatory recreation activities. For backpackers travelling in Southeast Asia, a typical route starts with Bangkok, through South Thailand and peninsular Malaysia, to Singapore (or across to Sumatra), Java, Bali, Eastern Indonesia and on to Australia. The route may be reversed or could include side trips to Vietnam or the Philippines (Hampton, 1998; Pearce, 1990).

The form of backpacking might also have changed. Cohen (2003a) drew a parallel between backpackers and the mass tourists wherein the contemporary backpackers spend significant periods of time in various backpacker enclaves or on the road from one such enclave to the other. These enclaves may serve as bases for trekking, riding or rafting trips and for tours or excursions to natural sights, ethnic communities or various events in the vicinity of the enclaves.

More recently, Jarvis (2004) identified a new subsegment of the 'holiday backpacker' in South-east Asia. The 'holiday backpacker' travels for a shorter period of time in a similar manner to mainstream tourists but utilises the infrastructure developed for long-term travellers. These travellers are typically older and are on paid annual leave from their full-time job. Jarvis contended that contrary to the popular perception of a backpacker overland route from Bali to Bangkok, this subsegment of traveller travels around specific airport locales (e.g. Bali or Bangkok). He called it 'hub backpacking'.

Backpacker Tourism and Developmental Impacts

The linkage between tourism and the economic development of a country is expounded in a rich source of academic literature, e.g. Hampton (1998), Hamzah (1997), Jarvis (2004), Riley (1988), Scheyvens (2002), Spreitzhofer (2002) and Visser (2004).

Infrastructure and ownership

It is frequently argued that backpacker tourists require only a 'minimalist' infrastructure that is less capital intensive. As described by Riley (1988: 323):

> Thus, this category of traveler is not so concerned about amenities (e.g. plumbing), restaurants (e.g. westernized food), and transportation (e.g. air conditioning) geared specifically to the tastes of the mass tourist. If a budget traveler place has an appeal to Western tastes (e.g. banana pancakes), it requires minimal infrastructure.

The infrastructures required for the mass tourists are often built using foreign-owned tourism capital. By contrast, many of the small-scale developments associated with backpacker tourism are owned and funded by local entrepreneurs and operated by members of their family. When backpackers patronise these establishments, they contribute to localised economic development. Moreover, as backpackers travel more widely than the package tourists, the multiplier effects are also spread across a wider geographic area. In this respect, the economic impact is much more direct and involves a lower level of leakages.

Sustainability

Backpacker tourism, with its low-budget and low-impact character-istics, may emphasise sustainability, both in an environmental and cultural sense. Being a relatively small-scale development, this form of tourism may allow for a more meaningful interaction to be fostered between tourists and local residents with less social and cultural disruption than in the case of large-scale tourism developments. It may also encourage community participation in planning and seeks to strengthen institutions designed to enhance local participation (Visser, 2004). This was also the case for Malaysia, as Hamzah (1997) reported that in Pulau Tioman there was involvement of the local community using expertise available at local universities and standard chalets provided by *Majlis Amanah Rakyat* (a semi-government agency).

However, this type of small-scale development also presents a dilemma for government planners. On one hand, the multiplier effect and other economic spin-offs help to uplift the socioeconomic well-being of the rural folk. On the other hand, when small-scale developments proliferate without control, sustainability is threatened. Hamzah (1997) highlighted Malaysia's experience of this, including depletion of marine habitats and ecosystem, economic leakage, displacement of the local community, breakdown of traditional values and conflict over limited resources. Nevertheless, Hamzah maintained that small-scale developments could still be viable if managed well. This could be achieved through better planning, conducting regular dialogues with local community and closer collaborations between government agencies and local cooperatives.

Backpackers spearhead mass tourism

Backpackers generally avoid places frequented by mass tourists or what they refer to as 'touristic' places. In their quest for novelty, variety and exoticism, backpackers usually seek out rural, off-the-beaten-track areas, thereby opening up new areas of tourism. This expansion occurs due to a very extensive traveller communication network that eventually results in a dramatic increase in the number of tourists in an area (Riley, 1988). Herein lies a paradox. By seeking new destinations, backpackers inadvertently spearhead mass tourism and expand the mass tourist destinations (Cohen, 1972). To a large extent, Malaysia's experience is consistent with this phenomenon, as noted by Hamzah (1997: 202):

> Destination areas such as Cherating, Pulau Tioman and Pulau Pangkor were merely an extension of a network of cheap lodgings...connected to each other by a cheap transportation system. Informal information boards at every destination helped to promote outlets at the other destinations within this network. As the pioneering *kampung* tourism areas expanded and began to attract more and more tourists, the 'drifters' moved on to new destinations such as Marang, Pulau Perhentian, Pulau Pemanggil, Pulau Aur and so forth.

Backpacker tourism and urban redevelopment

The 'minimalist' infrastructure demand of backpackers impacts the supply side not only in rural areas but also in urban areas. In some places, backpackers have acted as a catalyst for localised urban redevelopment within cities (Jarvis, 2004). Jarvis cited the case of St. Kilda in Melbourne (Australia), where its run-down red light district has been transformed into a backpacker centre:

> Old guesthouses, hotels and coffee palaces, which had been originally designed without en-suites, were converted cheaply to backpacker style accommodation with minimal investment required. Once the backpacker arrived, they brought economic activity and a vibrancy that helped stimulate the urban rejuvenation process.

Methodology

To achieve the objectives of the study, a quantitative survey was conducted from January to March 2005. In this study, the operational definition of a backpacker would be one who has a preference for budget accommodation and who identifies himself/herself as a 'backpacker' or a 'traveller'. Self-administered questionnaires were distributed to various backpacker hostels listed in the *Lonely Planet* guidebook or through popular Internet hostel booking portals such as Hostelword.com and Hostelz.com. The questionnaire consisted of basic questions related to identity, transportation, expenditure patterns, activities, information sources, motivations and personal attributes.

A quota sampling method was adopted to ensure that the samples were representative of the population. Quotas were assigned to the four main backpacker 'hubs' in Peninsular Malaysia, namely Kuala Lumpur, Georgetown (Penang), Melaka and Kota Bharu (Kelantan). The reasons why these towns/cities were chosen are briefly described below:

- Kuala Lumpur is the capital city of Malaysia.
- Georgetown (Penang) is the Northern gateway into Thailand.
- Melaka is the transit point between Singapore and Kuala Lumpur and a key tourist town on the West coast.
- Kota Bharu (Kelantan) is the Eastern gateway into Thailand and a base to the islands on the East coast.

A total of 403 self-administered questionnaires were distributed; 262 usable questionnaires were received, giving a response rate of 65.0%. Statistical data were then analysed using the SPSS Version 11 software.

Results

Demographic profile

The sample in this study had a larger proportion of males (60.3%) than females (39.7%). The majority of the respondents were young, with 71% of the sample under 30 years of age. The mean age was 29.2; the youngest being 17 and the oldest being 72. They were also well educated; 66.1% of the respondents possessed a degree qualification and above. Referring to Table 9.1, the majority of backpackers were from the European Union (64.6%). Backpackers from the UK/Ireland/Scotland constituted the largest group (33.2%), followed by Scandinavian (12.2%). By contrast, Asians, which account for 87.8% of all tourist arrivals to Malaysia in 2004, were represented by only 6.5% of the sample in this study.

The demographic profile of the respondents in this study corresponded closely with previous studies on backpackers and youth travellers such as Jarvis (1994), Loker-Murphy and Pearce (1995), Richards and Wilson (2003) and TNT Magazine (2003). However, the gender distribution tended to be more balanced in other studies. The higher percentage of males in this study is probably be due to sampling bias or simply because Malaysia appeals more to male backpackers.

Backpacker identity

The majority of the respondents, 71.4%, identified themselves as 'backpackers', while 26.0% and 2.7% saw themselves as 'travellers' and 'others' respectively. Among those who identified themselves as 'others', some described themselves as being 'connected', on a 'spiritual journey', 'culture' and 'both backpacker and traveller'. It should be highlighted that this was also a filter question. Hence, those who identified themselves as 'tourists' or 'business visitors' would have been excluded in the data analysis.

Cross-tabulation of backpacker identity against respondents' age groups revealed that the younger age groups (30 and under) tended to refer themselves as 'backpackers', whereas the older age groups (over 30) tended to refer to themselves as 'travellers' ($\chi^2 = 24.809$, $df = 4$, $p = 0.000$). However, the observation is not statistically significant against gender and nationality.

Transportation and travel characteristics

Among the sample respondents, 39.3% travelled alone, 42.3% travelled with a friend or partner and 18.3% travelled in a group of more

Table 9.1 Demographic profile of respondents

Demographic profile		Freq.	%	% (Cum.)	Mean	Min.	Max.
Gender	Male	158	60.3	60.3			
	Female	104	39.7	100.0			
	Total	262	100.0				
Age	≤ 20	25	9.5	9.5	29.2	17	72
	21 – 25	92	35.1	44.7			
	26 – 30	69	26.3	71.0			
	31 – 35	41	15.6	86.6			
	≥ 36	35	13.4	100.0			
	Total	262	100.0				
Education level	Completed postgraduate	29	11.1	11.1			
	Some post-graduate	19	7.3	18.4			
	Professional qualification	40	15.3	33.7			
	Completed degree	85	32.4	66.1			
	Some tertiary	43	16.4	82.5			
	High/secondary school	46	17.6	100.0			
	Total	262	100.0				
Work experience	> 20 years	19	7.3	7.3	8.04	0.0	60.0
	$10 < x \leq 20$ years	45	17.2	24.5			
	$5 < x \leq 10$ years	55	21.0	45.5			

Table 9.1 (*Continued*)							
Demographic profile		*Freq.*	*%*	*% (Cum.)*	*Mean*	*Min.*	*Max.*
	$0 < x \leq 5$ years	123	46.9	92.4			
	0 year	20	7.6	100.0			
	Total	262	100.0				
National-ity	UK/Ireland/ Scotland	87	33.2	33.2			
	Scandinavia	32	12.2	45.0			
	Europe (ex Germany and Scandi-navia)	31	11.8	57.3			
	Canada	24	9.2	66.4			
	Australia/ New Zeal-and	23	8.8	75.2			
	Germany	19	7.3	82.4			
	USA	18	6.9	88.9			
	Asia	17	6.5	95.8			
	Others	5	1.9	100.0			
	Total	262	100.0				
Identity	Backpacker	187	71.4	71.4			
	Traveller	68	26.0	97.3			
	Others	7	2.7	100.0			
	Total	262	100.0				

than 2. For 72.5% of the respondents, this was their first visit to Malaysia. However, Malaysia was not their only destination; 75.6% of respondents indicated that they had visited other countries on the way to Malaysia, while 79.8% intended to visit other countries after Malaysia. Thailand,

Table 9.2 Point of entry

Entry point	Freq.	%	Cumulative
Malaysia–Thailand border (North)	51	19.5	19.5
Malaysia–Thailand border (Rantau Panjang–Kelantan)	11	4.2	23.7
Malaysia–Singapore border	98	37.4	61.1
KLIA	94	35.9	96.9
Others	8	3.1	100.0
Total	262	100.0	

Singapore and Indonesia were frequently cited as the countries that they had visited or intended to visit. This appears to confirm the existence of a backpacker South-east Asia circuit, as discussed in Hampton (1998) and Pearce (1990).

Even though Malaysia is part of the South-east Asia circuit, it is not considered a transportation hub for the rest of the region. Referring to Table 9.2 and Table 9.3, 35.9% and 37.7% of the respondents used the Kuala Lumpur International Airport (KLIA) as the point of entry and exit respectively. In fact, 61.1% and 56.4% of the respondents entered and exited Malaysia respectively via the country's border with Thailand and Singapore using public buses, train or chartered vehicles (pooled with other backpackers). On average, the planned duration of the respondents'

Table 9.3 Point of exit

Exit point	Freq.	%	Cumulative
Malaysia–Thailand border (North)	57	22.2	22.2
Malaysia–Thailand border (Rantau Panjang– Kelantan)	17	6.6	28.8
Malaysia–Singapore border	71	27.6	56.4
KLIA	97	37.7	94.2
Others	11	5.9	100.0
Total	257	100.0	

trip in South-east Asia was 90 days, while that for Malaysia was 19.5 days (see Table 9.5).

For some nationalities, the decision to travel alone in Malaysia was more pronounced than other nationalities. The difference was statistically significant for backpackers from the USA (72.7%), Germany (47.4%) and UK/Ireland/Scotland (44.8%), who preferred to travel alone compared with only 39.3% of backpackers of other nationalities ($\chi^2 = 55.325$, $df = 32$, $p = 0.006$).

Information and planning

Although the backpackers maintained a flexible schedule while travelling, they planned ahead for their trips. On average, the respondents took 18.96 days to plan their trip to Malaysia. The top three sources of information that backpackers relied on for planning were guidebooks ($\mu = 2.02$), the Internet ($\mu = 2.36$) and recommendations from friends and relative ($\mu = 3.31$) (see Table 9.4). This finding is consistent with other studies by Richards and Wilson (2003) and TNT Magazine (2003) and allows tourism planners to direct their promotional activities in targeting the backpacker segment more effectively.

The popularity of the Internet should not be surprising given the age and education profiles of the respondents. Perhaps of greater concern to tourism planners would be the importance of guidebooks and word of mouth recommendations that backpackers relied on for their information. Unfortunately, these are sources that tourism planners have relatively weaker influence over.

The impact of word of mouth recommendations cannot be underestimated. When asked to what extent information provided by other travellers influenced their travel decisions, 95.4% of the respondents indicated 'sometimes', 'frequently' or 'often'. Only 4.6% indicated that they were not influenced at all by others. Nevertheless, service providers could encourage positive word of mouth from the backpackers. According to the respondents, the main factors that tourism operators should pay attention to in order to encourage positive word of mouth from backpackers were: 'having friendly and helpful staff and good service' ($\mu = 2.05$), 'providing a good, clean product and facility' ($\mu = 2.59$) and 'provide value for money' ($\mu = 2.85$).

Consumption patterns

To determine backpackers' consumption patterns, respondents were asked to provide a breakdown of what they spent the previous day and

Table 9.4 Information and planning

Variable	Mean	sd	N
No. of days required to plan	18.960	61.2871	262
Information source			
Guidebooks	2.02	1.479	262
Internet	2.36	1.351	262
Recommendations	3.31	1.586	262
Travel agents	5.08	1.260	262
Magazines	5.18	1.136	262
Tourism board	5.34	1.126	262
TV programmes	5.40	1.044	262
Newspaper	5.42	1.141	262
Airlines	5.53	0.900	262
Others	5.79	0.888	262
Word of mouth factors			
Staff and good service	2.05	1.016	262
Good, clean product	2.59	1.186	262
Value for money	2.85	1.141	262
Good atmosphere	3.38	0.923	262
Have a good time	3.39	0.991	262
Encourage social activities	3.89	0.466	262
Others	3.94	0.382	262

an estimate of their budget for the whole duration of their trip in Malaysia. The results are tabulated in Table 9.5.

The average daily expenditure was RM227.06 (US$59.75). Multiplying the average daily expenditure with the average duration of trip in Malaysia, i.e. 19.5 days, the estimated expenditure per person for the whole duration of their stay in Malaysia worked out to be RM4,427.67

Table 9.5 Descriptive statistics of expenditure components

Item	N	Min.	Max.	Mean	sd
Trip duration					
In South-east Asia	257	1	2,190	90.01	193.063
In Malaysia	256	1	365	19.54	28.552
Expenditures					
Accommodation	258	0	300	34.90	38.370
Souvenirs	257	0	300	7.95	29.648
Food	254	0	1500	36.62	99.217
Shopping	257	0	3800	77.81	306.014
Transportation	255	0	1000	26.33	89.606
Sightseeing	257	0	350	4.89	31.406
Entertainment	257	0	200	6.30	24.133
Drinks	256	0	500	20.77	56.054
Others	257	0	500	8.52	45.629
Total spent yesterday	251	0	3864	227.06	413.096
Estimated budget for whole trip	237	100	20,000	2014.73	2231.56

(US$1165). Based on earlier estimates, if 300,000 foreign backpackers visit Malaysia each year, then the backpacker industry in Malaysia could potentially be worth RM1.3 billion (US$342 million) a year. According to statistics from Tourism Malaysia, in 2004 the average length of stay per tourist in Malaysia was 6.0 days and the average per capita expenditure for all tourists was RM1888 (US$496.84). Hence, the backpacker's per capita expenditure was 2.3 times higher than the average of all tourists to Malaysia. This ratio compared well with the figures from the Australian Tourist Commission discussed earlier.

Referring to Figure 9.1, accommodation constituted 36.6% of the average tourist's expenditures in 2002 (EPU, 2001). By contrast, accommodation constituted only 15.6% of the total daily expenditure of the respondents. This is consistent with literature sources that suggest

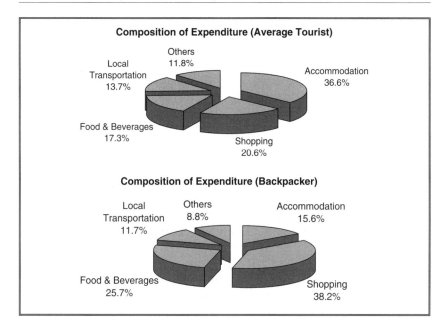

Figure 9.1 Comparison of expenditures between tourist and backpacker

backpackers require only a minimalist infrastructure (Riley, 1988). By staying in backpacker hostels and guesthouses, they were able to cut down their expenditure in accommodation and stretched their budget to justify the long periods of travel. On the other hand, backpackers spent 25.7% of their daily expenditure on food and beverages and 38.2% on shopping (compared with 17.3% and 20.6% respectively for the average tourist), possibly at small local establishments.

Conclusions

Several generalisations might be drawn from this study to describe the characteristics of the backpacker tourists to Malaysia as a market segment that is distinct from international mass tourists. The backpackers to Malaysia are predominantly male, young (under 30) and are highly educated. They are also likely to come from Europe, with the UK/Ireland/Scotland constituting the largest group. Malaysia is not their only destination but part of the backpacker's trip through South-east Asia. Most backpackers would enter or exit Malaysia through its border checkpoints near Thailand and Singapore using public buses, trains or chartered vehicles (shared with other travellers) rather than via the main gateway at the Kuala Lumpur International Airport (KLIA).

Although backpackers maintain a flexible schedule while travelling, they plan ahead for their trips using guidebooks, the Internet and the backpacker network as the main sources. Contrary to the perception of backpackers as small spenders, their total expenditure in Malaysia is more than twice that of the average tourist. What little backpackers spend on accommodation, they make up for by staying longer in the country and spending more on food and beverages and shopping, often patronising small local establishments.

An implication of this study might be how tourism planners could structure an appropriate marketing mix to meet the needs of this niche segment. Specifically, a key imperative for tourism planners would be how to adopt effective communication strategies to persuade back-packers to plan for a longer stay even prior to their trip. These strategies would require careful consideration of the content and delivery of the message, as well as the communications medium, taking cognisance of the sources of information used by backpackers.

This is relevant in view of the rapid development of low-cost carriers in the aviation industry in Asia. The low prices of air travel mean that backpackers will now have greater mobility into, within and out of Malaysia. It is reasonable to assume that there will be a greater influx of backpackers into the country. But it also implies that the average length of stay might be shortened if backpackers are not entirely satisfied with their travel experience here. The challenge for tourism planners is how to convince backpackers to stay longer by informing them appropriately and to encourage them to spend more by offering them more choices and value in terms of backpacker-specific products and services.

Apart from the marketing implications, this study could also shed some light on the impacts of the industry in infrastructure development. For instance, the urban rejuvenation experienced in Australia (Jarvis, 2004) is also beginning to take form around the Bukit Bintang area in Kuala Lumpur. Decrepit pre-war shop houses have been given a new lease of life through the establishment of 'concept' backpacker hostels. However, the common grievances expressed by the entrepreneurs of these establishments are bureaucracy and high handedness of the local authorities. Due to the size and nature of their operations, these backpacker hostels are classified as neither private dwellings nor hotels *per se*. Consequently, many do not operate with legitimate permits and do not display any prominent signboards in order not to attract unwarranted attention from the authorities.

Thus, a review of some of the existing policies is necessary. The authorities need to take a pragmatic approach in ensuring that infrastructure development is regulated in a way that does not stifle the industry's growth. Insights gained about backpackers would enable the authorities to deal objectively with the dilemma of planning for small-scale tourism developments in both urban and rural areas. These would also include issues related to host–guest interactions and sustainability.

To a certain extent, this study has achieved its primary purpose of describing the characteristics of foreign backpackers to Malaysia and the broad-ranging empirical data collected provide a useful tool for segmenting the tourist market here. However, it should be pointed out that while the choice of accommodation provides a convenient basis to distinguish the backpackers from the overall tourist market, it is also a relatively simplistic characterisation of them. Studies by Jarvis (2004), Mohsin and Ryan (2003) and Spreitzhofer (2002) have indicated that the backpacker market can be very heterogeneous.

Nevertheless, this study has opened up future research possibilities in a Malaysian context. Future research in Malaysia should include areas such as spatial travel patterns, travel motivations, activities and post-purchase behaviours among backpackers. It is hoped that continuous exploration of the various aspects of needs and wants of the backpackers in Malaysia will lead to a more balanced tourism development orientation, thus ensuring the industry's sustainability in the future.

Note

1. Based on figures of all inbound tourists to Malaysia (from Tourism Malaysia) but excluding tourists from Malaysia's neighbouring countries (i.e. Singapore, Indonesia, Thailand and Brunei).

Chapter 10

Exploring the Motivations of Backpackers: The Case of South Africa

CHRISTINE NIGGEL and ANGELA BENSON

Introduction

Backpacker tourism, a niche market of tourism, is a rapidly expanding phenomenon (Cohen, 2003a). An examination of the current literature on backpacker tourism highlights that studies tend to focus on the economic significance and impacts of backpacker tourism (for example, Hampton, 1998; Scheyvens, 2002), with little research conducted on aspects such as the motivations for backpacking. This view is supported by Loker-Murphy and Pearce (1995), who believe that the existing literature gives an insight into the influences on contemporary backpacking, but still, little systematic empirical research has been conducted to contribute to an understanding of the characteristics, motivations and behaviours of backpackers. Furthermore, studies have tended to relate to destinations such as Australia (for example, Mohsin & Ryan, 2003; Riley, 1988) and South-east Asia (for example, Hampton, 1998; Spreitzhofer, 1998), which have been fashionable backpacker destinations both in the past and the present.

Since South Africa became a democracy in 1994, it has become a popular backpacker destination and a well established infrastructure for backpacker tourists has been developed (Lonelyplanet.com, 2004). Therefore, this chapter aims to explore the motivations of backpacker tourists in South Africa. The analysis and evaluation of this data is focused towards contributing to the knowledge of the 'global nomad' (Richards & Wilson, 2004a).

Since the political course in South Africa has changed, the country has seen a growth in tourism arrivals. In 2002, South Africa surpassed the six-million mark in tourist arrivals for the first time. Approximately 6.4 million tourists visited the country; an 11% increase over 2001 (Smith,

2003). Moreover, backpacker tourism in South Africa is experiencing a growth rate of 21% per annum (Smith, 2003).

The average backpacker spends 6–12 weeks in southern Africa (Drakensberg Tourism Board, 2001). Tourists from the UK are the biggest market by far, followed by other Europeans, who include Germans, Dutch, Scandinavians and Spanish backpackers, as well as Australians and New Zealanders. Although aimed at the 18–35 market, the average age of the backpackers is between 25 and 28 (Delport, 2003). Due to the high growth rate of backpacker tourism, SATOUR, the official South African Tourism Board, developed their brochure 'Factfiler 2004', to give backpackers information on the infrastructure, transportation, accommodation, safety issues, activities and attractions in South Africa.

In addition to SATOUR, the independent body Backpacker Tourism South Africa (BTSA) was founded in order to promote backpacker tourism in South Africa. BTSA's main goal is marketing South Africa as a primary backpacker destination. The organisation supplies travellers with general information on backpacking in southern Africa, such as accommodation, transportation, information, adventure and tours/ safaris in the different regions of the country. Furthermore, it has established a notice board on the Internet where backpackers can look for travel companions, find information about special locations or inform themselves about the backpacker scene in general (Gregory, 2002). BTSA also produced a map of Southern Africa with the title 'Backpacking Southern Africa', which includes symbols of hostels and possible activities at different locations.

Hostels have been established so that backpackers can travel the whole length and breadth of the country staying only in hostels (SATOUR, 2001). Transportation around South Africa for backpackers is also organised for easy access and backpackers frequently use the Baz Bus. When using this service, passengers simply buy one ticket to their final destination, hopping on and off anywhere along the route, as many times as they want with no time limit. The Baz Bus offers a door-to-door service between 180 backpacker hostels nationwide and lodges around South Africa and Swaziland, with links to Lesotho and Mozambique (The Baz Bus, 2004).

Methodology

This study used a self-administered questionnaire that consisted of one page (two sides) and contained 14 questions. The questionnaire was in three parts: the first part examined general issues linked to backpacking and contained 9 questions. These reflected issues linked to: why South Africa; travelling with whom; budget and activity prior to backpacking. The second part examined the motivations aspects; this was subdivided into push and pull factors. The push factors consisted of 18 Likert-scaled statements with the respondent being given the opportunity to state any 'other motivations' that were not listed. The pull factors consisted of 16 Likert-scale statements with the opportunity for the respondent to outline any 'other motivations for wanting to visit South Africa'. A seven-point Likert scale was used, ranging from 0 (no significance) to 7 (high significance). This was the same scale used in a study of Australian backpackers (Mohsin & Ryan, 2003), thus enabling comparisons to be drawn. These are highlighted later in the discussion section. The third part of the questionnaire requested demographic information, namely nationality, sex, age and educational level.

The research was conducted during April 2004 in the Eastern parts of South Africa. The self-administered questionnaires were handed out to backpackers in buses or in backpacker hostels at four different location: Port Elizabeth, Durban (both located on the coast), Oudtshoorn and Queenstown (located in the inner country). There were no instances where a backpacker refused to complete the questionnaire and all questionnaires were completed fully; therefore the total number of usable questionnaires was 95. It is worth noting that Uriely *et al.* (2002) estimated that only 40% of all backpackers are females and it could be argued that female backpackers in this study, who completed 60% of all questionnaires, may be over-represented.

The statistical program Minitab13 was used to analyse the data from the questionnaire. In order to examine correlations between different variables, some of the data were collapsed and recoded. After the initial data set was established a series of cross-tabulations were run in order to establish the relationships between different variables.

Research Findings

Demographic information

Of the 95 questionnaires, 36 (40%) were completed by males and 57 (60%) were completed by females. They came from Europe, Australia, New Zealand, USA, Canada, Argentina and African countries and were on average 25 years old. Thirty backpackers (31%) and therefore the largest percentage came from the UK. This is in accordance with Delport (2003), who estimated that backpackers in South Africa are between 25 and 28 years old and that backpackers from the UK are the biggest market.

Profile of the backpackers

The length of stay varied considerably among the respondents. However, 87% of all respondents were travelling for less than a year and the average length was 18 weeks. Overall, 46.3% stated that South Africa was their only destination, whereas 53.7% were on a multiple-destination journey. Whilst travelling, 41.1% backpackers travelled with one companion, 33.7% travelled on their own, whilst 25.2% travelled with two or more companions. These findings are not in accordance with Mohsin and Ryan (2003), who claim that the majority of backpackers travel on their own. The majority of backpackers (77.9%) were travelling by bus. Other modes of travelling were not very popular, as only 26.3% were using a car and 11.6% were hitchhiking. Nearly 12% said that they were using other forms of transport such as local taxis or a lift by friends. On average they spent £18.9/day. In comparison, conventional tourists spend about £80/day in South Africa. This corresponds with Loker-Murphy and Pearce's (1995) findings that backpackers travel on a low budget.

A third of the backpackers (33.3%) took leave from study to go backpacking; 23.7% had taken holiday from a full-time job and 19.4% had quit their career in order to go backpacking. In order to apply Mohsin and Ryan's (2003) two models of backpacker motivations, the categories listed under the 'previous activity' question were merged. The previous activities 'have quit my career', 'quit my part time job' and 'took leave without pay' were collapsed into one category, as in these cases the backpacker was proactive (i.e. an opportunity for travel was created). The previous activities 'taken holiday from full time job', 'unemployed/ retired', 'taken leave from study', 'retrenched' and 'other' were collapsed into a second group, as in these cases the backpacker was reactive (i.e. an opportunity for travel is taken). In the study by Mohsin and Ryan (2003), 30.1% of the respondents were proactive, whereas 69.9% were reactive; in this study the proactive percentage, 41.7%, was considerably higher.

A large proportion of the sample (82.1%) of the respondents spent or wanted to spend time off the beaten track. This high percentage supports Riley's (1988) and Richards and Wilson's (2004a) findings that back-packers seek adventure in exotic or at least different settings and therefore travel 'off the beaten track'.

Furthermore, the study revealed that 68.4% of backpackers consider themselves as tourists. This is not in accordance with Spreitzhofer (1998) and Welk (2004), who claim that most backpackers seek to maintain a distinction between the tourist (the others) and the backpacker or traveller (themselves). The reasons given as to why they are not tourists (31.6%) were very similar among the respondents and were similar to those presented in other studies. Further reasons given by the backpackers are summarised in Figure 10.1.

Motivations of Backpackers in South Africa

Push factors

The ranking of the push motivations for this study are illustrated in Table 10.1. The most important motivation, 'to discover new places and things', scored 6.3. However, it was closely followed by the motivation to 'broaden the knowledge about the world' (6.2). 'Escape from everyday work, home and leisure scene/monotony of the daily routine', 'to have a good time with friends', 'preference of the travelling lifestyle' and 'to relax physically and mentally' were also quite significant motivations with scores from 4.6 to 5.2. 'To challenge abilities', 'self-testing' and 'to make new friends' were of medium significance, with scores from 3.8 to 4.0, whereas 'confusion about future plans', 'advice of friends and

---

"Off the beaten track. No package tours" (23 year old South African female)

"Tourist = Holiday, Traveller = Backpacker" (24 year old British male)

"Prefer to try and blend in and be involved in culture rather than living apart from it" (34 year old British female)

"Trying to do least amount of "touristy" things" (22 year old British male).

"Cheap ways, rarely use tour operations." (26 year old British male).

"Tourist (for weeks away) Traveller (ongoing travel)" (30 year old Australian male)

"We've planned everything ourselves, we've taken black taxis all the time" (21 year old German male)

"I am a Peace Corps Volunteer from USA since Jan 2003 in SA" (62 year old female from the USA)

Figure 10.1 Reasons for 'not being tourists' stated by backpackers

Table 10.1 Ranking of push motivations

Push factors	
1. To discover new places and things	6.3
2. To broaden knowledge about the world	6.2
3. Escape from everyday work, home and leisure scene/monotony of the daily routine	5.2
4. To have a good time with friends	4.9
5. Preference of travelling lifestyle	4.6
6. To relax physically and mentally	4.6
7. To challenge abilities	4.0
8. Self-testing	3.9
9. To make new friends	3.8
10. Confusion about future plans	2.2
11. Advice of friends and relatives	2.1
12. To gain a feeling of belonging	1.8
13. The completion of study commitments	1.6
14. To improve status	1.4
15. To postpone current commitments	0.8
16. The completion of work commitments	0.7
17. In search of employment	0.5
18. In search of the right partner	0.5

relatives', 'to gain a feeling of belonging', 'the completion of study commitments' and 'to improve status' were of low significance, with scores from 2.2 to 1.4. Below an average score of 1 and therefore of no significance were the motivations 'to postpone current commitments', 'the completion of work commitments', 'in search of employment' and 'in search of the right partner'.

Pull factors

Table 10.2 illustrates that with a score of 5.5, the most important pull factor to go backpacking in South Africa was a 'unique mix of adventure, cultural and wildlife attractions'. However, 'to get to know native cultures', 'to see the big five (elephant, rhino, leopard, lion, buffalo) and wild animals', 'in South Africa there are lots of facilities for backpackers', 'the climate of South Africa', 'friendly people', 'the history of the place', 'the beaches of South Africa', 'positive word of mouth', 'wide range of adventure and outdoor sports' and 'to visit a National Park' were also quite significant motivations, with scores between 4.9 and 4.0. 'The vastness of the place', 'to go on safari', 'value for money'

Table 10.2 Ranking of pull motivations

Particular motivations to visit South Africa	
Unique mix of adventure, cultural and wildlife attractions	5.5
To get to know native cultures	4.9
To see the big five and wild animals	4.8
In South Africa there are lots of facilities for backpackers	4.7
The climate of South Africa	4.6
Friendly people	4.6
The history of the place	4.6
Beaches of South Africa	4.4
Positive word of mouth	4.1
Wide range of adventure and outdoor sports	4.0
To visit a National Park	4.0
The vastness of the place	3.9
To go on safari	3.6
Value for money	3.2
The low value of the Rand	2.9
Price of backpacker accommodation in South Africa	2.6
Reasonable car hire rates	1.2

and 'the low value of the Rand (South African currency)' were not very significant, with scores between 2.6 and 3.9. The least important motivation was 'reasonable car hire rates', with a score of 1.2. (This can be explained by the fact that only 26.3% of the backpackers were travelling by car.)

Overall, it can be stated that the features that SATOUR markets in order to motivate backpackers to come to South Africa were highly significant to fairly significant (5.5–2.6) to the backpackers of this sample. 'Reasonable car hire rates' was the only exception. The backpackers were exclusively interested in tribal culture, such as the Zulus or Xhosas, which are native populations of South Africa.

'Other' motivations

The questionnaire identified 19 backpackers who indicated 'other' motivations to those that were listed. The motivational themes stated by backpackers were 'to learn more about myself, to find myself, to educate myself about the world', 'shark diving' and 'to experience Nelson Mandela and the post-apartheid South Africa, white versus black'. The motivation 'to learn about myself, to find myself' can explain the backpacking trip as a 'rite de passage', a motivation that has been identified by Sørensen (2003). 'Shark diving' was one example of backpackers seeking adventure in exotic or at least different settings (Richards & Wilson, 2004a; Riley, 1988). 'To experience Nelson Mandela and the post-apartheid South Africa,' as well as the high scores of 'to get to know native cultures' (4.9) and 'the history of the place' (4.6), confirms the argument by Riley (1988) that backpackers show an interest in the culture and history of the country they are visiting.

Relationships Between Different Variables

Relationship between 'backpacked before'/'not backpacked before' and 'to travel off the beaten track'

Whereas 71.4% of the backpackers with no experience wanted to spend time off the beaten track, the share was considerably higher among the backpackers with experience (88.1%). Certainly, it could be argued that spending time off the main track is a self-esteem and development motive, which is a higher-level need, as identified by Pearce (1993 as cited in Burns & Holden, 1995: 42). As only one relationship and no others could be identified, and all other motivations had the same ranking among backpackers with and without experience, Pearce's career ladder (1993) was not confirmed by this study.

Relationships between gender and motivations

A relationship between gender and the significance of the motivation 'the price of the backpacker accommodation in South Africa' was explored. It is confirmed by the chi-square test, which shows that only 23.7% of all males considered the price of backpacker accommodation in South Africa as a significant motivation, compared to 43.9% of the females.

Relationships between educational level and motivations

The chi-square test confirmed that there is a relationship between educational level and the motivations 'the completion of study commitments' and 'the climate of South Africa'. Only 12.5% of the backpackers who had finished their education stated that the completion of study commitments was a significant motivation for them; 29.8% of the backpackers who were still in education considered it as significant. Furthermore, the climate of South Africa was much more significant to backpackers who were still in school (83.0%) compared to those who had finished their education (64.6%).

Relationship between age and motivations

Several correlations could be identified between the age of the respondents and the different motivations. Whereas only 8.7% of the backpackers who were at least 24 years old stated that the completion of study commitments was a significant motivation to them, 32.7% in the age group of up to 23 years of age stated that it was significant. This can be explained by the fact that in the older age group, more respondents have already finished their studies or their education in general. Furthermore, there is a relationship between age and the pull-motivation 'the vastness of the place'; 75.5% of the backpackers up to 23 years of age responded that it was an important motivation to them, whereas in the age group of 24 and above it was only 50%. The climate is another motivation that was more significant to the younger age group. Whereas 87.7% of the younger backpackers said that the climate of South Africa was a significant motivation, only 58.7% in the age group of 24 and above shared this view.

Relationships between nationalities and motivations

Several relationships related to nationalities were also identified. Nationalities were grouped accordingly: Nationality 1 were backpackers from the UK, Australia and New Zealand; Nationality 2 were backpackers from continental Europe; and Nationality 3 were backpackers from the USA, Canada, African countries and Argentina.

The backpackers (97.5%) from the UK, Australia and New Zealand (Nationality 1) stated that they spent or would like to spend time off the beaten track. Among the backpackers from the USA, Canada, Africa and Argentina (Nationality 3) the number was 80%. However, the back-packers from continental Europe (Nationality 2), with a percentage of 65.7%, were the least interested group in terms of spending time off the beaten track.

With regard to the 'confusion about future plans', 25.0% of the backpackers from Canada, the USA, Africa and Argentina said that it was a significant motivation for them; only 11.4% of the continental European backpackers stated that this was important. However, among the backpackers from Britain, Australia and New Zealand, 40% responded that this motivation was significant. Therefore, it could be argued that although Riley's (1988) statement about being at a crossroads in life and confused about the future are backpackers' main motivations is not confirmed by the majority of the backpackers, it is most significant to the backpackers from the UK, Australia and New Zealand.

The final relationship was identified between nationality and the motivation 'to go on safari'. This motivation was mainly significant to the backpackers from the UK, New Zealand and Australia (65.0%), and the backpackers from continental Europe (57.1%). However, only 25% of the backpackers from the USA, Canada, Africa and Argentina considered it significant.

Overall, it can be stated that there were no relationships related to the most significant push motivations 'to discover new places and things', 'to broaden knowledge about the world', 'escape from everyday work, home and leisure scene/monotony of daily routine' and the pull motivations 'unique mix of adventure, cultural and wildlife attractions', 'to get to know native cultures' and 'to see the big five (elephant, rhino, leopard, lion, buffalo) and wild animals' identified in this study. These motivations were equally significant among the different nationalities, age groups, educational levels and gender.

Discussion

Table 10.3 presents the push factors that were tested in the Mohsin and Ryan's (2003) study, as well as in this research project. The comparison was facilitated by the fact that a Likert-scale from 0 to 7 was applied in both studies. As illustrated in Table 10.3, the motivation 'to broaden the knowledge about the world' was highly significant to the backpackers of both research projects. The motivation 'preference of travelling lifestyle' achieved an almost identical score as well. However, all other motivations illustrated above were of lower significance to the sample of backpackers in South Africa compared to the backpackers in the Northern Territory. The biggest differences were between the significance of the motivations 'to postpone current commitments' (South African backpackers 0.8, Australian backpackers 3.46) and 'the completion of work commitments' (South African backpackers 0.7, Australian backpackers 3.55). However, although there were considerable differences in the scores, the hierarchy of the motivations was very similar in both studies.

Table 10.3 Comparison of backpacker push motivations

Push motivations	South Africa (Benson & Niggel, 2005)	Australia (Mohsin & Ryan, 2003)
To broaden knowledge about the world	6.2	6.08
Preference of travelling lifestyle	4.6	4.76
Self-testing	3.9	4.61
To make new friends	3.8	5.22
Confusion about future plans	2.2	4.12
Advice of friends and relatives	2.1	4.33
The completion of study commitments	1.6	3.61
To postpone current commitments	0.8	3.46
The completion of work commitments	0.7	3.55
In search of employment	0.5	2.84
In search of the right partner	0.5	2.54

When comparing the findings of the study with the motivations found in the literature, it is clear that the need to explore and learn as well as curiosity and the search for the meaning of the world, which was identified by Andrzej and Buchanan (2001) and Luthans (1995) as innate and central drives or motives, proved to be most significant to the backpackers. Furthermore, the escapism motive, which has been identified by numerous studies (Cohen, 2003a; Loker-Murphy & Pearce, 1995; Riley, 1988; Spreitzhofer, 1998; Vance, 2004), was highly significant to the sample and the third most important push motive overall. As the motive 'to have a good time with friends' had a high score of 4.9, it confirmed Burns and Holden (1995) and Riley's (1988) claim that enjoyment and fun are important tourism motivations. Furthermore, the motive of seeking adventure and excitement (Richards & Wilson, 2004a; Riley, 1988) and activity motives (Andrzej & Buchanan, 2001; Luthans, 1995) were not only confirmed by the wish to go shark diving but also by the high rankings of the motivations related to the adventurous character (including the wildlife) of South Africa.

However, the need for certainty, as identified by Pettinger (1996), was not a significant motivation in this research. Moreover, whereas Binder (2004) and Luthans (1995) argue that power, achievement, security and status are the most significant motivations in modern societies, the relatively low scores of the motivations 'to improve status', 'self-testing' and 'to challenge my abilities' proved that this was not the case within the sample population. The low scores of the motivations 'to gain a feeling of belonging' and 'in search of the right partner' are in contradiction with Richards and Wilson's (2004a) and Luthans' (1995) statements that the affection motivation has a growing significance in modern societies.

However, most of the historical tourism motivations, such as relaxation, to improve knowledge about the world, to improve social contacts as well as education after finishing school, which have been identified in the literature (Pearce, 1982; Riley, 1988), were highly significant to the sample of this study. Beard and Ragheb's (1993) contemporary approach to tourism motivation as cited in Ryan (1997) is also confirmed by this study. This is due to the fact that the significant motivations that were identified included intellectual components such as 'to discover new places and things', social components such as 'to make new friends', competence mastery components such as 'self-testing', as well as stimulus avoidance components such as 'to escape from everyday work, home and leisure scene'.

Conclusions

As the backpackers were mainly young budget tourists on an extended holiday, on a multiple-destination journey, mostly of Western origin and with an average length of journey of 18 weeks, it can be stated that the sample corresponded to the profile of backpackers that has been identified in the literature on backpackers (Loker-Murphy & Pearce, 1995; Mohsin & Ryan, 2003; Riley, 1988; Sørensen, 2003; Uriely *et al.*, 2002). A comparison with the findings of Mohsin and Ryan's (2003) study about the motives, behaviours and satisfactions of backpackers in the Northern Territory, Australia, revealed that the hierarchy of the motivations was very similar in both studies, albeit the sample for this study was smaller.

Many of the push and pull motivations in the survey were identified by SATOUR as 'features' that are communicated to 'would-be' back-packers in South Africa. Many of these motivations had a score between 5.5 and 2.6 and, therefore, were moderately significant to the sample. A large proportion of the motivations identified in the literature were confirmed by the findings of this study. However, it is also evident that a few theories and motivations identified as significant in the literature were of no significance to the sample of this research; in particular, Pearce's (1993) career ladder could not be confirmed by this study as backpackers with and without experience had the same ranking of the motivations. There was only one relationship of backpackers 'with backpacking experience' and 'backpackers without experience' related to their motivations.

Although several relationships between motivations and different variables were identified, there were no relationships related to the most significant motivations. The main motivations as discussed in the findings were equally significant to all backpackers regardless of nationality, age, educational level and gender.

Chapter 11

Study Backpackers: Australia's Short-stay International Student Travellers

JEFF JARVIS and VICTORIA PEEL

Introduction

In many parts of the world, Cohen (2004) argues, backpackers are often condemned for their appearance, conduct, superficiality, stinginess and seclusion in backpacker enclaves. In response, tourism officials of many developing countries are encouraged to upgrade facilities to attract perceived 'quality' tourists. In stark contrast to this, in 1995, the Australian federal government launched its 'National Backpacker Tourism Development Strategy' (Bureau of Tourism Research, 1995), the first targeted policy of its kind in the world. The strategy relied on original work conducted by Australian tourism researchers (Jarvis, 1994; Loker, 1993a; Pearce, 1990), which paved the way in identifying the backpacker as a distinctive and economically beneficial market segment for the nation. The economic development power of the segment has been further emphasised in studies by Hampton (1998), Scheyvens (2002) and Visser (2004). Since implementation of the strategy in the mid-1990s, market response has been overwhelmingly positive, as indicated by growth in international backpacker numbers to Australia[1] from just over 160,000 in 1994 to over 485,000 in 2004 (Bureau of Tourism Research, 2005). In 2002 it was calculated that the Australian 'Backpacking Industry' was worth $A2.5 billion to the Australian economy or approximately 22% of earnings for the entire tourism industry (Bureau of Tourism Research, 2002). As a result, the strategic importance of the segment within Australia's overall tourism marketing context continues to be recognised in government policy (Department of Industry, Tourism and Resources, Tourism Green Paper, 2003: 23):

> While backpackers constitute 10 per cent of visitors to Australia they contribute 22 per cent of expenditure by international visitors ... they

visit more regional areas than other international visitors and hence can provide a boost to local economies which might not benefit significantly from the growth in inbound tourism.

Growth in the long-stay, high-yield backpacker market has encouraged a tentative interest in the affiliated long-stay international student market by Australian government tourism agencies. The federal government's 2004 *Tourism White Paper* (Department of Industry, Tourism and Resources, Tourism White Paper, 2004) noted the forecast growth in international students to Australia who are estimated to spend more and stay longer than other segments of comparable size. In 2003, while a modest 6% of all international visitors came to Australia for education purposes, the student sector accounted for 29% of total nights spent in the destination (Bureau of Tourism Research, International Visitor Survey, March quarter, 2003). According to the federal government's Tourism White Paper (DITR, Tourism White Paper, 2004: 11), these students spend an estimated A$13,448 per capita, making them worth over A$3 billion per annum. Nominating student tourists as a 'key niche market' in the Tourism White Paper (DITR, 2004), policy makers have also highlighted the benefits of student spending-power for hinterland regions that support tertiary institutions.

The commensurate growth in yield associated with international students in Australia has exceeded that of the backpacker segment with which it is sometimes compared (DITR, 2003b: 11). Since 1990, the international education market has grown eightfold (Marginson, 2005) and Australia claims the largest ratio of international to local students among English-speaking countries (Australian Education Institute, May, 2003: 6). In 2002, education and training was valued at approximately $5 billion to Australia's economy and is the nation's third largest services export (DEST, 2002). Economic pressure on universities is partially driving this growth on the supply side. Easing of government restrictions on international student access to Australian higher education, and decreasing public funding for the tertiary education sector, coupled with government inducements for universities to strengthen international academic linkages and find economies of scale, have stimulated the expansion of overseas enrolments (Gallagher, 2002).

Cohen (2004) has emphasised the heterogeneous nature of backpacking, and as the market matures in Australia, it can be seen that new segments are emerging to rival the traditional dominance of the 'long-term' budget traveller (Riley, 1988). Yet while the Australian government has correctly identified the fiscal benefits of both international students and international backpackers, policy has so far failed to address segmentation of both markets and their inter-related potential. This chapter aims to achieve a more nuanced understanding of the connections between the international student and backpacker markets through a study of the travel patterns and motivations of Australia's short-stay tertiary student population. Short-stay students are defined as those who spend one or two semesters at an Australian university compared with the several years required for a full degree. A quantitative survey of short-stay international students at Monash University in Victoria, Australia, was used to assess, firstly, motivations to study abroad, secondly, reasons for choosing Australia as a study destination, thirdly, information sources used in trip planning, fourthly, propensity to travel while in the host country and, fifthly, expenditure patterns. The significant tourism imperative shown by the group in their decision to study abroad, to choose Australia as a destination and in the use of leisure time while visiting shows them to be a lucrative niche market spanning both the larger backpacker and international student populations.

Australia's Short-term Student Market

Despite the paucity of academic analysis of student tourists, observed by Litvin (2003), research in this sector increasingly reveals a segmentation approach (Carr, 2003; Chen & Kerstetter, 1999; Cohen, 2003b, Hawkins & Bransgrove, 1998; Hsu & Sung, 1996). Building on the foundation work of Chadee and Cutler (1996) and Hsu and Sung (1996), Field (1999) determined differences between the travel propensity of domestic and international students in an American study, which demonstrated that international students were less likely to undertake leisure travel than their local peers. Of particular significance in the context of this chapter, Field's work identified travel differences between student groups according to nationality, demonstrating that Australian and New Zealand students visiting North America showed the greatest propensity for travel while visiting Indian students showed the least (Field, 1999: 379). Similar findings were also borne out in a study of university students in Australia conducted by Ritchie and Priddle (2000). As Carr (2003: 187) suggests, cultural origin and associated demographic factors such as gender, age and marital status have significant bearing on the nature of student travel patterns. Yet little research has segmented student travel patterns in host destinations according to their motivation to travel for study purposes.

Students from Asian countries comprise 80% of the total international tertiary student enrolment in Australia and the majority of these are clustered in the Information Technology, Business and Commerce fields (DEST, 2002). Gallagher (2002) has attributed the phenomenon in part to the youthful populations of these countries combined with modernising economies and the need for skills in a changing workplace. Relaxation of government policy in China, and the substantial demand for an English-language education out of that country, has also resulted in demand for Australian university places. Yet, despite the importance of North and South-east Asia as source countries in fuelling the general boom in demand for Australian education, student arrivals from Europe and North America are also rapidly increasing. Between 1999 and 2001, the number of American students studying in Australia nearly tripled (Bureau of Tourism Research, *International Visitor Survey, 1999–2002*). While in 2003 the number of European students at Australian universities represented only about 7% of the total international university student cohort, the market shows similarly significant growth. Students from Norway, Germany and Sweden in particular accounted for over 61% of all European student arrivals in 2004 (DEST International Student Statistics, 2004).

The conditions under which American and European students come to Australia, and their motivations for doing so, differ substantially from the majority of their Asian counterparts. American and European students are less likely to pursue full-degree study while in Australia, choosing to remain short-term for one or two semesters. Australian universities host these students either on a fee-paying basis as a 'study abroad' student, or on exchange where an Australian student is provided with a replacement position at the sending institution. Grades achieved while in Australia contribute towards the student's degree at their home institution. In 2003, Australia hosted 6387 study-abroad students of which the six leading source countries in rank order comprise the USA, Canada, France, Germany, Sweden and the UK (IDP, 2003).

Changed student recruitment practices in Australian universities are facilitating this process. As Gallagher (2002) notes, the atypical informal connections made between institutions and individual academics that once formed the only conduit for study abroad are now largely formalised and controlled by university marketing offices. Study-abroad students can purchase a range of services such as tuition, housing, food and travel from Australian universities through arrangements brokered with the sending institution. Trade in study abroad in particular is highly commercialised and competitive. In North America, universities and colleges frequently promote diversity of study-abroad destinations and programme style as a point of difference in the competition for students.

The intense marketing of Australian universities to fee-paying students has frequently relied on the deployment of tourism stereotypes and popular icons, particularly in the American and Scandinavian markets (Peel, 2004). In April 2001, the *New York Times Higher Education Supplement* reported on the marketing strategy of the University of the Sunshine Coast, located north of Brisbane, which is based on Steve Irwin, best known to viewers of the Animal Planet channel in North America as 'The Crocodile Hunter'. Irwin's name and image appears on posters and large cardboard cut-outs used by recruiters to publicise the institution, while brochures depicting Irwin and a crocodile announce: 'What a beaut base the Sunshine Coast is for you to plan your future from' (*New York Times, Higher Education Supplement*, 8 April, 2001). The strategy builds unashamedly on Australia's established position in the American outbound tourism market, which was successfully created two decades before by Paul Hogan's Australian Tourist Commission (ATC) advertising campaign.

The packaging of semester break travel opportunities confirms the promotional power of tourism in the selling of Australian education (Peel, 2004). Tours purchased independently by students or prepackaged by the host university are widely used in advertising to study-abroad students. Funded by the universities and the Australian Embassy, the Washington-based Australian Education Office (AEO) has promoted links between American and Australian higher education since 1992. AEO's *Study Abroad Guide to Australian Universities* includes information on the extracurricular travel offered by individual universities and the tourism possibilities of campus location. Bond University's Gold Coast location is thus described as 'renowned for its magnificent beaches, waterways, beautiful national parks and warm subtropical climate'(AEO, n.d.: 18). In *Study Downunder*, the International Development Program (IDP) Education Australia promotional magazine, images depict typical backpacker activities such as bushwalking and bungee jumping while the text and accompanying advertisements reinforce offers of the kind of stereotypical travel experiences anticipated by the international backpacker. One example of a Western Australian university advertisement offers students the chance to 'experience the real downunder' through a 10-day camping expedition to remote corners of the state, while another promoting a regional institution in New South Wales exhorts students to 'hit the books then hit outback Australia'.

Methodology

Between June 1998 and June 2005 a survey was administered to short-stay international students enrolled at Monash University for one or two semesters only. All students in the sample had elected to take an undergraduate unit in Australian studies from the National Centre of Australian Studies, which was designed for visiting international students, as part of their study programme. A quantitative methodology was used via a voluntary self-completion questionnaire distributed at the end of each semester of study. After collection, the data were collated and analysed using the SPSS statistical package. At the conclusion of the data-collection period, 912 useable surveys had been collected.

Findings

The population comprised students from 25 nationalities and was evenly divided between fee-paying study-abroad students and non-fee-paying exchange students. The age of the sample ranged from 18 to 38, with an average age of 21.3. American students were slightly younger at 20.5 years as compared with European students averaging 22.9 years. Female students comprised just over two thirds of the sample. In terms of region of origin, 64% came from North America, of which Canadians comprised 4% and Americans 60% ($n = 547$). Europeans comprised 29% ($n = 264$) and Asian students numbered just 7%. A national breakdown of the European sample shows that Germany, Scandinavia and the Netherlands each accounted for 8% of the total.

Stop-overs before and after study in Australia

Respondents' travel patterns were significantly multidestinational, with 20% of the cohort reporting having visited another country before arrival, and 58% planning to stop over on completion of their Australian journey. New Zealand proved particularly popular as a stopover destination for 21% prior to arrival in Australia and for 40% at the conclusion of their studies. A majority of the sample (81%) arrived directly in Melbourne, with 18% landing in Sydney, indicating some pre-semester travel may have also occurred. Like backpackers, short-term students are long-stay visitors, with an average 188 days spent in Australia of an average total of 198 days spent away from home. American short-term students overwhelmingly prefer one semester away (95%), while Europeans are more inclined to stay for two semesters. In consequence, the American length of stay is slightly

Table 11.1 Overseas enrolments in universities in Australia by region, 2004

Region	
Americas	11,823
Southern and Eastern Europe	1424
Northern and Western Europe	9446

Source: www.AEI.dest.gov.au

shorter, at 155 days, compared to 238 days for European students. Only 7% of the population had previously visited Australia, of which Europeans were the most prominent repeat visitors.

Pre-departure information source

In terms of information sources on Australia, students were asked to rate in terms of importance a range of options from 0 to 10. Like backpackers (Jarvis, 1994), short-term students regard guidebooks (6.8), the Internet (6.3) and advice from friends and relatives (5.9) as the most important pre-departure information sources.

Table 11.2 shows that, like the backpacker market, travel agents rate poorly as a pre-departure information source (score = 3.4) while over 52% rated guidebooks as extremely important (score = 8+). In considering

Table 11.2 Information sources on Australia accessed prior to arrival (rated 0–10)

	Total%	USA%	European%
Guidebooks	6.8	6.7	7.0
The Internet	6.3	6.5	5.7
Friends who had travelled in Australia	5.9	5.9	6.0
Print media articles on Australia	4.1	3.9	4.1
TV programmes/documentaries seen on Australia	4.0	3.6	4.7
Travel agent at home	3.4	3.5	3.0
Tourism information provided by the ATC	2.5	2.5	2.2
Australian Embassy	2.0	1.5	2.7

specific study information sources, 66% of the cohort rated the international office at their home university extremely highly (score = 10), followed by the Internet (score = 6.6) and personal advice from friends who had studied abroad (score = 5.1), a result that emphasises the value of word of mouth information in this segment.

Motivation to study abroad

In exploring factors influencing the decision to study abroad, students were asked to rate statements that included long-term desire to travel and study, positive feedback on the experience from friends, the personal challenge of the experience, the opportunity to broaden their awareness of the world, the opportunity to meet people, the opportunity to achieve a change from everyday life, the opportunity to experience another culture and the opportunity to enhance career prospects.

As shown in Table 11.3, the top five responses in order of their mean value closely match previous studies on the motivation of backpackers to Australia (Jarvis, 1994). In rank order, these comprise 'desire to broaden awareness of the world' (score = 8.7) combined with 'a long desire to travel/study in another country' (score = 8.5), the 'desire to meet people' (score = 8.3) and the 'desire to experience another culture' (score = 8.3). It is notable that career enhancement as a motivation for studying abroad was slightly less influential in decision-making (score = 6.7), with Americans less influenced by this aspect than Europeans.

As shown in Table 11.4, motivation to study specifically in Australia explicitly identified a desire to understand the host culture on a deeper level than the average 'tourist'. 'Desire to experience more about life in Australia than being a tourist' was rated highly (score = 7.3) together with the 'desire to travel to use study as an excuse to travel to Australia' (score = 7.2) and as a result of 'positive advice from friends who had travelled in Australia' (score = 7.1). This finding highlights the significant role of tourism as a motivator in the choice of Australia by this group in association with the academic benefits of studying in the country. European students rated the 'size of Australia' and commensurate diversity of travel experience as the second most important reason for country selection after the desire to experience more about Australian culture than is possible as a tourist.

Travel patterns in-country

Concomitant with the importance of travel opportunities in the motivation to visit Australia, respondents undertook intense in-country

Table 11.3 Study cohort motivation to study in another country

	Total cohort	USA subgroup	European subgroup
I wanted to broaden my awareness of the world	8.7	8.8	8.5
I have been wanting to travel/study in another country for a long period of time	8.5	8.6	8.4
I saw studying abroad as a challenging experience	7.9	7.7	8.3
I wanted to experience another culture	8.5	8.7	8.1
I wanted to meet people	8.3	8.5	7.9
I wanted a change/break from everyday life at home	8.0	8.4	7.3
I saw studying overseas as an opportunity to enhance my career prospects once I return home	6.7	6.5	7.2
I heard a lot of positive things about studying in another country from friends	8.0	8.7	6.8

travel. A trip for one or more nights outside Melbourne during a mid-semester break for an average of nine nights was undertaken by 89% of the population. With regard to travel in various Australian states during this break, 43% of the cohort claimed to spend the majority of their time in Queensland, 15% in New South Wales and 13% in Victoria. A significant variation between student nationalities in this regard showed that American (64%) students were more likely than Europeans (12%) to take a mid-semester break in Queensland where the backpacker hub of Cairns/Far North Queensland was the most popular destination. The European subgroup preferred travel closer to Melbourne, to the Southern states of Tasmania (23%), New South Wales (20%) and Victoria (20%).

With regard to travel intensity during semester, 68% of the sample took more than three trips away of at least one night's duration. While 63% chose to visit Sydney, which is easily accessible from Melbourne by air, road and rail, study constraints ensured that the majority of these

Table 11.4 Study cohort reasons for studying in Australia

	Total cohort	USA subgroup	European subgroup
I wanted to study and travel so that I could experience more about life in Australia than I could by just being a tourist.	7.3	7.5	7.2
I have always wanted to travel to Australia and studying here gave me a good excuse to come.	7.2	7.6	6.7
Many other friends and travellers have told me positive things about travelling in Australia.	7.1	7.6	6.5
I heard a lot of positive things about studying in Australia from friends.	6.6	7.4	5.4
The size of Australia means that there are a lot of different things to experience and see while here.	6.5	6.6	6.8
Australia is a safe destination to study/travel in.	6.3	6.9	5.1
Australia is very different from home.	4.8	4.4	5.3

trips were conducted close to Melbourne within the state of Victoria. The four most visited destinations in the state of Victoria were the Great Ocean Road (71%), the Grampians National Park (40%), Wilson's Promontory (33%) and Phillip Island (29%).

At the conclusion of their studies 76% of the cohort planned to travel in Australia for an average of 27 days with an average budget of A$1701. European students were more likely to travel post-semester in Australia (88% for an average stay of 40 nights with a budget of A$2325) than American students (68% for an average trip of 19 nights with a budget of A$1401). Of those who travel at semester end, the most popular destinations corresponded with the significant backpacker locations of Sydney (50%), Cairns (47%), Brisbane/Gold Coast (47%), Ayers Rock/Alice Springs, (32%), Sunshine Coast/Fraser Island (32%), Whitsunday Islands (29%) and Byron Bay (29%). The European subgroup were far more travel active at semester end and therefore more likely than Americans to visit a range of destinations, with 32% visiting Darwin (as opposed to just 13% of the American subgroup), 17% visiting Tasmania, 15% visiting South Australia and 13% visiting Perth.

In terms of transport used to travel around Australia, the cohort emulated the backpacker market, employing a mix of modes. Flying was the dominant means (84%), followed by intercity coach (62%), intercity train (56%), rental car (53%), private car (40%), boat (33%) and a 'backpacker tour' bus such as OZ Experience (23%).

Expenditure patterns

The expenditure patterns identified in Table 11.5 demonstrate that these short-term students are decidedly high yield, spending approximately A$7766 exclusive of university fees during a semester of study in Australia. Yield is significantly increased with the addition of university tuition fees, which can be in excess of A$11,000 for a semester study abroad (University of Melbourne Study Abroad Fee Schedule, 2005). A breakdown of expenditure showed that 39% of an individual budget was spent on travel in Australia, either during the mid-semester break or at the end of semester, further highlighting travel intensity. Differences between national subgroups showed that the European cohort averaged A$912 in eight days during a mid-semester trip compared with the American average of A$1498 in ten days. Mean expenditure on each mid-semester trip was A$1296.

Average weekly expenditure during the period at university was A$298. Rent comprised 38% of that figure, food and drink 28%, entertainment 14%, general shopping 14% and public transport 7%. For an estimated 16-week stay in Melbourne including 13 weeks of classes, a one-week orientation period and a two-week exam period, average expenditure for each participant was estimated at $4769.

Visiting friends and relatives

The strategic importance of the market was further emphasised by the 55% of the cohort who attracted friends or relatives to visit Australia while they were studying.

Each student in the population attracted an additional 1.3 visitors with an average stay of 31 days in Australia. Europeans as a whole attracted more VFR traffic, with 72% having one or more visitors who stay for an average of 40 days compared with 45% of Americans who have guests staying for 19 days. Of those who host visitors, on average an additional 2.4 guests arrive in the country.

Table 11.5 Study cohort expenditure

	Full cohort	*USA sub*	*European sub*
Weekly expenditure $A			
Accommodation	112.52	116.72	105.62
Food and drinks	84.11	89.51	76.86
Entertainment	41.45	42.13	40.28
Transport/travel	19.39	20.83	17.41
General Shopping	40.60	41.88	39.38
Total weekly expend	298.07	311.07	279.55
Total spend for 16 weeks	4769.12	4977.12	4472.80
Travel expenditure $A			
Mid-semester trip	1296.24	1497.75	911.60
End of semester trip	1701.01	1401.60	2325.43
Total travel expenditure	2997.25	2899.45	3237.03
Total expenditure (excluding university fees)	7766.37	7876.47	7709.83
Percentage of total expenditure on travel, mid- and post-semester	39%	37%	42%

Discussion and Recommendations

Cohen (2004) calls for research to cease from referring to backpacking as a homogenous phenomenon and pay more attention to its diverse manifestations. The empirical evidence of this study suggests that short-term students can be identified as a uniquely high-yielding subsection of the increasingly heterogeneous backpacker market or 'study backpackers'. This group is primarily motivated by the packaged and independent travel opportunities associated with study in Australia ahead of academic outcomes. In essence, the market is being driven by Australia's tourism 'pull' as a youth destination, assisted by the policy 'push' to internationalise university campuses. This is occurring through either the development of exchange programmes under the influence of globalisa-tion or the recruitment of financially lucrative study-abroad fee-paying students for one or two semesters.

Study backpackers are travel intensive and will spend 39% of their estimated total expenditure on travel, with Europeans spending more on travel than Americans. The high-yield practices of the broader back-packer market are apparent in the subsegment, which spends an average $7766 per semester in Australia, excluding tuition fees paid to the university. Similarities to the broader backpacker market also exist in that study backpackers are multidestinational travellers with one fifth of the respondents reporting side trips to another country before arrival in Australia and more than half planning stopovers on the return home. Clearly, there are advantages in this traffic for the tourism industries of Fiji, Thailand, Singapore, Tahiti and particularly New Zealand, which is the most preferred secondary destination (Jarvis, 2004). Study back-packers also share the same information source characteristics identified in the backpacker market, with a strong emphasis on guidebooks and word of mouth information. They rely on their home university's international office in terms of sourcing specific study information.

Like the broader backpacker market to Australia, the study back-packer subgroup is dominated by Americans and Europeans, with an over-representation of the latter. One rationale for the strong connection between travel and study for American students can be traced to their particular work–life cycle (Jarvis & Peel, 2005). Diverting from estab-lished pathways to employment by undertaking extensive travel during university studies is culturally challenging for this group. This hurdle to long-haul travel was also identified by Riley (1988), who hypothesised that sociocultural conditions in source markets influence the take-up rate of backpackers. The results of this study suggest that the desire of young Americans to travel is being converted into study-abroad programmes that serve to legitimate travel motivation within the home culture.

While sharing a range of characteristics with the general international backpacker population, the study backpacker shows distinctive and strategically attractive traits for host destinations. The subsegment is economically beneficial in ways similar to working holiday makers in that their day-to-day living expenses are contained within the host city. The subsegment can therefore be presumed to contribute significantly to the dispersal of backpacker expenditure in regional destinations that possess universities. The economic benefits of this segment are dispersed into the local economy rather than the established tourist economy via students either staying in university accommodation or renting private apartments, purchasing goods in local supermarkets and visiting local entertainment venues frequented by Australian students. The timing of this expenditure is typically constrained by the study timetable and concentrated during the academic year.

Despite long length of stay (188 days average), educational require-ments cause study backpackers to be relatively travel time poor, prompting travel in a hub and spoke pattern from the home base. Generally short-stay student travel in Australia is confined to three types. Firstly, in short breaks during semester weekends to nearby destinations; secondly, as a longer trip during the mid-semester holiday of around nine days usually to one or two states; and finally, as an extended trip at the conclusion of the semester of approximately 27 days in a pattern that echoes that of traditional backpackers. This localised travel pattern around the study hub presents significant opportunities for suitable product development for the regional hinterlands surrounding univer-sities. The lucrative mid-semester travel market, where the average spend is $1296 over nine days, has already stimulated some universities and private companies in Australia to offer specialised international 'spring break packages' to established backpacker destinations such as Northern Queensland and Central Australia. The more extensive post-semester travel needs of the segment are more than adequately met by the existing backpacker network in Australia.

In addition, the sub-segment stimulates lucrative long-haul VFR traffic to the host country. While over half of the study cohort attracted VFR, with an average stay of 31 days, this trend was significantly expressed by European short-stay students, of whom 75% in the study population brought one or more visitors to Australia with an extended average length of stay of 40 days. It can be hypothesised that parents, siblings, friends and partners are using the study backpacker relative as a trigger to visit Australia. Anecdotal evidence also indicates that European study backpackers prompt non-studying friends to apply for a 12-month working holiday maker visa in order to meet and travel together. These findings support the significant strategic benefit of this segment as the host destination directly benefits from their expenditure while each study backpacker attracts an additional 1.3 international visitors to the host destination. Further study into the travel behaviour and economic impact of this VFR group is encouraged.

Overall, these findings suggest the need for a more nuanced approach in government and industry marketing to the study backpacker that recognises their specific travel patterns and product interests. While some preliminary cooperative marketing to student travellers has been

Table 11.6 Study cohort generation of VFR to Australia

	Total study cohort	*USA subsegment*	*European subsegment*
Percentage who have a visitor from home	54.9	45.0	72.3
Average number of VFRs per study backpacker	1.3	1.0	1.9
Average number of VFRs for those who had visitors	2.4	2.3	2.6
Average estimated length of stay in Australia per visitor	30.8 nights	19.4 nights	40.2 nights

undertaken by Australian government tourism and education sectors, it would appear that larger opportunities exist. At present, university marketing units are at the forefront in understanding the nexus between tourism and education for this group and are actively developing products to meet their needs. One example is the 'Melbourne Welcome' programme offered at the University of Melbourne. This five-day programme conducted prior to the commencement of semester, packages day trips to wildlife parks and Melbourne's rural hinterland together with surfing lessons (University of Melbourne, 2004). In addition, there are promising signs that pedagogical approaches in individual institutions are also recognising and using this connection in the classroom (Peel, 2004). This is particularly evident in the discipline of Australian studies at a number of institutions where intensive short field trips use students' tourist interest to engage them practically and theoretically with the social, historical and environmental themes studied in the course. With increasing pressure on Australian universities to attract fee-paying international students, significant opportunities exist to further develop intellectually challenging field-based programmes.

This use of study at an Australian University as a vehicle for deeper cultural immersion is perhaps the defining characteristic of the study backpacker identified in this chapter. A substantial body of research on backpacker motivation has shown the central role played by status attainment in this form of travel (Allon, 2004; Richards & Wilson, 2004a; Riley, 1988; Sørensen, 1999; Vogt, 1976). Backpackers gain status by priding themselves on their ability to penetrate the host culture more deeply than mainstream tourists as a result of their being 'time rich'

(Sørensen, 1999) and through the belief that they 'live' in the destination rather than merely visit (Allon, 2004). Studying as a visiting short-term student in Australia gives backpackers an opportunity to penetrate the host culture and engage in further status-building through interacting with locals (Australian university students) away from the backpacker 'bubble' in the local hostel. In this way, as Welk (2004) argues, they seek to differentiate themselves from conventional tourists, or in this case conventional backpackers. In this context they seek to become anti-backpackers. In this regard, studying in a host destination provides an escape from the backpacker scene and plays a similar role in status attainment to the opportunity to work in the host country. In 2005, the Working Holiday Maker Visa Scheme (WHM) enables nationals from 19 countries aged 18–30 to work for 12 months in Australia and has significantly promoted backpacker market growth in recent years. Between 1999/2000 and 2003/2004, the number of WHM visas distributed has increased by 26% to a figure of 93,760 (http://www.immi.gov.au/media/fact-sheets/49whm.htm).

Finally, while Australian government interests have identified a broad backpacker market and encouraged the packaging of the backpacker product to meet demand, the impact of rising commodification of backpacking on particular segments of the market is yet to be recognised. As Cohen (2004) has observed, the increasing commercialisation of backpacking has created an 'ideology gap' between travellers' desires to emulate the experience and culture more associated with the counter-culture drifter, and their ability to do so within the restrictions of a commercial backpacker industry. This need is well recognised by university recruiters in America and Europe as this quote from a University of Melbourne study abroad brochure highlights:

> Studying abroad is an exciting and rewarding experience, giving you the opportunity to discover the intellectual, social and cultural life of another country. (University of Melbourne, 2004)

The rapid growth in backpacker consumption of study and work opportunities in Australia suggests young travellers are seeking alternative forms of travel in response to the commodification of backpacker travel in Australia. Young Americans are also adapting to the cultural constraints within their society, which demands the validation of longer periods of travel through study. The opportunity to either work or study in Australia is perceived by this group to permit a deeper and more authentic interaction with the host society, thereby enabling status attainment, and provides financial support for further travel or possible career enhancement. This positions these 'study backpackers' somewhere in a newly defined globalised world between long-term tourists and short-term immigrants.

Note

1. As defined by the Bureau of Tourism Research as an international visitor to Australia who spent at least one night in a youth or backpackers' hostel.

Chapter 12

Women as Backpacker Tourists: A Feminist Analysis of Destination Choice and Social Identities from the UK

LINDA MYERS and KEVIN HANNAM

Introduction

A growing number of women worldwide are making the most of their increasing independence and becoming motivated to travel. Women are grasping the opportunity to be tourists in their own right; for their own pleasure and satisfaction, breaking away from their hybrid identities of 'the wife', 'mother', 'girlfriend' or the 'housewife'. Women of all ages are beginning to become empowered and to travel together in close female friendship groups, in two's or alone, and are able to independently self-organise their trips.

This chapter reviews literature that contextualises the position of Western women in a patriarchal society; the social advances that have been achieved during recent history, leading to greater freedom and hence travel opportunity. It considers the problems of male attitudes and cultural differences that relate to women backpackers but also highlights the associated benefits of such travel experiences and the potentially liberating experience for women as they gain the freedom to express and extend their identities.

Secondly, it considers the position of qualitative research in tourism studies and explains and justifies the use of these methods in this study. Focus group interview techniques and textual analysis are employed, along with personal photographic evidence and semiotic analysis to explore women's views and experiences of backpacker tourism. Small groups of women were interviewed in friendship groups, hoping to produce a more relaxed intimate atmosphere from which to collect personal data. The added dimension of three separate age groups, ranging from 20 to 69 years, gave a broad base from which to draw evidence. The chapter then focuses on the transcribed results from the six focus group interviews and presents the results in a themed discussion section, including individual and conversational quotes and photographic evidence from the women's own travel experiences. It explores women backpackers' perceptions of tourist destinations, travel motivations and tourism experiences.

Despite the tendency to assume that male appeals are universal, research suggests that female and male perceptions and experiences of space differ substantially. Women are much more concerned with the quality of the experience and its processes, whereas men are more orientated towards the activity and the visit (Wearing & Wearing, 1996). Humberstone and Collins' (1998: 137) study of women's experiences of landscape compares the competitive, exploitative 'experience of men with the more reflective and spiritual perceptions of women'.

Henderson *et al.* (1996: 214) has argued that: 'Feminist research is based on the outcomes of the research and not the methods.' Such qualitative research provides greater opportunity for feminist sensitivity to go to the fore; it allows women's voices to be heard and women not to be treated as objects to be controlled by the researchers' procedures. It is generally agreed that the method for studying women needs to be one in which women can present their thoughts and feelings in their own words rather than the words of the research.

As members of a particular society or social group will share meanings and knowledge, women's knowledge and reality will be different from that of a man. 'Rather than being a "woman's way of knowing", there are women's ways of knowing' (Reinharz, 1992: 4), depending upon the cultural background of the women in question.

The UK has a long tradition of intrepid women from the upper classes travelling to places that were dangerous and very different from their own. These women were not only experiencing physical adventure; they were also challenging the ideas of their time about the role of women in society. By strength of character they were accepted in many countries and cultures where women were rarely seen in public by outsiders. Often these women seem to have been successful travellers because they were prepared to assimilate some of their host's culture, motivated by the desire to escape the conventions of their home environment and romantic Orientalist notions (see Pratt, 1992). The role of women today is clearly different to that of previous centuries and a female adventure traveller is no longer an unusual sight. However, women still face particular challenges when visiting some parts of the world where indigenous male attitudes to them are very different from those they are used to at home (Swarbrooke *et al.*, 2003).

The chapter concludes that women do have a tendency to be attracted to destinations and places that give them the opportunity to escape from everyday life, relax, shop and enjoy cultural and experiential tourism with other females. The associated accumulation of cultural capital coupled with many positive physical and emotional experiences liberates and empowers women, often leading to new identity formations. Conversely, the research finds that issues such as safety, host male attitudes and differing cultural values cause women to be very cautious about certain destinations due to their perceived image, which can be constraining and limiting for them.

Gender and Tourism Research

In her classic book, *Bananas, Beaches and Bases*, Enloe (1989: 40–41) concludes that 'tourism is profoundly gendered, based in ... ideas about masculinity and femininity – and the enforcement of both – in the societies of departure and the societies of destination'. Gender is now being taken seriously as a variable in tourism studies. It has been noted that there is a prevailing male bias in tourism research where few allowances are made for gender differences and female behaviour is subsumed into that of the dominant the male pattern (Breathnach, 1994; Pritchard & Morgan, 1998).

Nevertheless, the growing feminist scholarship in tourism (Aitchison and Reeves, 1998; Craik, 1997; Davidson, 1996; Deem, 1996; Kinnaird & Hall, 1994, 1996; Richter, 1994; Swain, 1995) offers a reconstructed and reinterpreted analysis of tourism from a gendered standpoint. The most notable publication was undoubtedly Kinnaird and Hall's (1994) *Tourism: A Gendered Analysis*, which drew together a collection of gender issues in tourism. They identify three issues central to the conceptual framework for understanding gender in tourism. First, tourism processes are constructed from gendered societies ordered by gender relations. Second, gender relations over time inform and are informed by the interconnected economic, political, social, cultural and environmental dimensions of all societies engaged in tourism development. Third, control, power and equality issues are articulated through race, class and gender relations in tourism practices.

However, relatively little research has focused on distinguishing between motivations of male and female tourists (Kinnaird & Hall, 1994). Kinnaird and Hall (1994) discerned a wide range of triggering factors including the need to: (a) escape from domestic chores or a routine job, (b) overcome a loss of emotional ties, (c) experience the thrill of danger, (d) demonstrate women's abilities and (e) undertake scientific discovery. In a study of young, educated, long-term, budget travellers, Riley (1988) found that women more than men said they wanted to travel to establish independence from their families and to feel comfortable with doing things alone. Older female holidaymakers in the UK meanwhile were studied by Stone and Nicol (1999), including the needs and motivations of single women (aged 30–55). Their findings indicated that this group displays specific holiday needs as to justify separate treatment by the tourist industry.

Backpacker Tourism

Backpacker journeys can be described as 'Self-imposed transitional periods, and for many self-imposed rites of passage' (Sørensen, 2003: 849). 'Many Backpackers are at a crossroads in their life: recently graduated, married or divorced and between jobs' (Riley, 1988: 325). In research literature and in general, backpackers are often characterised as self-organised pleasure tourists on a prolonged multidestination journey with a flexible itinerary, extending beyond that which it is usually possible to fit into a cyclical holiday pattern. Such a description serves as a guideline only and cannot be used to objectively distinguish backpackers from other tourists, for only a few match all the parameters throughout the trip. Thus, there exists a continuum of backpacker types that differ with age. Pearce (2005b: 14) meanwhile has argued that 'backpackers are best defined in social rather than demographic or economic terms, and points to a criteria for budget accommodation, an emphasis on meeting other backpackers and locals and independent flexible travel plans'. As Sørensen (2003) suggests, recent fieldwork data and information from specialised travel agents indicate a strong growth of the short-term backpacker segment.

Some studies report on backpacker gender distribution (Loker-Murphy, 1996; Pearce, 2005b). Australian data suggests an even male/female split, whilst authors from the developing world suggest a 60 percent male/40 percent female mix (Sørensen, 2003). The vast majority are aged between 18 and 33 years. Other than this literature, there is little academic literature on women backpackers as a serious phenomenon. Richards and Wilson (2004c: 264) point out that: 'Perhaps because of the additional restrictions place upon their movement and behaviour, women see backpacking differently. Compared with their male counterparts, females consider backpacking to be less sexy, less thrilling, less drug-related and less of a lonely pursuit ... women are significantly more likely than men to be travelling in order to develop friendships with other(s) ...' However, it has also been recognised that there has been an increase in the number of female backpackers taking trips across Africa, Asia and South America.

Moreover, increasingly it is argued that backpacker travel is of benefit to and motivated by a person's self-identity. In particular, the home-coming experience is important where tourists' stories and photographic evidence are used to present new self-identities. According to Giddens (1991: 53), 'self-identity is not a distinctive trait, or even a collection of traits possessed by the individual. It is the self as reflexively understood by the person in terms of his or her biography.' He argues that because self-identities are no longer firmly structured in advance by social hierarchies and traditional authorities, the modern individual faces a diversity of possible selves. The choices available in modernity mean that it is nowadays the task of the individual to maintain a sense of continuity in 'who I am' and 'how am I to live'. Tourist experiences and hence reflective biography can enhance the process of self-identity and assist in future lifestyle choice. All life spans involve significant transitions, from work to retirement, where identities have to be renegotiated, recon-structed, and new trajectories set. Often such transitional circumstances lead to the motivation to travel. Sociologists thus note that feelings and ideas about self are partly formed when we react to the cultural expectations attached to the multiple roles we acquire during our lives. Our sense of self is also partly structured by how others see and interpret our behaviour. 'Identity depends on how people see themselves, which in turn is influenced by how others (that is, society) see them' (Marshall, 1998: 6).

The relationship between tourism and identity is discussed in a recent collection by Abram *et al.* (1997). In an important shift in the conceptualisation of identity, they see tourism as caught up in an on-going and never-ending process of identification for both guests and hosts. This flexible and constructive conceptualisation of identity is mirrored in the work of Munt (1994), who concentrates more on tourism consumption. He considers the role of the increasingly popular 'alter-native' tourism to new Third World destinations in the construction of new middle class identities. He argues that these destinations are imaged and encountered as places where individual achievements, strength of character, adaptability and worldliness can be performed and narrated, particularly among young tourists accumulating cultural capital to assert a middle class identity. 'Travelling has emerged as an important informal qualification with the passport acting, as so to speak, as professional certification; a record of achievement and experience' and 'The relative popularity of new and far-distant destinations lies in the accumulation of cultural capital or the ability to demonstrate taste (Bourdieu, 1984) – where long-haul tourism is used to construct the identities of new class fractions among the middle class of the first world' (Munt, 1994: 112). Munt maintains that if the decision to go away is about investing in tourism for self-identity, then coming back home again should be one way of reaping the rewards of the experience.

For example, in her recent book *Questions of Travel*, Kaplan (2000) states that: 'Like most moderns in the west, I was brought up to believe that distance gives needed perspective, that difference leads to insight, and that travel is quite figuratively "broadening"'. Similarly, Desforges (2000) work argues that 'the full process of anticipation of holidays, the act of travel, the narration of the holiday stories on return are all tied up into an imagination and performance which enables tourists to think of themselves as particular sorts of person'. Thus various tourism sites, attractions, landmarks, destinations and landscapes can be seen as spaces through which power, identity, meaning and behaviour are constructed, negotiated and renegotiated according to sociocultural dynamics.

Methodology

A research method for women needs to be one in which women can present their thoughts and feelings in their own words rather than in the words of classical scientific research. As Reinharz (1992: 9) explains: 'this asset is particularly important for the study of women because in this way learning from women is an antidote to centuries of ignoring women's ideas altogether or having men speak for the women'. Feminist scholars, disenchanted with the disengagement and aloofness of positivistic research and its inability to explore women's experiences and life situations, have begun to advocate a more integrative, experiential approach to research. Such an approach regards women's everyday experiences as an important area of study that necessitates alternative methods of scrutiny.

Feminist researchers thus share a common need of a centring and 'problematising' woman's diversity of views and life experiences. A group interview or focus group, as used in this study, offers a viable feminist qualitative research method. As Madriz (1998: 369) argues: 'Group interviews are particularly suited to uncovering women's daily experience through the collective stories and resistance narratives that are filled with cultural symbols, words, signs and ideological representations that reflect the different mentions of power and domination that frame women's quotidian experiences.' Such focus groups offer a safe environment where people can share ideas, beliefs and attitudes in the company of people from the same socioeconomic, ethnic and gender backgrounds. Some studies conducted on focus groups show group participants find the experience more gratifying and stimulating than individual interviews (Morgan, 1998; Wilkinson, 1998). The advantage that a focus group has over an individual depth interview 'is respondents or informants involved . . . react to one another . . . more naturally' (Priest, 1996: 66). Using this approach 'a richer picture of how information is processed and conclusions are drawn can be constructed in comparison to . . . an interview situation' (Priest, 1996: 56). Moreover, women gathering together and sharing experiences with women have the potential to result in actions and movements for social change; in theory they gain power.

In this particular study, the criteria used to select the respondents were first and foremost that they were women who had backpacker tourism experiences who would be willing to give up their time to share experiences and opinions. Secondly, to give breadth to the study, it was decided to recruit three age groups: respondents in their 20s, 40s and 60s. Having fairly homogenous groups is important in establishing psychological comfort for the respondents. To permit good information exchanges, good interaction and a lively discussion, all participants must feel comfortable presenting their views during a discussion. This was a further deciding factor in group formation and selection.

Three separate age groups were selected, each group consisting of 4 members and the researcher, and each group was interviewed twice. The 20 year olds were tourism students who had been close friends for a number of years, the group of 40 year olds consisted of mature students who had met some months earlier, and finally the group of 60 year olds were all retired teachers who coincidentally were all widowed. In the selected groups a social structure already existed, due to the participants being fairly close associates. Therefore, conversational ground rules were already established and the groups operated smoothly and in a positive, friendly, jovial manner. Also, two of the groups (the oldest and youngest) had had travel experience(s) together specifically as groups. Participants afterwards commented upon the enjoyment they got from the sessions, how they were made to think about ideas more carefully and would have been willing to continue as they were comfortable and motivated by the experience.

The first group sessions were exploratory in nature and considered opinions, perceptions, expectations, experiences and behaviours of the women. Once the first session was transcribed and analysed, the information gained was used to construct a semi-structured questioning route for the researcher, to be used during the second interview. Photographic evidence was also collected and served as a means of backing up the verbal data gathered. At the end of the introductory session all participants were asked, firstly, to bring with them to the next session three photographs from their personal collection that symbolised and represented their experiences. Photographs have meanings and stories that are unique to the individual and give an insight into what it is about the destination or attraction or interaction with either, that is important. They can, therefore, provide added information about the motivations and destination choice and personal enjoyment of the women in the focus groups. For the purposes of this study, the photographic image choices were then individually presented to the group at the beginning of the second session, and the reasons for choice were given, which also served to stimulate further discussion. The groups really enjoyed this task, and some brought more photographs than requested as they found the numerical restriction limiting.

Women's Destination Choices

Evidence showed that women are increasingly making the most of their independence, and beginning to identify and satisfy their own needs when it comes to tourism. Women visit destinations with their families and their partners but also increasingly visit different types of destinations with female friends, in small groups or pairs, or even alone. Destinations chosen are usually a result of word-of-mouth recommendations from other friends' experiences, or as a result of Internet research, individual research in travel guides and a small amount of advice sought from travel agents. Interestingly, women search for information on the destinations themselves but do not search for companies that might provide what they want. If travelling together as females, as this study suggests, their visits are much more likely to be self-organised. This is an enjoyable challenge, particularly for the older women, who have the time, skill and discipline to thoroughly organise their own trips.

The women tended not to choose a destination purely because it had a good image; they chose destinations dependent upon whether they fit the criteria of the group with which they were travelling at that time. The women's age appears to be an important variable and destination choice did vary accordingly. The women tended to travel with other women in their age group, reinforcing their sense of 'identity' and giving them the confidence to go off as a group to do things they would not have the confidence to do alone. Other associated variables were social expectation, financial flexibility, personality and ambition.

When the women were asked to select an 'ideal destination', there was much less of an age-related distinction. A beautiful beach landscape, with palm trees, tranquil water, luxury accommodation and restaurants to have meals and have pleasant conversations, or a place to escape and relax. A destination that could also provide a shopping experience and some authentic local activities related to local culture. This idealistic picture was common to all age groups, providing affordability was not a decisive factor. As Wearing and Wearing (1996) discovered, women are more concerned with the quality of their tourism experiences. The focus groups related experiences that were emotive, in-depth and awe-inspiring, as the following examples suggest.

May (60s) (with reference to China): For me it's the wonder of climbing the Great Wall of China at Madaling. I just could not envisage, like the whole thing. When you read about something and then imagine it, but then the reality is just exciting. And I was doing something that I thought I would never ever in my life experience. It goes on forever, you can't see where it begins or ends and it's just a section that you're at. I was just nervous the whole time I was there, that was the effect it had, it was just amazing.

Pat (60's) (with reference to Kenya): I can remember the heat haze, the landscape all of a wobble. I can remember all the noises, the wind, the trees, the birds, the animals, the breeze in your face and the feeling of freedom.

Nevertheless male attitudes were important to all the age groups and a negative attitude or perceived negative attitude was seen as an important factor in destination choice. General knowledge, previous experience and word-of-mouth stories were all influential factors in 'destination image' construction. 'Image forms the basis of the valuation or selection process and does provide a link between motivations and destination selection' (Goodall, 1992: 7), thus, a negative image resulting from the cultural values and codes of behaviour of the men at a particular destination does deter women travellers.

Jo (40s): You want to go on holiday and feel free, and you're not there, you're restricted ... Its is really nice to go and see a different culture and see how different people live at the same time I like to feel free and comfortable and safe on holiday.

May (60s): We have found that in Mediterranean and South American countries they are lagging behind us with equal rights ... We have definitely experienced a difference in attitude from men (and sometimes women) of different cultures.

Kat (20s): I would be frightened to go to Turkey because of the Turkish men, they come up to you in the street and stroke your hair and try to grab your hand, they pester you, and try to buy you for camels.

Travelling as a group seemed to dilute the women's concerns, to give them power and control; 'safety in numbers' seemed to compensate for not travelling with a man, and gave them a sense of real freedom. Some destinations were perceived as being specifically 'male places', with Thailand singled out, in particular, as a male-orientated destination with its associations of sex tourism. Various 'spaces' were also identified as being specifically male domains such as bars or pubs and sporting activities. Silent disapproval, confrontation, teasing, joking and sexual harassment and innuendo as well as threat of violence were all concerns of the women. They sought to avoid places and spaces where they feel vulnerable, and choose environments where they are not treated as 'second-class citizens' and places where they have freedom of dress and are able to physically move about and explore as they wish.

Personal safety was a constant daily issue for the women interviewed, and even more exaggerated in the unfamiliar surroundings of a tourist destination. The older age groups made intricate plans to ensure their safety. As Valentine (1989) has showed, women 'map' certain places mentally and plan routes through cities making decisions based on safety and risk. Concerns about vulnerability and personal safety appeared often during the focus group discussion. Rape, robbery, mugging and being 'taken advantage of' were all discussed and a surprising number of actual incidents were presented considering the group size, especially from the older and younger single women.

May (60s): Safety and confidence are important factors in the selection of a destination for a woman. We were persuaded not to visit Amsterdam due to the myth or reality of drug pushers in the streets and in the cafe.

Ali (20s): You do hear about women being raped on holiday. I know sometimes I have been on holiday and you do forget and find yourself walking around the streets at night, sometimes alone if you're tired and want to get back to your accommodation before the others, but it does not cross your mind at the time because you're on holiday and your defences are relaxed more.

Dot (60s): Derelict buildings and narrow streets are also potentially scarier places. And in those places you tend to get fewer people so you are less protected by the crowds.

Pat (60s): The other thing is we always plan the night before what we are going to do the next day. We check transport, underground routes for example, so we look like we know where we are, so we are not hanging about street corners looking 'lost' and checking maps and therefore vulnerable.

Again these data confirm findings by other researchers in tourism and leisure studies. As Richards and Wilson (2004c: 264–265) have pointed out: 'The supposed freedom of backpacker travel is probably more curtailed for women by the need to preserve personal safety.' Women were found to be constrained by fear of male violence in public areas, especially after dark. The more mature women found planning a very useful device, to attempt to minimise their fear and safety. They planned routes, such as transfers from airports, in advance and carefully selected hotels in good safe locations close to areas that were easily accessible and where it was relatively safe at night to go out for a meal; they felt that all this minimised safety risks. They took city tours during the day specifically to orientate them and to make decisions about where the unsafe areas were and were not. This gave them confidence. They avoided underground metro systems, backstreets and poorly lit areas whenever possible and always stuck together. This is a good example of how women 'map' certain places mentally in relation to their fears of possible violence (Valentine, 1989).

Women's Backpacker Identities

Travel is one means of the individual re-imaging the self. For many of the women interviewed, the decision to start travelling was closely linked to transitional periods in their lives. The younger participants in their 20s were leaving their home environment for the first time and beginning to create their own identity away from that of being, for instance, that of a student and a daughter.

Kat (20s): Holidays and travel are a real novelty when you are young, it's like having your own place, and you have your own space, it's great.

Gen (20s): Then you first get away from your parents, it's the freedom; you're a different person, not behaving like someone else expects you to. No one knows you, so you can have your own space. It's great.

For the middle age group the transition period was from being depended upon by children, partners and ties with domestic duties, to the freedom of putting their own needs as a woman first. The women from this age group had previously or still were identifying themselves as wives, mother, housewives and carers. But through the discussion they began to realise they were entering a new phase of their lives and were developing new identities. Until the children are older the overwhelming consensus was that the woman's needs and wants were put 'on hold' for the sake of the children and the husband. Only when the children have flown the nest is the woman able to relax and enjoy an independent holiday, looking for pleasure and experiences to suit her personal needs.

Jo (40s): When we had the kids when they were younger, you are very aware that you have to go somewhere where they are going to be entertained, really I don't think what the woman wants really comes into it.

Finally, for the older women the transition from being a wife and mother to being free to pursue their own interests was important. All the women in this group coincidentally were widowed and had taken the opportunity to strengthen female friendships and travel together without family. Travelling provided a new set of experiences that contrasted with those at home in the everyday domestic routine. The opportunity to travel overcame previous restrictions tolerated by women in their earlier lives and gave them the opportunity to develop or construct a new self-image, a self-worth and importance to carry on to the next period of their lives.

M (60s): China was a different thing to me. I thought it was absolutely amazing; I had read about it and said to myself one day I am going to go there. I took me lots of years but I have done it. Achieving an ambition is really satisfying. There was one point when I stopped and put my hand on the stone wall and looked out over the landscape, I can still bring back that memory. I took a deep breath in so I could always remember the smell, I could feel the heat in the stones on my hands. And now I can nearly bring back how it felt, just the enormity of it. Such a tremendous landscape.

The older women in particular were extremely enthusiastic about their achievements, managing without their husbands and travelling to places that they had never dreamed possible in their lifetimes. They displayed enormous enthusiasm to continue to travel and gain all the associated benefits. They were by far the most passionate and enthusiastic interviewees about their previous and future independent travel experiences. Their stories contained descriptions of how they had been touched both physically and emotionally and their close friendships were further intensified through the shared meanings and experiences of travel. An air of confidence was apparent within this group, of strong meaning and direction of their lives in the future through travel.

The focus groups also identified several factors related to social change and its benefits and consequences for women as tourists; namely, increased freedom, opportunity and power in society. The younger women, in particular, felt financial independence, greater earning potential and greater disposable income were major factors.

Kat (20s):   Women haven't changed physically or mentally. I think in the past women will have been interested in travelling the world but they had no opportunity. I don't think women were on this earth just to be mothers and housewives, I think they've always wanted to do other things, it's just society has kept them in a place where they didn't think they could do it. The ones who did in the past were classed as strange and oddball. I admire those that did.

Ali (20s):   Women in the past really have been held down by society and politics. Men have led the way and made the rules. It is only recently that women are gaining more power and changing things.

The younger women in this study felt lucky that they have witnessed progressive changes in equality in their society. They appreciated having the freedom to travel independently and not be as oppressed and exploited as other women.

Gen (20s):   Nowadays a lot of women travel and move about the globe as part of their job. This really shows how things have changed for the better for women. There are much greater opportunities. In the 1950s women would only be travelling within the same town usually as part of their job, they had much more stereotypical roles in the house mainly doing domestic chores. There were no women as the head of the households but now a woman can be head of household, in fact some can earn more money than the men...

Conclusion

This study attempts to add to the body of backpacker tourism research by demonstrating some understanding of women and their specific needs and wants. We have argued that a feminist approach using qualitative research methods is conducive to attaining in-depth information into women's experiences and opinions. During the research process itself, the discussions at times caused the women to reflect on themselves and their own behaviour and needs as a tourist. This self-realisation and exchange of views and information was an enjoyable learning experience for some of the women. The group situation stimulated further discussion as ideas were exchanged and explanations sought.

Destination choice was usually a result of word-of-mouth recommendations from other friends with experiences, or as a result of Internet research, individual research in travel guides and a small amount of advice sought from travel agents. Other key factors included the age and interests of the women, the amount of time they had available and the determination of the women to overcome a general lack of confidence about going out into the world to explore. Affordability as well as the host male attitudes towards Western women and different cultural values were all found to be constraining factors.

Some of the reasons women go backpacking are easily expressed: the challenge, the opportunity to experience different cultures, to escape normal routine and duties, simply to relax, to experience the fun and camaraderie of being with other women and to create new lasting friendships. It can bring a sense of exhilaration, freedom and escape from the everyday world. Some experiences seemed to transcend mere language as they are fundamentally embodied. Some of the quotes from the focus groups to a certain extent describe these special moments when the women could experience and feel within themselves.

Chapter 13

The Backpacking Journey of Israeli Women in Mid-life

DARYA MAOZ

Introduction

This chapter examines Israeli women in their 40s to mid-50s that travel to India as backpackers in a phase of mid-life transition. It analyses whether there is a relation between their touristic experiences and the phase they are going through, as well as their gender identity. Tourism is known to have an important role in the search for identity and construction of it. Journeying is considered an ideal way in which to achieve a distance from the old and exposure to the new. It offers a period during which it is permissible and possible to self-consciously and deliberately remove the signs of one's old identity (Cohen, 1979: 189, 1984: 377; White & White, 2004). This is mostly true in *rite of passage* tourism, undertaken during transitions in life (Graburn, 1983). The effect that tourism has on dealing with transitions throughout the life span has hardly been studied (Desforges, 2000; Hastings, 1998; Maoz, 2006b; Riley, 1988); this may be an opportunity to do so. India was chosen as the travel destination because of its image as a place that enables the tourist to go through spiritual experiences and deal with existential quests (Maoz, 2005, 2006a, 2007; Riley, 1988).

Backpackers have formed the subject of numerous studies. Those dealing with Israeli backpackers studied young people in their 20s, just released from army service (Avrahami, 2001; Maoz, 2007). Other studies have investigated Western backpackers in their 20s and 30s (Ateljevic & Doorne, 2000b; Loker-Murphy & Pearce, 1995; Riley, 1988). This chapter is based on a first attempt to study older backpackers in general and older women in particular. Tourism studies have claimed that a young age is more suited to travelling, and indeed younger people have been found to travel more, and greater distances (Oppermann, 1995). Older age imposes barriers on travelling, such as poor health, children, lack of time, etc. (Lansing & Blood, 1964). But lately more and more older people have started to choose the mode of alternative tourism and to prefer it to mass tourism. The extension of life expectancy, the blurring distinction between ages, the rise of equality between genders, the increase of free time and other factors accelerate this process.

In Israel too a process of democratisation and popularisation of travel is apparent. About 50,000 Israelis travel to India as backpackers each year, most of them in their early 20s after demobilisation. This phenomenon, which emerged in the late 1970s–early 1980s (Uriely *et al.*, 2002) and became a trend during the past decade, now includes more and more older people. But only the young are encouraged by their society to conduct what is called *ha-tiyul ha-gadol* (the big trip), while older people who choose to travel as backpackers are seen as exceptional. The women investigated here described reactions of open criticism concerning their decision to embark on a backpacking journey. Long periods of absence from a permanent home clearly violate social norms and expectations of stability (White & White, 2004).

Studies on tourism usually regard the 'tourist' as a homogeneous gender, and few have distinguished tourists according to gender (MacCannell, 1999: xxiii) and stage of life (Gibson & Yiannakis, 2002; Maoz, 2006b). Nevertheless, tourists engage in a variety of behaviours or tourist roles, and their needs, wants and expectations vary (Cohen, 1979; Maoz, 2007: Pearce, 1982). Touristic behaviour is related to characteristics such as life stage, gender, education, income and marital status (Ryan, 1995a; Shoemaker, 2000).

Women's tourism is a fairly new phenomenon. The term 'tourist' initially defined only men, and it was not until the 19th century that women started travelling in large numbers. The Grand Tour phenomenon, starting in the late 16th century and symbolising the beginning of tourism in the modern sense, was an affair of young aristocratic men in their 20s who acquired a European education on their travels (Pearce, 1982: 55). Unless eloping with a lover or hired by a touring aristocratic family, middle-class women had no real chance to wander. It was not until the 18th century that aristocratic women joined Grand Tour journeys. The Grand Tour and travel in general enabled women to escape the domestic sphere, their roles and obligations and their identity of mother and wife and to create a new identity (Dolan, 2002).

I examine how Israeli women in mid-life interpret the journey to India and construct it in accordance with the needs that arise in the phase of transition they are undergoing. The proposition that tourism provides individuals with opportunities to satisfy a variety of psychological needs is not new. Since the 1970s researchers have begun to link touristic behaviour with psychological needs. Wagner (1977), in a study of tourists in Gambia, and Lett (1983), in a study of Caribbean charter yacht tourism, found that vacations provide individuals with opportunities to satisfy needs that constraints at home leave unsatisfied.

Why do the women investigated tell their travel stories in the way they do, and what is the purpose of their doing so; do they try to construct a new identity through their stories (Giddens, 1991); and what does this identity consist of? It seems as if in spite of describing a successful life, these women construct their journey to India as designated to compensate for deficiencies – a journey of change, escape from a former identity and a chance to construct a new one, more attached to suppressed aspirations and needs. The backpacking journey is grasped as an inner journey intended to respond to questions, needs and problems that arise in the mid-life passage.

Methodology

The study is based on 25 semi-structured in-depth interviews lasting from 90 minutes to three hours with Israeli women of 40–55 who conducted a backpacking journey of a month or more in India. For all the women this was their first backpacking experience. I found that most of the women had another common feature: 19 out of the 25 interviewees were successful career women who held a high-ranking position to which they devoted most of their time and efforts. All except one were mothers; sixteen of them were married, seven divorced, one widowed and one unmarried.

Some interviews were conducted during participant observation in India in 2001 and 2002, in the course of which the author acquired much knowledge about the phenomenon. This in turn helped shape the interviews and create intimacy and closeness with the interviewees (Fetterman, 1990: 48). Other interviews were retrospective, conducted in Israel not more than two years after the journey. In these latter interviews the women were able to talk about their experiences from a perspective of time and to describe the journey's influence on their lives.

The semi-structured interviews began with a few general questions about the backpackers' lives prior to the journey, their family, childhood and adult experiences such as marriage, parenthood and career. The main focus was on the journey itself, the chronicle of meaningful events and experiences, the feelings and thoughts that arose during the journey, the living conditions, the targets of the journey etc. The women cooperated enthusiastically with the researcher in India as well as in Israel, where they showed the author albums, diaries and letters. The fact that the author is a woman certainly helped create a friendly and intimate atmosphere.

The interviews were conducted in different places. Those in Israel took place mainly in the interviewees' homes, and those in India in their rooms or in the interviewer's room, rarely in a public place or in the company of others. All interviews were taped and transcribed without any editing or correcting. Analysis of the interviews was carried out with the aim to categorise the interviewees' responses to questions and topics in the interviews into several themes that were defined while the interviews were being read together (Hammersley & Atkinson, 1995).

Discussion

The women studied introduced themselves as successful career women, ambitious, responsible and conformist, with a strong desire to fit in with their surroundings. They had formerly worked long hours, aspiring to progress and advance their careers, and claimed that since an early age they had had much responsibility, overloading themselves with many assignments and pursuing their goals intensively. In her early 20s, Dalia, 53 (all names are fabricated), was pushed to marry a man because '... the parents said "you stayed with him, lived with him, and how would people react, and how does it look?" ... I felt their pressure to get married, that they are uncomfortable with what people would say, so I got married ... I wanted to shout "no!" during the wedding ceremony, but nothing came out.' Perla, 49, went to an officers' course 'because my dad told me "you are about to get married and you have a mortgage".' She developed an ambitious military career in which she gradually climbed the ranks to a colonel. According to their stories these women could be termed foreclosures or guardians (Josselson, 1996: 45–70). They viewed themselves as successful, ambitious, perfectionist women who took on responsibilities and duties from their youth and pursued them under parental pressure without first considering if they really wanted them.

In mid-life most of the women studied (21 out of 25) reported experiencing the crisis termed 'mid-life/middle-age crisis' (Helson & Wink, 1992: 53). The crisis was introduced as triggered by exhaustion and an awareness of something having ended. There were various immediate causes – a combination of career pressure with functioning as a mother and a spouse; marital problems; the death of someone close, inducing fears of old age and death; feelings of alienation from society; the empty nest syndrome etc. (see similar findings in White & White, 2004).

Gila, 53, for example, experienced a crisis related to her career: 'I couldn't go on, enough, [I am] fed up. I worked as a donkey ... I said "either this, or I leave." The reaction was "Sure, sure, at your age you'll leave? What will you do?"' Zila, 48, associated the crisis she went through mainly with the separation from her husband: 'my husband and I got separated a year ago. I am in crisis ... The crisis has to do with the separation. It arouses questions about myself. Part of my identity − I am the wife of. Who am I if not the wife of? Who am I if not me, whom I have known until now?' And others, like Sara, 51, introduced the crisis as related to many factors: 'The routine tired me. The work stressed me out ... I had a mid-life crisis due to the divorce, it scared me financially ... The children left home, it was very tough. ... there is also the fear of getting old ...'

The career women who tried to function also as spouses and mothers and whose self-image was that of a superwoman who has it all, realised there were things missing in their lives. Mainly their work troubled them, and for the first time they stopped to ask whether they were satisfied with it. Jung talked about depression, crisis and an inclination to nervous breakdown in mid-life, mainly among people who lead a life he defined as a 'masculine style of life' (Jung, 1976: 16). Levinson (1996: 372) found crisis elements among almost all the career women he studied.

The women experienced what was termed a 'fateful moment', in which 'consequential decisions have to be taken or courses of action initiated' (Giddens, 1991: 243). This fateful moment made them realise that they had expressed only a part of their identity − the ambitious, competitive, practical and rational part. The women felt that because of their inclination to conformism and responsibility they had given up on other parts of their personality and on fulfilling their 'true' desires, which stem from the soul and not from society's command.

The journey to India in mid-life was introduced as a way to overcome crisis and to provide an opportunity to construct a new self while struggling with the old one, shaped by the societal influence. The journey was seen as a means of connecting to suppressed parts of their personality. This process described in detail in their stories is very reminiscent of the reversal process that is supposed to occur in mid-life (Helson & Wink, 1992). The women present themselves as becoming more connected in mid-life to suppressed parts of their personality − the less ambitious and competitive parts. It was the journey, in their perception, that enabled them to do so. Indeed, tourism has been found to enable and promote the experience of reversal (Gottlieb, 1982; Graburn, 1983) because of its liminality (Turner, 1987), among other reasons. This is true especially in the mode of tourism that functions as a rite of passage, considered to facilitate self-reflection (Hastings, 1998; Stein & Stein, 1987).

The journey to India was experienced by the women researched as their first moratorium (Erikson, 1959: 202), a time of release from duties, of freedom from responsibilities and of searching by trial and error, all of which led them in their perception to the crystallisation of a new identity. The journey to India was seen as an act that brought some personal answers to the deficiencies and frustrations arising in a mid-life transition.

A Reversal

I shall go on to examine some of the central themes of the women's stories of their new selves. They tell of a struggle against the old self, shaped by the influence of society, and the birth of a new one. Themes of the awakening of repressed parts of their identity arise in their stories, and are seen as a reversal of the parts prominent in the first half of their lives.

Careerism and activity versus repose

Most of the women indicated that they were very career-minded from an early age; ambitious, hard working and wishing to succeed in their work. They worked around the clock and some called themselves 'workaholics'. The journey cut the intensive continuity of doing. In the journey the women concentrated on repose and on being (Wang, 1999). They moved along slowly, settled in one place for a long period and concentrated on freedom.

Significant changes may occur in the careers of women around the age of 40 (Levinson, 1996: 376). Among many career-minded women a tendency may occur to acknowledge their inability to be a superwoman, and a process of slowing down may follow. Some of the women investigated here had carried out some changes in their career prior to the journey, thus making the journey possible. Four of them decided on an early retirement and three resigned. Five others considered retiring or resigning or at least decreasing the amount of work. Those who left their jobs declared a feeling of happiness and even euphoria.

Conformism and responsibility versus irresponsibility and rebellion

Most of the women declared they had been responsible, conformist and considerate since childhood. They reported a sense of rising frustration because of their need to satisfy others' needs and not ever daring to rebel. Due to toeing the line and a high consideration for surrounding expectations and norms, the decision to embark on a journey is introduced as exceptional and as the first forerunner sign of establishing a new identity. The women left a family, children and a successful career and travelled for a few weeks or months. Travelling to India at this age is not a normative phenomenon in Israel, let alone for these women, and they stressed this in their interviews. The social reaction was described as amazement and criticism. 'Have you gone nuts?' and 'Did you fall on your head?' were only some of the reactions.

In India the women became even more light-headed, as they perceive it. From what they describe as anxious, responsible and worried people, they became careless and even egoistic. Their stories tell about abandoning the activity, responsibility and agency they had manifested until then, replacing them with irresponsibility and a light attitude towards life. Part of being irresponsible, in their perception, is carrying on spontaneously, as opposed to the rigid and planned life they had always led. Spontaneity is presented as having started with the decision to embark on a journey. Many women grasped their journey to India as spontaneous, unplanned and even accidental, as opposed to the agency they saw as their main characteristic until then. Most said they simply happened to decide to travel to India, and implemented their decision within a few days. They grasped the journey resulting from a passive process, not initiated, and even as a kind of destiny. The spontaneity continued in the journey as well, described as relaxed, not planned or organised. Spontaneity, as they see it, is losing control, and they attribute this new process to the travel destination – to India.

Anxiety versus 'everything will be just fine'

The tendency to be responsible, conformist and well organised is described as stemming from anxiety. The women claim to have changed during the journey or shortly prior to it and to have become more optimistic and careless. The feeling is not accompanied by concrete acts intended to relieve anxieties, but is described as part of a new spontaneous, emotional self that values flowing with life. It included relying on the journey to India to be successful though it is characterised by lack of planning. Most women reported not being worried anymore by the factors that induced the crisis, such as separation from a mate, career problems, etc. There is a kind of passivity, acceptance and even fatalism in the new attitude these women proclaim, which stands in contrast to what was described as the former organised and active attitude.

Outward versus inward inclination

Spontaneity and slowing down are part of a wider process in which the women, who grasp themselves as ambitious, rational and planned, report converting such traits and connecting to their emotional side – to intuition and gut feelings. They slow down the race they were involved in, the ambitious career striving and move to another phase – calmer, more relaxed, less ambitious. One of the central insights they say they reached prior to their journey and mainly in the journey itself is that hard work is not necessary anymore. There is no need to exert oneself, to aspire and to advance. Instead, one should concentrate on inner wishes and on self-awareness. For that purpose some of the women turned to engage in spirituality and reflexive examination of the self.

Twenty-one out of the 25 women investigated turned to spirituality in mid-life, and this was presented as one of the central interests in their journey. Engaging in spirituality helped them, in their perception, to deal with the crisis that occurred in mid-life. Concern with spirituality is described in the stories of the women as a reversal of their previous lives. It is introduced as including changes in perceptions and in behaviour. For them spirituality means slowing down the race, but also abandoning the rational side and moving to focusing on the soul, the feelings and the present.

The process of turning from focusing on the outside world to introspection and reflexivity, while sharpening self-awareness, happened to these women, as the studies expected, in mid-life (Jung, 1976: 17). This phase serves as a suitable opportunity to engage in a liminal experience that enables self-examination, arising from high self-awareness (Turner, 1987). The journey, which is considered as enabling self-examination and reflexivity, is a tool to create an experience of change under detachment from familiar surroundings (Cohen, 1984: 377).

A queen versus a peasant for a day

Gottlieb (1982) terms the process people go through in tourism 'reversal', and she labels a middle to upper class person who settles for little in his/her journeys a 'peasant for a day'. Like Gottlieb's 'peasants', the Israeli women settled for simple houses, cheap food and local transport. They exchanged their comfortable, well-to-do lives for poor conditions. These middle to upper class women decided to invert their status as well as their appearance. In Israel they dressed according to their status and their occupation, with suits, high heels, makeup and elaborate hairstyles. During the journey they wore no make up or scent, and they dressed in sportswear and *sharwals* [Indian trousers]. Dress is a status symbol. Once the women changed their appearance, they thought they changed their status too (Turner, 1973).

Ageing versus regressing to childhood

Their new look and appearance symbolise the women's will to regress in time − back to youth − instead of proceeding to the next phase in life. Preservation of youth or the will to return to it is a typical phenomenon of mid-life (Jung, 1976: 14, 19). It is a desire stemming from fear of ageing and dying and from an aspiration to stop the biological and sociological clock (Neugarten, 1968) that is related among women to menopause and the empty nest. This is a phase of no return as it is a biological process of ending fertility. The journey, on the other hand, may delay the perceived passage to the next phase and even induce regression to youth. This apparent delay is made possible due to the fact that the transition is taking place in a place mentally and physically remote from one's own society, a place where the rules, expectations and sociological clock are different. Regression to youth becomes possible through the touristic journey, described as enabling people to experience regression to narcissism and to childhood, without responsibilities and anxieties (Dann, 1998: 8, 13).

Conservatism versus sexual openness

In the movie screened in her head she was a young light-headed girl and he an exotic sensual man, and in the next scene they should have kissed. And so they did. (Maoz, 2002: 145)

An unsatisfied need for some women at this age was a sexual one (see also Gibson & Yiannakis, 2002). Eight out of 25 women talked about affairs they had in India with men younger than themselves, and in six cases local. Another woman had an affair with a married man prior to her journey and three more told of their interest in men during the journey but with no realisation of it. Conducting an affair was another aspect of the construction of a new self-alternative and different to the one before the journey. The women made a point of stressing that until the journey they would never have conducted affairs of this kind. Gila, 53, sent me an e-mail about her affair with an Indian guy and claimed she wouldn't have conducted this kind of affair in Israel. A sense of pride emanates from her words: 'I never thought I would do something like this ... but I have been having an affair with X, 34 years old ... What fun!!! Can't believe I am actually doing this.'

The story is usually told as a love story and not just sex, similar to what is termed 'romance tourism', regarded as different from 'sex tourism', which is attributed mainly to men, and is based upon sex only. The Israeli women studied here conducted affairs similar to those described in the literature with a younger man who was the initiator and who met them through his work, connected with tourism. He offered them sexual satisfaction, confidence and friendship and they gave him direct or indirect financial support (Pruitt & LaFont, 1995: 436).

Conclusion

In their narratives the women construct the journey as a transforma-tive experience that has changed them. The journey is described as an answer to the problems that arise in mid-life and as an experience that enabled them to cope with frustrations, crisis and unwanted traits by creating a new and different identity. The women presented a story of change and construction of a new and reversed identity. As we saw, the women studied preferred to see the journey as a reversal of their previous lives. The journey was initiated spontaneously, continued cheerfully and irresponsibly and in their perception indicated attachment to their childlike, light side. It caused, as they see it, a considerable change in their selves, presented as a binary change. But one could wonder whether the new image these women constructed for themselves does not ignore another side of the story – the fact that the journey to a large extent also indicated continuity of their former identity?

These women would rather see their journey as a spontaneous act, something that simply happened and was not planned as the tasks of their lives were. But the actual choice in dealing with stress by an act and not by passively accepting fate could indicate that these women continue to show control over their lives. Even though they grasp the journey as a 'spontaneous' act, they in fact describe an act of agency – a doing which takes responsibility for life, that does not let life lead them. The choice of a backpacking journey to India continues the line of agency that has governed their lives. They embark on an adventurous and daring journey, exceptional for women their age, to a Third World country with poor living conditions. But this side of their story rarely appears in their narratives, in which they rather emphasise the passive, accepting, flowing and spontaneous side of their new self.

The experience of forming a new self is introduced mainly as connected to the journey and thus it usually comes to an end when the women return to Israel – to family, work, habits and norms. They are expected to end the crisis and the 'little game' they were playing with their identity (far from home) and to go back on track. The women talk about a certain change they bought back from India, but all admit to have returned to their 'old self' in most domains. Most women concluded that in order to re-experience the dormant part of their self they would have to travel to India again. India is grasped as a place to regain strength and to take a moratoric time off when things get tight. That is why many of the women studied continue to travel to India on a regular basis after their first visit.

Those women represent a transit generation. They live between two poles in a liminal state – between the model of the traditional woman and the expectation to function as wife, mother and housewife, and the emerging norms that allow and even demand of them to work, develop a career and function as independent, assertive and liberated women. The only way as they see it to rebel against roles, expectations and social norms is tourism, perceived as enabling a change of the self. But this new self is limited to the liminal phase of the journey, which facilitates temporary reversal and moratorium; it cannot last in daily life. These women are existential tourists (Cohen, 1979), who return to India on a regular basis in order to experience a side of their self that they feel cannot be expressed in Israel.

Chapter 14

Intracommunity Tensions in Backpacker Enclaves: Sydney's Bondi Beach

JULIE WILSON, GREG RICHARDS and IAN MACDONNELL

Introduction

Backpacker tourism has become an increasingly important part of the international tourism industry, thanks to the growing propensity of young people to travel, rising incomes and an increased desire for intercultural experiences. Australia has become a particularly popular destination due to its rich mix of natural and cultural assets, relative lack of language barriers and temporary work opportunities. Australia has also gained a competitive advantage in the global backpacker market because of its rapid and extensive institutionalisation and commercialisation of back-packer travel. It not only represents a destination that is relatively safe for young travellers and as such is popular with first-time backpackers (Clarke, 2003), but also it is appealing in that many travellers already have friends or family resident there. The Australian tourist industry, local employers and communities looking for alternative sources of economic development have generally welcomed backpackers.

This has led to a growth in 'enclaves' where backpackers tend to congregate, particularly where there are natural and/or cultural attractions, employment opportunities and dedicated infrastructure. Sydney, the largest and best known of Australian cities, in particular has experienced this growth. Expansion of backpacker enclaves in the city has arguably had positive impacts in terms of employment and income for local businesses. However, it has also caused problems for local residents living near backpacker hostels, and for local authorities who have to deal with the increased financial and administrative burden of the additional temporary residents. This situation has led to tension not only between the backpackers and the host community, but also between different stakeholders within the community.

This chapter considers such tensions in Sydney's iconic suburb, Bondi Beach. In Bondi, the rapid influx of visitors has raised serious concerns about potential negative social and environmental impacts on the local community. While the district has seen a large increase in designated hostel accommodation, the main problem has tended to be the parallel growth of illegal hostels that has responded to the fluctuating seasonal demand for budget accommodation. In extreme cases, this has led to anti-backpacker attitudes on the part of Bondi residents. These anti-backpacker narratives contrast greatly with the positive view espoused by the national government and backpacker interest groups. In the following analysis, we examine how the tensions arising from the development of backpacker enclaves manifest themselves in the community of Bondi Beach.

Tourism and the Community

Tourism implies both benefits and costs for the local communities in which it takes place. Backpackers, like other tourists, contribute to the places they visit in economic terms, but they can also generate social and environmental costs in terms of pressure on local services, noise, litter and disruptive behaviour.

One of the problems in dealing conceptually and practically with such issues is the fact that the notion of 'community' is far from clear. As Richards and Hall (2000) argue, the word community can be applied to a wide range of different social groups, including the residents of a specific area, a coherent social group or even a global imagined community. In this sense, while the local community in which backpackers stay might be considered the primary element of analysis in any discussion of community impacts of tourism, it should not be forgotten that the backpackers themselves also constitute a community. For many of the backpackers in Australia, they may even stay long enough to consider themselves 'locals'.

The other problem is that even when we can agree on a geographic or social basic for analysing the community, this by no means implies that the local community will be homogenous. Local communities every-where are becoming more diverse, and local residents also vary widely in their relationship to tourism, backpacking and the impacts of backpacker travel. Those living next to an illegal hostel, which is therefore not congruent with the planning regulations, may largely suffer the negative consequences of such development, but the hostel owners and residents living further away may not see the problem.

Backpacker travel may therefore not only cause impacts that pit 'locals' against backpackers, but there may also be considerable tension between different members of the community as well. In analysing such problems, stakeholder theory may offer a useful framework. Stakeholder theory considers the groups and individuals that can affect an issue. Freeman (1984: 46) defines a stakeholder as 'any group or individual who can affect or is affected by the achievement of the organisation's objectives'. The various groups of stakeholders in a host community of course have differing stakes and degrees of influence. Broadly, they can be seen as 'voluntary' stakeholders who have made some form of investment in the development of backpacker tourism, or involuntary stakeholders who stand to be affected by the activities or outcomes of its development.

According to Mitchell *et al.* (1997), stakeholders vary in terms of their possession of one or more of three relationship attributes: power, legitimacy and urgency. Power enables stakeholders to impose their will on a relationship, while legitimacy reflects the extent to which stakeholders are seen by others as having a justified claim on power or resources (Larson & Wikström, 2001). Urgency reflects the extent to which stakeholders can make a claim on immediate attention. Each stakeholder in a given situation will have differing degrees of these three attributes, and the most important will tend to have high levels of all three. In the case of backpacker tourism, those involved directly in tourism services tend to base their power claims on the economic impacts of tourism, and particularly job creation. In addition to the tourism industry, the tendency for backpackers to work casually in many sectors of the economy, including agriculture, means that employers' associations in other industries have also become important advocates of backpacker tourism. The local authority is usually also a powerful stakeholder by virtue of planning controls and regulation of the industry. Many local residents' groups, on the other hand, tend to base the legitimacy of their opposition to backpacker tourism on problems of public order, public health and nuisance caused by hostels. The level of power claimed by each group can be radically affected by external events. In Australia, this was dramatically demonstrated by the Childers incident in 2000, where a backpackers' hostel fire in Queensland claimed 15 lives. This brought an increase in planning controls for hostels at national level, and also strengthened local opposition to the location of hostels in residential areas.

One important factor in the application of stakeholder theory to backpacker enclaves in Australia is also the fact that backpackers themselves remain in the local community for a relatively long period. In many cases, therefore, the backpackers themselves can also be seen as a stakeholder group. Their ability to exert pressure through the political process may be limited, but their economic impact gives them important leverage with local suppliers and therefore indirectly with the local authority, particularly as they often work in jobs in which there is a severe labour shortage, such as seasonal crop harvesting and hospitality work. Backpackers may therefore be considered as indirect stakeholders whose legitimacy derives from their expenditure, their labour and also their long length of stay in the local community.

The following analysis attempts to trace the positions of the different stakeholders in a specific enclave in Bondi Beach, Sydney, and to highlight areas of conflict and the emergence of new coalitions around the backpacker issue. Before analysing the local situation, a broader context of backpacker tourism in Australia is outlined.

Backpacker Tourism in Australia

Backpacker tourism is perhaps better researched in the Australian context than in any other destination, largely due to the economic importance of this market. Australia's Bureau of Tourism Research (BTR) defines a backpacker as aged 15 years or over and spending at least one night at a backpacker or youth hostel (Commonwealth Department of Tourism, 1995). According to this definition, the number of backpackers visiting Australia has grown significantly in recent years and now accounts for about 10% of visitor arrivals, but more importantly about 25% of all bed-nights.

It has been argued that the preferred 'travel styles' of young independent travellers in Australia differ significantly from those travelling in other parts of the world (Richards *et al*., 2004) (Table 14.1). Whereas

Table 14.1 Travel style (self-definition) for respondents in Australia and elsewhere (Richards *et al*., 2004)

Type	Australia (%)	All respondents (%)
Backpacker	49.5	31.2
Traveller	38.3	51.6
Tourist	12.1	17.2
Total	100.0	100.0

less than a third of those visiting other countries saw themselves as backpackers, in Australia this proportion was almost 50%. This is at least in part accounted for by the fact that the well developed backpacker industry (and its infrastructure) in Australia brings travellers into contact with the concept of backpacker travel more often than in most other destinations.

According to a recent fact sheet issued by Tourism New South Wales (1997: 1), backpackers are 'active adventure seekers' seeking out 'activities that are authentically Australian, and removed from the mainstream tourist experiences' (cited in Allon, 2004). Many of the backpackers interviewed by Allon (2004) confirmed this definition of travel style, and particularly the preference for seeking out experiences that are seen as 'authentically Australian'. Many backpackers also distinguished themselves from tourists by a particular claim on their authenticity of experience. As one backpacker said, 'Travellers and backpackers have a "different way of viewing things"'. They 'sink into the surroundings' and 'take things in'. They 'go to see other cultures' and also 'want to know more about local communities' (Allon, 2004).

This claim to authentic experience is at least partly based on the length of stay in the destination. Numerous market studies have indicated that the average length of stay in Australia for a backpacker is around 6–7 months, depending on the type of visitor (Slaughter, 2004). Indeed, among all young independent travellers surveyed by ATLAS/ISTC, those who saw themselves as 'backpackers' tended to stay longer than other visitors (Richards & Wilson, 2003).

Research conducted by Giesbers (2002) with backpackers in Australia indicates that backpackers want to know something about Australian culture and history, and more importantly to meet local people. Meeting new people in general was the strongest motivation in Giesbers' study, but mixing with other travellers seemed slightly less important than meeting local people. This social link with the local community is reinforced by their economic contribution. Recent studies have consistently shown that backpackers who stay longer in the destination spend more in total than other 'leisure' tourists, and because they spend more of their money directly with local businesses, they also produce a greater economic spin-off for the local community. For example, the Australian BTR estimated that 'backpackers' in Australia spent around AUS$6130 per head compared with an average spend of AUS$4005 for all visitors in 2002.

The large amounts of money spent by young independent travellers during their stay are at least in part due to the fact that many work during their trip. The availability of work in service and agricultural jobs

Table 14.2 Working holiday visas granted by Australia

1999–00	2000–01	2001–02	2002–03	2003–04
74,450	76,570	85,200	88,758	93,760

Table 14.3 The principal source countries, 2003–04

UK	35,061
Ireland	12,260
Japan	9943
Germany	9700
Canada	6517
The Netherlands	3036

Source: http://www.immi.gov.au/media/fact-sheets/49whm.htm

is one of the reasons why Australia is an attractive backpacking destination, particularly for those coming from countries that participate in the Working Holidaymaker scheme (WHM). Table 14.2 and Table 14.3 give details of the scheme.

The aim of the WHM programme in Australia is to 'promote international understanding' (Clarke, 2003), providing opportunities for resourceful, self-reliant and adaptable young people to holiday in Australia and to supplement their funds through incidental employment.

Activities in Australia

Although most travellers say they are motivated to visit Australia to find out something about the country and its people, the actual activities undertaken by backpackers and other independent travellers differ little from the classic pattern of tourist activities (Table 14.4).

Even though Australia is perceived as a destination that offers a wide range of landscapes and relatively 'wild' areas to explore, most back-packers actually tend to stick to the beaten track. For example, Giesbers' (2002) study indicated that almost 90% of his respondents had visited Sydney and over 80% had visited Melbourne but less than one third had been to Perth. Allon (2004) notes that, although travelling throughout Australia is the goal for many backpackers, Sydney, in particular, is the favoured destination. The city is promoted as a cosmopolitan global city with a highly developed tourism infrastructure, as well as the setting for

Table 14.4 Activities of respondents in Australia (Richards & Wilson, 2003)

Activity	%Respondents
Walking, trekking	88.0
Hanging out on the beach	84.5
Nature, wildlife	84.5
Sitting in cafes, restaurants	81.2
Shopping	79.8
Cultural events	73.8
Nightclubs	73.1
Visiting historic sites	70.2
Visiting museums	65.5
Playing sport, adrenaline activities	61.9
Watching sport	42.9
Learning a language	25.0
Academic study	20.2
Working as volunteer	8.3

a range of unique and culturally distinctive experiences, places and lifestyles, and has many opportunities for casual work.

Giesbers' survey also specifically dealt with the amount of contact that backpackers had with local people and other travellers. These data indicate that about a third of backpackers felt they had had a lot of contact with local people, but the majority only had limited contact, implying that the desire to interact with local people is often not met in practice. In general, backpackers tended to have almost twice as much contact with fellow travellers as with locals, indicating that backpackers have much greater social contact with each other than with the local community. However, backpackers who had been to Australia before were significantly more likely to seek contact with local people than first-time visitors.

There was no difference in the degree of contact with local people or fellow travellers according to accommodation form, which suggests that those staying in backpacker hostels have just as much contact with local people, for example, as those staying with friends or relatives. Figures from the ATLAS/ISTC study of work exchange visits to Australia in 2004 indicated that a third of those visiting Australia had friends or relatives there, and 73% expected to be staying in a hostel.

The Spatial Context of the Independent Traveller Scene in Sydney

The widespread use of hostel accommodation by both short-term and long-term visitors to Sydney has seen a dramatic increase in backpacker hostel supply in recent years. For example, the backpacker reservation website   http://reservations.bookhostels.com/travelhops.com/finda-bed.php has 114 hostels in the Sydney region available, whereas 20 years ago there were virtually none. While its city centre backpacker enclaves such as Kings Cross have been able to absorb the impact of the travellers' presence more readily, others outside of Sydney's CBD have experienced considerable resident opposition to the rapid growth of traveller-oriented facilities. It is mainly the coastal eastern suburb communities of Sydney (with easy access to surf and beach cultures) that have the highest proportion of backpacker hostels, budget accommodation facilities, short-term rental accommodation and housing used illegally as backpacker premises (Allon, 2004). As such, these areas tend to experience the highest degree of backpacker visibility within local communities.

The growth of the industry has also stimulated the creation of national, regional and local stakeholder groups to further the interests of backpacker operators. For example, the New South Wales Backpacker Operators' Association (BOA) includes members operating accommodation (being the major percentage), travel agents, tour operators, publications and communication. The major issues that the BOA deals with include hostel room size regulations, advertising and brochure distribution, ethical standards, brochure misrepresentation, touting and hostel standards. The number of BOA members has increased to over 100 in regional NSW and Sydney. It works in conjunction with local authorities to stamp out unauthorised backpacker accommodation, liaises with the NSW Police Service in regard to backpacker safety and is fighting for the exemption of bed tax for the hostel industry.

The backpacker industry stakeholders see themselves as involved in a fight to be considered a 'legitimate' part of the tourism industry:

> Backpackers are considered a dirty word by the upmarket end of the hotel sector, [but] that doesn't make it right. They are the highest

yielding customers in Australia. Today's backpackers are tomorrow's convention delegates; backpackers are the rich young kids of the world. (Allen, 2002: 6, cited in Allon, 2004)

With this professionalisation of the backpacker industry more generally, so hostels have tended to become larger and more professional. For example, Sydney Central YHA opened in 1996 with 570 beds, a travel agency, information desk, bar, shop, swimming pool, sauna, games room, cinema, book exchange, kitchens, laundries, public telephones, barbecues and a general manager (Clarke, 2003). Generally speaking, the YHA hostels have become bigger, with more twin rooms and en-suite bathrooms, giving fewer opportunities for different people to mix. This is one of the reasons why it is seen as very important to provide communal spaces in hostel developments to provide an opportunity to interact with other travellers. This can also minimise disruption to local residents as well as generating more income for the hostels. However, it also serves to increase the gap between the backpackers' desire for adventure and the reality of socialising largely within the confines of the enclave.

Sydney's Bondi Beach

The broader struggles for recognition of backpacking as a legitimate activity are played out at a local level in communities such as Bondi Beach in Eastern Sydney. Bondi is perhaps the most famous of the backpacker enclaves that have developed in Sydney's coastal communities, where backpackers have easy access to surf and beach cultures. As one Sydney backpacker commented, 'The name Bondi says it all. When you say Bondi Beach everyone says "Oh my God, you're staying at Bondi". Bondi is world renowned. Everyone knows Bondi Beach. Wherever you are in the world, everyone knows Bondi Beach' (Allon, 2002). The eastern suburbs tend to have the highest proportion of backpacker hostels, budget accommodation facilities, short-term rental accommodation and also housing used illegally as backpacker premises (Allon, 2002).

One newspaper article titled 'Southern Exposure as Backpackers Flood in Seeking Jobs, Surf and Sun' described the 'human migration' to the east coast of Sydney that takes place at the start of summer every year: 'The beaches are packed on a weekday, the barman has an Irish accent and houses overlooking the beach are fitting five Brits to a bedroom. Yep, it's backpacker season again. The human migration takes place each year. Backpackers arrive armed with working visas, shorts, sandals and singlets. They spend the winter in the north, but arrive in Sydney en masse in spring.' (Thompson *et al.*, 2002: 5, cited in Allon, 2004).

In Bondi, part of the Waverley Local Government area that houses 65,675 permanent residents (http://www.waverley.nsw.gov.au/area/census/), the rapid influx of visitors has raised serious concerns about potential negative social and environmental impacts on the local community. This presents a dilemma for local planning authorities in that they must deal with increasing complaints from residents and settle disputes arising, for example, between residents, backpackers, budget-accommodation proprietors/managers and illegal premises, while continuing to promote the suburb as a desirable tourist destination.

The Stakeholders

The visitors

Over 2 million people a year visit Bondi beach, including an estimated 860,000 overseas visitors. Backpacker arrivals were estimated at 150,000 per annum in 1999 through a survey undertaken for the Visitor and Tourist Management Strategy. The usual pattern for Sydney backpackers is to stay an average of three nights in the city centre, then move to a less expensive area outside the CBD. In a study of 92 independent travellers in Sydney, Byron Bay, Cairns, Darwin and Melbourne in 2002, Sydney was most associated with the sun/beach and iconic sights. It was also seen as a fast-paced, energetic centre. Its energy and beauty were seen to be unrivalled by other Australian cities (ATC, 2002). The same study found that less experienced and less adventurous travellers were likely to focus their trip on Sydney and the East Coast of Australia, and that over 48% of backpackers staying in Sydney visit Bondi Beach.

In spite of the high level of visits, there is limited tourist accommodation. Backpacker hostels provided 520 beds in 2002 even though the 2001 census indicated that about 1906 visitors were staying in Waverley, or 3% of the total population, compared with 1.2% for Sydney as a whole. The 'surplus' backpackers are staying with friends or relatives, or are using other forms of accommodation, including illegal backpacker hostels.

Independent travellers in Bondi and other Sydney enclaves have previously indicated that those calling themselves 'backpackers' were more likely to disagree that 'backpackers don't give anything back to the places they visit' and more likely to agree that 'backpackers want to help local people'. 'Backpackers' also tended to disagree that 'backpackers can go and do whatever they want', indicating that there is an awareness of a need to be respectful and limit behaviour in some way. This indicates that backpackers see themselves are being relatively integrated into the local community and that they have a relatively positive view of the impact they have. However, 'backpackers' were also more likely to agree that 'backpackers are lazy' and to agree that 'thrill seeking is important' and that 'extreme experiences are important' than others.

The backpacker industry

The division of backpackers' self-image seems to echo Clarke's (2003) study of 'backpacker industry' members in Sydney, which suggested it is possible to differentiate between the 'vomit backpackers' and those very conscientious, casually minded, slightly more refined, probably slightly older travellers who really want to explore the city and the country. It could be argued that the former contingent has increased in numbers in areas such as Bondi principally thanks to the growth of illegal hostel accommodation in residential properties. The illegal hostels do not adhere to health and safety regulations (a big issue since the Childers fire) nor do they make much effort to ameliorate the impact of their clients on the locality.

The growing numbers of such operations have also stimulated legal hostel owners to try and differentiate their operations as much as possible from their illegal counterparts. This strategy also seems to be paying off for some hostels. For example, when the YHA-affiliated Bondi Beachouse opened in 1998, all the neighbours registered complaints. Twelve months later one neighbour dropped in to apologise and the neighbourhood now openly acknowledges how much nicer the business is now. It's a more modern, clean, well kept building rather than the previous run-down one, and, to everyone's surprise, less noisy. Marketing statistics show that 18% of all guests are relatives of local residents, showing how difficult it is to make hard and fast distinctions between 'locals' and 'backpackers'.

However, not all the legal operations are so welcome. Plans to open new hostels are often met with vociferous opposition from residents, who argue that Bondi already has enough backpacker accommodation, in spite of the apparent excess demand mopped up by the illegal hostels. Such opposition makes it difficult for new, professionally managed hostels to open (see the Stop the Hostel campaign, below), while the illegal hostels continue to expand.

Residents

Richards and Wilson (2003) found some significant differences among local residents and backpacker service providers interviewed, depending on which area of Sydney they live and/or work in. Residents and providers from Bondi Beach/Bondi junction were significantly more likely to agree that 'backpackers are a nuisance' – a finding that is understandable, given that there appear to be more illegal hostels in operation in this area than in either the City Centre or King's Cross/ Darlinghurst.

These concerns have manifested themselves in the growth of local pressure groups aimed at stemming the growth of backpacker accom- modation. One example is the 'Stop the Hostel' campaign, which was created in direct opposition to proposed plans for a 360-bed hostel in a residential street one block from the beach in Bondi. This group successfully lobbied against the plans, arguing that the proposed densities were too high and that the negative impacts on local residents would be too great. This has now been followed by a 'Stop the Hostel Again' campaign ranged against revised plans for the same site. Although the density has been reduced and the total number of backpacker beds has been more than halved in the new plans, the campaigners still argue that the negative impacts of the development will be unacceptable.

On closer inspection it seems that the direct source of local objections to the development lie in the fact that the building that previously occupied the site was used for a time as an illegal hostel, which generated 'two in the morning five-a-side football matches and street parties', according to the campaigners. However, their sophisticated website does not make any distinction between the problems caused by illegal hostels (which are run by fellow residents of Bondi) and the development of a legal hostel with a well developed management plan. In fact, it is clear from council reports that most of the problems reported by residents relate to illegal hostels.

The local authority

The problems related to backpacker accommodation have led to growing calls for tougher local regulation of backpacker accommodation. Waverley Council has responded to this by adopting a number of policies and measures aimed at legal and illegal hostels.

Since the late 1980s, the Waverley community and Council have been concerned about the environmental and amenity impacts of high visitor numbers. Many are sensitive to the noise that is generated by alleged illegal backpacker establishments. While some residents question whether visitors are or should remain a part of the character of the area at all, Council is faced with the need to provide ongoing management of tourism in a way that maximises the benefits and minimises any negative impacts.

The key policy document regulating backpacker accommodation is Waverley DCP No. 12 – Guidelines for Boarding Houses, Backpacker Accommodation and Bed and Breakfast Establishments. Section 3.0 provides guidelines for backpacker accommodation. The guidelines are based on the national standards laid down in *Building for Backpacker Accommodation* (Commonwealth Department of Tourism, 1996).

In 2001, an amendment to these guidelines indicated that 'mechanisms for more stringent regulation and enforcement of management and operating guidelines for backpacker accommodation should be investigated' (Amendment to Waverley DCP no. 12: 1). The proposed changes to the regulations included increasing the amount of space available to each hostel guest from 3.25 to 5.5 m^2. Industry representatives countered that this would make the hostels uneconomic and more akin to hotel accommodation, encouraging the provision of cheaper, illegal hostels. The document concluded that an increase in room size would be likely to stimulate the provision of illegal hostels. It also expressed concern that the council did not have sufficient resources to police regulations or to prevent the operation of illegal hostels, of which there were 72 identified in Bondi in 2001 (and probably more unidentified).

One of the main aims of the Visitor Management Scheme (VMS) introduced in 2002 was therefore to tackle the problem of illegal hostels. The council appointed a dedicated member of staff to deal with backpacker issues and process enforcement notices against illegal hostels. This seems to have met with some success, as complaints about hostels decreased by a third between 2002 and 2003. However, the report notes that there is continuing concern about organised groups of illegal hostel operators. One of the problems is that properties on long tenancies may actually be used by a large number of short-term visitors, with or without the knowledge of the property owner. It is also difficult to prove that premises are being used as an illegal hostel. The report suggested implementing a publicity campaign directed at local residents, hostel owners and backpackers about the problems.

The VMS report also identified a number of other problems stemming from increased visitor pressure, including noise, litter, pressure on council services and the loss of 'character'. This latter point not only referred to a growth in services aimed at visitors, but also the replacement of family homes by backpacker accommodation, leading to 'a more homogeneous, less socially diverse community'. Allon (2004) argues that this is one of the main concerns for local residents in this predominantly working-class area.

Despite the considerable economic benefits that backpackers bring to the city, some Sydney-siders still regard the growing backpacker communities and cultures as a problem, citing abandoned cars and rubbish dumping; excessive noise and large groups of 'disruptive youth' at beaches and other public spaces; overcrowded, unsafe hostels and inadequate budget accommodation; and an incompatible degree of 'cultural difference' (Allon, 2004). A number of local government areas in the eastern and inner-western suburbs of Sydney, for example, have been identified as particular problem areas. Councils in these areas face considerable challenges. On one hand, they must deal with increasing numbers of complaints from residents and settle disputes arising, for example, between residents, backpackers, and budget-accommodation proprietors and managers. On the other, they must continue to promote their areas as highly desirable tourist destinations with distinctive and recognisable cultural profiles.

The complaints made to Waverley Council in general relate to one of the following issues:

- dumped vehicles;
- increased rubbish collection costs; or
- noise.

However, based on a review of council documentation, newspaper articles and interviews conducted in the Bondi area (Allon, 2004), the source of the bulk of these complaints is illegal backpacker hostels. As the illegal hostels are usually owned and/or managed by local residents, this creates direct conflict between the different stakeholder groups in the community about how the problem should be dealt with. As indicated above, the legal hostel owners are keen to align themselves with local residents pressing for action against illegal hostels, as long as they are not tarred with the same brush. Most local residents, however, seem to have a fairly general view of backpackers and backpacker accommodation, which does not usually discriminate between legal and illegal operations, or between long- and short-stay backpackers.

Creating Consensus?

The areas of conflict between the main stakeholders in backpacker tourism in Bondi make it clear that all parties have much to gain from resolving these problems. Bondi already has a number of initiatives that focus on bringing residents, the visitor industry and backpackers together in a positive way. This has been achieved through a targeted social marketing campaign, funded by the NSW Stormwater Trust, which aimed to promote awareness of the negative environmental impact that can occur in high-use visitor destinations. As well as a cooperative volunteer beach cleanup event, run to unite backpackers and residents in cleaning up the beach and the park areas, specific target groups were identified and a poster campaign developed to promote awareness of environmental impacts. 'Backpacker' posters were placed in specific locations (e.g. hostel bedrooms, Internet cafes) and more general 'impact' posters were placed around the public areas (beach and parks). A range of media were used, including radio and magazine articles and commercials. An innovative approach that specifically targeted the transient backpacker group involved a 'welcome kit', which was given to all new hostel guests in the target area. Importantly, this kit included materials that the target audience would find useful (attractive postcards, a pen, a condom) with subtle environmental messages incorporated. Materials were market tested and developed to maximise effectiveness for each target audience.

Conclusions

Backpacking is a major growth market, which is stimulated by the desire for experience and learning about other places and cultures. One potential result of this is that backpackers tend to have more contact with the local communities in which they stay than other tourists. In working-oriented enclaves such as Bondi, they stay in relatively small accommodation units that are often located in residential areas, which some visions of sustainable tourism may see as infinitely preferable to the development of homogeneous resort complexes.

However, the structure of suburban backpacker enclaves produces new challenges that may arguably impact more on local residents and their environment than resort-based tourism. The experience desired by backpackers is one of some integration into the local community, and more contact with local people. This however contrasts with their actual activities in the enclave, which are usually undertaken with fellow travellers rather than 'locals'. These activities also tend to generate negative impacts such as noise and litter, which impinge on the quality of life in the areas they live in.

The growing resistance to backpacker tourism in enclaves such as Bondi has tended to polarise the position of the major stakeholders in the backpacker 'scene'. The major division is between the voluntary stakeholders who benefit from the industry, largely the hostel owners and other businesses in the area, and the involuntary stakeholders, usually characterised as local residents. The local authority, trying to balance as it does the benefits and costs of backpacker tourism for other stakeholders, has both a voluntary and involuntary interest. The public sector is a voluntary stakeholder in terms of the income derived from the development of backpacker tourism, and an involuntary stakeholder in terms of its duty to deal with the physical and social problems arising from backpacking.

The evident tensions between the stakeholder groups in the Bondi community particularly raise questions of legitimacy. Who should have the 'right' to decide the form and scale of backpacker tourism development in the area? At a basic level, the local authority has a statutory duty to police the operation of hostels, but the many illegal hostel operations place considerable limits on this power. It is often difficult to prove the existence of an illegal hostel, which allows them to operate with relative impunity. In the backpacker 'industry', legitimacy for the expansion of legal hostel operations is based on the important economic impacts of backpacker tourism and the growing professionalism of hostel operations. The problem for the legal hostel owners, however, is to differentiate themselves from illegal hostels (and to distance themselves from 'vomit backpackers'). If they fail to do so, then new legal hostels will continue to be opposed by residents, exacerbating the shortage of backpacker accommodation and fuelling the growth of illegal hostels. For the residents, one of the main issues is that the growth of illegal hostels is stimulated by the active or passive involvement of a number of fellow residents. Their apparent inability to distinguish between different types of hostels and different types of backpackers means that they are also unable to direct their full energy to rooting out the main source of problems: illegal hostels. Instead of resisting any form of hostel development, they may have more success if they form a coalition with legal hostel owners (and long-stay backpackers, who are at least a temporary part of the community) to oppose illegal operations. In this sense it is clear that Bondi not only suffers from tensions between stakeholder groups, but also within stakeholder groups as well.

Chapter 15

Perceptions of Backpacker Accommodation Facilities: A Comparative Study of Scotland and New Zealand

JENNY CAVE, MAREE THYNE and CHRIS RYAN

Introduction

The intent of this chapter is to compare the characteristics of facilities and traveller attitudes to services in backpacker/hostel accommodation from two geographically dispersed locations – New Zealand and Scotland. Research indicates that backpacker profiles may be evolving globally towards a wider age-inclusive demographic and use by short-break users, in a market that was once typified as the preserve of youthful, international travellers. It appears that accommodation providers may be adapting their products to meet these changes; but to what extent is the posited change actually in line with the facilities and services expected by travellers? Is there a difference in response that accords with demographic age profile? Until now, there has been no comparison of: hypothesised changes in demographic profiles; or of backpacker traveller attitudes towards the supply of backpacker accommodation between the two countries. This chapter aims to address these gaps in order to elucidate the changing requirements of this significant tourism and hospitality market and implications of such change for the future design of backpacker facilities. The comparisons also enable contrasts to be drawn between a developing destination in need of a clearer understanding of the attitudes of this market in Scotland (Shipway, 2000), and the more developed 'backpacker' destination of New Zealand.

The chapter is structured as follows. First, it outlines a theoretical context which serves to introduce some of the key variables that appear to influence attitudes and behaviour in the backpacker sector. Second, the research contexts of New Zealand and Scottish markets are described. Methodological issues are then outlined and findings from the comparative study are presented. Finally their implications are assessed in the light of future industry needs.

Literature Review

Issues regarding service quality and facility supply in the tourist experience have been researched in a number of areas including: alpine ski resorts (Weiermair & Fuchs, 1999), Hong Kong cruise sector (Qu & Ping, 1999), heritage attractions (Beeho & Prentice, 1997), the development of visitor attractions (Bigne & Andreu, 2004; Cave & Ryan, 2004), destination image (Ryan & Cave, 2004), boutique accommodation (McIntosh & Siggs, 2005), food service (Almanza et al., 1994), dining (Kivela et al., 1999) and in restaurants or cafes (Lockyer, 2005; Mohsin et al., 2005). An online database search of research published from 1997 to 2005 specific to the accommodation sector (over 70 items) emphasises the hotel sector. A few of these studies examine small accommodation businesses such as B&Bs, home stays or small country hotels and a handful relate to farm tourism and conferences. Specific issues investigated by research to date are: repeat choice of accommodation (Richard & Sundaram, 1994), employee training (Taylor & Davies, 2004), classification and grading schemes (Callan & Lefebve, 1997; Ingram, 1996), business guest perceptions (Lockyer, 2002), on-line booking systems (Fam et al., 2004) and host–guest psychographic matching (Tucker & Lynch, 2004).

Published research into the supply-side of the backpacker accommodation industry, however, is sparse, with the exception of Ross (1992, 1995) and recent work by Obenour et al. (2006) and Nash et al. (2006). Several studies on the wider issue of the backpacker industry, however, do contain material relevant to this question of facility requirements. As Elsrud (2001: 606) says, 'typifications and routines, internalized in the process of socialization at home do not necessarily give a puzzled traveller in a new situation the right answers'. Weber (1995) highlights the liminal experience of being away from home. Sørensen (2003) talks of the distinctive subculture created by backpackers as evidenced by 'road status' symbols (worn equipment, clothes and attitudes) and reinforced by guidebooks such as the *Lonely Planet*. These hint at a 'special' backpacker experience. In fact, Riley (1988) claims that backpackers are less concerned about amenities (e.g. plumbing), restaurants (e.g. Westernised food) or transportation.

Ross (1997) argues that achievement/control needs are high among backpackers, and the existence of and achievement of these needs form a symbiotic relationship with perceptions of satisfaction. In terms of decision-making, a prime influencer for the choice of backpacker accommodation is price. Another influencer is the location of the facility, and concerns about the services and facilities provided are placed last. Decisions appear however to be only marginally influenced by traveller's values such as eco-friendly practices (Riley, 1988).

Positive recommendations from travellers about backpacker accommodation are known to be profoundly influenced by the staff and the environmental setting (hostel design). The staff and facility design are key drivers of satisfaction with the opportunities for social interaction and whether the dynamics of both long-term and short-term stay residents are managed well (Murphy, 2001: 65). Accommodation services and food/drink are negative motivators of enjoyment, but the positives are friendships/relationships and personal fulfilment (Ross, 1992). Recent research by Obenour *et al.* (2006) in the USA addresses the issues of distinctiveness in backpacker accommodation, stressing the importance of social interaction, user independence and iconic symbols. Recommendations are made in that study for the redesign of backpacker accommodation as a means to improve social interaction, or distance if desired, among travellers. For example, social interaction would be enhanced by a larger kitchen and dorm rooms being allocated according to the size and nature of the travel party (i.e. solitary or partnership) (Obenour *et al.*, 2006). We know that the intentional construction of *communitas* adds value and extends the service experience (Arnould & Price, 1993). These findings are supported by Nash *et al.* (2006) and the broader research of Loker-Murphy (1996), Loker-Murphy and Pearce (1995) and Murphy (2001).

Recent Scottish Youth Hostel research suggests that facility design should be altered to respond to two distinct age groups who are now commonly represented in backpacker accommodation – those aged under 30 and over 50 years. For the under 30s, design improvements should entail: developing the 'fun' element such as themed hostels; more liberal attitudes towards licensing of properties, sale and consumption of alcohol, even bars and discos; and increased provision of activities, trained activity leaders/personnel and equipment hire (Nash *et al.*, 2006). In contrast, the over-50s group look for smaller rooms with en-suite facilities and shared facilities such as kitchens and dining/social areas that offer opportunities for both socialising as well as privacy. This current research will establish whether such needs are apparent in a cross-cultural comparison.

The backpacker market segment is identified as one that impacts on host communities and upon nature, in particular: localised ways (Cohen, 2004; Huxley, 2004), and frequenting both urban and rural destinations (Elliott, 2002). Activity participation of backpackers emphasises 'adventure in nature' but it is now known to include mainstream tourism products (Duffy, 2002; Wearing *et al.*, 2002), extending its value more widely in local and national economies. It is a sector with high value for rural areas, as backpackers seek out new destinations and have a penchant for remote and unusual places (Scheyvens, 2002). Various definitions and discussions of the composition of the backpacker market have been offered (Cave & Ryan, 2005; Loker, 1991; Loker-Murphy, 1996; Mohsin & Ryan, 2003; Murphy, 2001; Ryan & Mohsin, 2001; Thyne *et al.*, 2004). Yet increasingly research is in agreement that the most significant commonality within this 'backpacker' market is their accommodation choice (Mohsin & Ryan, 2003; Nash *et al.*, 2006; Thyne *et al.*, 2004). Demographic characteristics and criteria such as length of stay, travel patterns and activities and shared motivations have been used throughout the years as defining characteristics of the backpacker (Loker, 1991, Loker-Murphy, 1996; Murphy, 2001; Mohsin & Ryan, 2003).

In North America, human constructs of quest and adventure deepen backpacker travel but are associated with the need for solitary experience (Cole, 1998; Cole & Stewart, 2002; Hammitt & Madden, 1989; Hammitt & Patterson, 1991, 1993; Patterson & Hammitt, 1990; Stewart & Cole, 2001). In Australasia, Pearce (1990) defines the backpacker as a traveller with a preference for budget accommodation, an emphasis on meeting other travellers, someone who is independently organised but retains a predilection for flexible travel schedules, whose travel durations are not brief, and who maintains a clear emphasis on informal and participatory activities during the holiday period. Loker (1991) typifies the backpacker as an 18–30 year old, who stays in a country for a minimum of four months and for whom holiday is the main purpose of the trip. But worldwide, awareness is growing of the presence in backpacker research of older age groups; the impacts of globalisation and worldwide socio-economic change are radically shifting the demographic characteristics observed in backpacker travellers (Cave & Ryan, 2005; Keeley, 2001). The 'ageing adolescents' are also described as 'baby boomers' who seek adventure (Patterson, 2002) and return to favourite destinations with their children, or they 'trade down' as a result of global economic downturn, increased demand for value for money accommodation and/or no-frills travel. Research shows that amongst users of budget accommodation the trend towards increased usage of the facilities by older travellers is having the effects of extending the travel season, encouraging accommodation providers to remove their communal sleeping facilities and also to install smaller rooms with en-suite amenities (Cave & Ryan, 2005; Mohsin & Ryan, 2003). In the Wet Tropics of Northern Australia, the features that align with the highest service quality expectations for backpacker accommodation are age and higher education (Ross, 1995). Aramberri (1991) also notes that youth backpacker travellers are ready to put up with a lesser degree of comfort than older generations. Perhaps then, if older and younger travellers who use backpacker accommodation are compared, might one expect to see very different preferences exhibited, or will these be the same? This will be the main crux of this chapter, along with providing an international comparative dimension.

To summarise, it is notable in the context of this chapter that age disparity appears as a significant demographic factor affecting segment responses in studies such as those of Loker-Murphy (1996), Mohsin and Ryan (2003), Nash *et al*. (2006) and Obenour *et al*. (2006). Further, that price, facility location, and services and environment (design) are key determinants of service satisfaction for backpackers. However, previous literature has not addressed the gap in our understanding as to the differences in attitudes to accommodation facilities amongst the ever increasingly diverse age groups using the facilities. Thus the aim of this research is to determine whether or not accommodation providers are meeting the demands of these groups, using an international comparison to do so. Before this is addressed however, both case study regions will be discussed, with a particular emphasis on the value of the backpacker market to each destination.

Research Context: The New Zealand and Scottish Backpacker Markets

New Zealand

New Zealand's tourism market comprises visitors who want to interact with the landscape and culture, and consume a broad range of activities and high levels of nature/adventure-based products. Similar products are used regardless of country of origin, and consumption is determined by travel style, life stage and budget (Tourism Research Council, New Zealand, 2004). Most tourists have a clear idea of what they want to see and do in New Zealand. Camping tourists want to see mountains and glaciers, backpackers seem more attracted to iconic natural and cultural sites, whereas budget tours from Australia want to see as much as possible in the time available; 'up-market' tours want to indulge themselves and the Asian market want to see a lot in a short time (Becken & Butcher, 2004).

The backpacker market in New Zealand reached 4,341,536 guest nights in the year ending May 2005 (Tourism Research Council New Zealand, 2005), continuing its faster annual increase than other sectors, and noted as having grown by 67% since 1997 (Tourism Research Council New Zealand, 2004). Backpackers stay in a range of other accommodation, for longer periods than other international tourists. Backpackers have an estimated annual spend of up to $NZ3533 per person, much higher than the average international tourist, and were estimated in 2002 to be worth $NZ701 million annually to the New Zealand economy (Newlands, 2004). Economic multipliers calculated by Becken and Butcher (2004) indicate that backpacker tourism generates an employment yield of 2.3 employees and $133 per day. This would result in figures of $4.09 million dollars generated in 2005 from backpacker accommodation use in New Zealand. A significant portion of backpacker accommodation is used by domestic New Zealanders, reinforcing the trend for an increased proportion of short-break travel periods amongst backpacker travellers. The country is well known for its clean, green image and an extensive tourism industry spanning cultural, wine, eco- and adventure tourism that is well supported by a sophisticated infrastructure of transportation, tours, travel agents, offshore accommodation, event, tour and attractions wholesalers and governmental investment. It exhibits many of the features of a mature and well developed destination such as infrastructure, governmental support and value-added services such as associated merchandising, transportation and activities. In the backpacking sector this is evidenced by strong linkages between adventure activities and backpacker accommodation, as well as in links to more mainstream activities in recent years (Ryan *et al.*, 2003); the Kiwi-Experience network of buses and range of tour options, which are well marketed offshore; and the newly established Qualmark quality accreditation standards that have been developed specifically for the backpacker sector.

Research into backpackers in New Zealand is varied, covering a wide span of issues such as: the activities and accommodation preferences of YHA and backpacker lodges in New Zealand undertaken by Ware (1992); examinations of the Kiwi-Experience bus tours (Moran, 2000); the backpacker hostel network (Garnham, 1993); information sources used (Pearce & Schott, 2005); the relationship of backpackers within local communities (Doorne, 1994); the link between backpacker industries and entrepreneurship (Ateljevic & Doorne, 2000a); pre-travel decisions (Farrell, 1999); Korean pleasure travellers (Cha & Jeong, 1998); service quality expectations (Toxward, 1999); backpacker profile (Ateljevic & Doorne, 2001); energy consumption (Becken, 2001; Becken *et al*., 2003); waste minimisation by suppliers (Thampson & Mooney, 1998); and a Tourism New Zealand in-depth interview study of 24 backpackers (Tourism New Zealand, 1999). Before now, however, what has been missing in the research is a comparison of facility characteristics with another country, and no distinction has been made between the preferences of different age groups, hence the research outlined in this chapter.

Scotland

Duffield and Long (1981) and Fennell (1996) both postulate that formative factors for tourism in Scotland have been the processes of economic centralisation in the UK, leading to a depleted economic base and an undeveloped social infrastructure, which ironically contributes to the positive tourism resource of Scotland's unspoiled landscapes and distinctive local culture. The backpacker market has been recognised in wider Britain as an important and growing market (Keeley, 2001). Keeley estimates that the backpacker market accounts for 10% of overseas visitors to the UK and those 2.5 million travellers come to Britain for a three- to four-week backpacking trip. Further, he suggests that there is a potential market worldwide of 20 million young people who at any given time have the resources to visit Britain. Britain's appeal to the backpacker market includes its history, cultural diversity, visual images and the use of the English language (Shipway, 2000). Yet the characteristics of this segment in Scotland are largely anecdotal (Keeley, 1995, 2001) and specific information on the backpacking phenomenon across Scotland as a whole is incomplete and sporadic.

According to VisitScotland, the number of hostels in Scotland has doubled since 1990 to 227 in 2000 and occupancy levels in hostels at 49% are higher than in all forms of accommodation, with the exception of self-catering (VisitScotland, 2000). These results may reflect a steady growth of backpacker type tourists who tend to favour this type of accommodation. However, recent studies have deepened the understanding of Scottish backpacker lifestyles, in terms of: the attractions they visit, activities undertaken and motivations (Thyne *et al*., 2004); importance and satisfaction of the backpacker experience (Nash *et al*., 2006); and their economic worth to the local economy (Foster, 1990; Scottish National Party, 2000; Scottish Office, 1999). Research points to the backpacker/hostel sector in Scotland as being one with potential, but that has not yet developed an extensive support, marketing and sales infrastructure and one which is perceived by travellers as a less developed locale (Duffield & Long, 1981; Fennell, 1996).

Methodology

The research presented in this chapter therefore addresses a specific comparison between the attitudes of users of backpacker accommodation in the two backpacker contexts outlined above. This comparison addresses a call made by Pearce and Butler (1993) for more comparative tourism research – although over 10 years on, destination comparative research is still lacking in the tourism literature. The validity of a comparative approach between these specific countries has been established by two recent studies. Page *et al*. (2005), in their research on tourist injuries, argue that New Zealand and Scotland are fruitful comparative destinations; mainly due to both countries exhibiting similar inherent environmental qualities and volume of international and domestic tourism. Also, Tucker and Lynch (2004) compared Scottish and New Zealand home-hosted accommodation. Page *et al*. (2005) further argue that such comparative research enhances our understanding of the processes of development and change in tourism at different geographical scales. In the case of this research, such comparisons also enable contrasts to be drawn between a more developed 'backpacker' destination (New Zealand) and a less commodified destination (Scotland), together with intra-country contrasts.

A common questionnaire was adopted in both countries, with some local variations. Similar research dimensions have been used in Australia, but will be reported elsewhere.

New Zealand methodology

The New Zealand questionnaire consisted of five main sections, based upon prior research undertaken in the Australian backpacker market (Ryan & Mohsin, 2001; Ryan *et al*., 2003). These are: an importance scale relating to the selected attributes and activities found within New Zealand (including adventure sports and cultural/social activities); a satisfaction scale using the same items; a section on desired accommodation facility and service attributes; an assessment of satisfaction with accommodation; and finally open-ended questions regarding choice of activities. Scale items were chosen to represent the nature of activities and attractions thought to appeal to backpackers, evidenced by previous research undertaken (e.g. Ryan *et al*., 2003).

Respondents were approached at the Hamilton bus station and backpacker accommodation in Hamilton and Raglan (New Zealand). The sample then comprised 494 usable responses from face-to-face interviews, from 600 respondent approaches.

Scottish methodology

The methodology for the Scottish study was a two-stage process: in-depth interviews, after which a more extensive questionnaire was developed. In-depth interviews ($n = 22$) were undertaken with visitors staying at hostels throughout Scotland to gather exploratory information and aid in the design of the questionnaire. The interview results were contrasted with the literature to determine the items that needed to be included in the questionnaire. There were seven sections to the questionnaire: details of respondents' holiday in Scotland (length of stay, regions visited, travel party); reasons for travel (motivations, activities undertaken); transportation; accommodation (types used, importance satisfaction of accommodation facilities); spending behaviour; information sources used; and demographics. Questionnaires were distributed to 12 Scottish Youth Hostel Association hostels and 12 Independent Hostels throughout Scotland (2400 questionnaires were distributed in total), ensuring an even split between urban and rural hostels. In total, 309 usable questionnaires were returned from the SYHA hostels and 191 were returned from the Independent Hostels for a combined total of 500 responses, 419 of which are usable in this analysis.

Analysis

As this chapter focuses on the comparison of attitudes toward the facilities and services of backpacker accommodation, only the questions relevant to that issue will be included in the analysis and discussion sections in this chapter, along with an outline of the profiles of both samples.

The authors have adopted a model for this study that is based on personal construct theory and the theory of reasoned action – permitting the construction of Likert scales utilising variables that reflect attributes considered important by actual or potential users of a resort or tourist zone (Ryan, 1995b). While some of the attributes are different between the samples, a common core of 12 allows comparison for each country of the factors that are deemed to be important from precursor studies. An additional attribute in the New Zealand sample is 'linked to adventure'; and in the Scottish sample additional attributes are 'no-smoking policy', 'single/double/twin accommodation available' and 'value for money'.

Analysis of these attributes is conducted as follows: descriptive statistics and measures of central tendency and dispersion are generated for each attribute. First as combined samples for both the Importance and Satisfaction Components, then as subsample comparisons.

The model of attitude satisfaction adopted by the authors is built upon a modified version of Fishbein's (1967) theory of reasoned action, which reflects the dimensions of importance and satisfaction of predefined accommodation attributes. Such mechanisms allow researchers to describe beliefs about the nature of personal experience, as well as an evaluation of the importance of that belief to the individual (Ryan, 1995b). Fishbein argues that there are two dimensions of attitude, the evaluative component and the importance of that belief (Fishbein, 1967). According to the theory then, an individual's attitude toward any object is a function of (1) the strength of his beliefs about the object and (2) the evaluative aspect of those beliefs (Cohen et al., 1972). Thus, attitude is a sum of the product of the evaluative reaction to a salient property and the strength of belief connecting the property to the attitude object or event across all salient properties (Ahtola, 1975). A Fishbein matrix maps the degree of importance dimension against the satisfaction dimension using a Likert-type scale rating of each attribute. The aggregate means for each attribute can be arrayed on a matrix whose axes are formed by the respective Grand Means of each component. This allows researchers to map the attributes into four quadrants that show clearly the (un)/ importance of an attribute to individuals in the sample; and the attributes that are (not)/perceived to be present by individuals at the destination or service facility. A criticism of this method is that it describes reasoned behaviour but not those that are unconscious, routine or mindless. Consequently, caution may be needed in extending this model beyond its original theoretical tenets by its use in wider contexts (Ahtola, 1975). Nonetheless, it offers some real advantages in the understanding of tourist behaviours, in the sense that it allows researchers to know the relative position of each attribute and to make recommendations for management in industry based on the quadrant in which an attribute is located by the sample of respondents. Adapting Ryan (1995b), if the attribute is in Quadrant 1: not present and highly valued (an operations manager may see this as an opportunity for improvement?); Quadrant 2: present and highly valued (keep doing this); Quadrant 3: present and not valued (why do this?); Quadrant 4: not present and not valued (is it needed?). This method continues to be used in marketing, service industries, hospitality (Alexandris *et al.*, 2002; Buttle & Bok, 1996; Kivela *et al.*, 1999; Lee-Ross, 1998, 2000; Lee-Ross & Pryce, 2005) and in tourism (Saleh & Ryan, 1992; Wen, 1998).

The analysis concludes with a *t*-test for significant differences between age groups in attitudes towards the accommodation facilities.

Findings

The earlier literature review notes that age disparity and nationality appear as significant demographic factors affecting segment responses in backpacker research, the most significant of which is age. Therefore, this results section will begin with a summary of the age groups within each sample, along with a gender breakdown (see Table 15.1 and Table 15.2).

A more mature backpacker is represented in both samples, although less so in the New Zealand sample (80% under 30 years, compared to only 50% in the Scottish sample), confirming the views of Keeley (2001), Mohsin and Ryan (2003) and Newlands (2004) in previous literature, that a change in age structure of the backpacker composition has taken place over time. The proportion of males and females in each sample is quite similar: 46% male to 54% female (New Zealand); and 48% male to 52% female (Scottish).

Table 15.1 Sample of users of New Zealand backpacker accommodation

		Gender			
		Male	*Female*	*Total*	*%*
Age	Under 18 years	14	21	35	7
	19–24	99	137	236	48
	25–30	70	53	123	25
	31–40	20	26	46	9
	41–50	12	10	22	4
	51–60	7	13	20	4
	Over 60	3	9	12	2
	Total	225	269	494	100

Table 15.2 Sample of users of Scottish hostel accommodation

		Gender			
		Male	Female	Total	%
Age	Under 20 years	10	21	31	7
	20 – 24	46	41	87	21
	25 – 29	45	47	92	22
	30 – 34	24	18	42	10
	35 – 39	17	21	38	9
	40 – 44	14	20	34	8
	45 – 49	13	12	25	6
	50 – 54	6	11	17	4
	55 – 59	12	14	26	6
	60 – 64	5	6	11	3
	65 or over	9	7	16	4
	Total	201	218	419	100

Although previous literature has suggested that alterations should be made to accommodation facilities and amenities to accommodate varying age groups (e.g. Nash *et al.*, 2006), there has not until now been any analysis that confirms whether there are in fact distinct requirements and differences in preferences between these varying ages. Such an analysis will be outlined later in this section.

Table 15.3 begins the analysis of the accommodation facilities. Both samples are combined and their overall importance levels for 22 accommodation facilities are outlined (Likert scale measure: 1 = not at all important; 7 = extremely important).

As shown in Table 15.3, for the combined samples, the most important accommodation attributes are cleanliness, the availability of cooking/self catering facilities, the availability of additional travel information, private showers and bathrooms, and the availability of clothes-washing facilities. These findings appear to contradict the belief of Riley (1988) that the backpacker is not concerned about amenities, and Obenour *et al*.

Table 15.3 Overall importance levels for accommodation attributes (combined samples)

Rank	Attribute	N	Mean	sd
1	Clean rooms (NZ and Scottish samples)	822	6.11	1.285
2	Value for money (Scottish samples)	369	6.07	1.260
3	Self-catering/cooking facilities (NZ and Scottish samples)	809	5.33	1.759
4	Lots of travel information (NZ and Scottish samples)	795	5.10	1.860
5	Private showers and bathrooms (NZ and Scottish samples)	809	4.97	1.901
6	Suitable heating/air conditioning (Scottish Independent Hostels)	115	4.93	1.761
7	Staff present and available (Scottish Independent Hostels)	117	4.91	1.771
8	No-smoking rule (Scottish samples)	365	4.85	2.342
9	Clothes-washing facilities (NZ and Scottish samples)	786	4.83	2.023
10	Close to city centre (NZ and Scottish samples)	773	4.80	2.034
11	No-noise rule after a certain time (NZ and Scottish samples)	654	4.30	2.151
12	Less rules and restrictions (Scottish Independent Hostels)	114	4.29	1.890
13	Dormitory accommodation at budget prices (NZ and Scottish samples)	780	4.28	2.011
14	Single/double/twin accommodation (Scottish samples)	353	4.25	2.374
15	Drying facilities (Scottish Independent Hostels)	117	4.21	2.189
16	Booking office for local trips (NZ and Scottish samples)	752	4.16	2.217

Table 15.3 (*Continued*)

Rank	Attribute	N	Mean	sd
17	Pick-up/collection service (NZ and Scottish samples)	740	3.94	2.295
18	TV room (NZ and Scottish samples)	783	3.62	2.165
19	Private study area (NZ and Scottish samples)	766	3.54	2.130
20	Access for disabled (Scottish Independent Hostels)	101	2.79	2.304
21	Access to the internet (Scottish Independent Hostels)	108	2.87	2.158
22	Catering to children (Scottish Independent Hostels)	105	2.64	2.254

(2006), who suggest that the opportunities for social interaction especially need to be considered when developing accommodation facilities. This current research shows that the respondents do value creature comforts, such as clean rooms and private bathroom facilities, suggesting a higher level of demand from this target market than has previously been documented. These results also suggest that this market may be moving more in line with mainstream tourists in respect to their accommodation demands, proposing that a greater degree of comfort is now sought than previously thought (Aramberri, 1991).

As can be seen from Table 15.3, not all of the attributes are identical in each study, thus Table 15.4 presents only those attributes that are common to both the New Zealand and Scottish samples. The purpose of Table 15.4 is to show only significant differences between the perceptions of the Scottish sample and the New Zealand sample regarding accommodation facilities. Again, the attributes were measured on a Likert scale (1–7).

All of the attributes show significant differences in importance ratings between the two samples ('clean rooms' has a significance value of 0.52, but due to its proximity to 0.50, it is also included in this discussion). Without exception, the Scottish sample rate each attribute of lower importance than the New Zealand sample. The biggest contrasts are between clothes-washing facilities (New Zealand mean = 5.57; Scottish mean = 3.98); the availability of a TV room (New Zealand mean = 4.59, Scottish mean = 2.53); a pick-up service from bus/train stations (New Zealand mean = 5.09, Scottish mean = 2.54); and the provision of a booking office for local trips (New Zealand mean = 5.31, Scottish mean = 2.76). These major differences may be attributed to such factors as the timing of the research in each destination; the New Zealand data was collected in mid-winter, thus adverse weather may affect the activities that can be undertaken, so a TV room may become more important, as would a pick-up service from bus/train stations (if the weather is too bad to walk in for example). The Scottish data were collected during the UK summer period. Also, in the Scottish sample, 60% of people used their own car or a rental car for transportation, hence they were not likely to need a pick-up service if the weather was unfavourable, and instead of relying on entertainment within the hostel (such as a television), they had more freedom to leave the hostel to perhaps visit a castle, museum or cathedral for example.

These results do suggest that the New Zealand sample is more demanding and expect more from backpacker accommodation than the Scottish sample. One possible reason could have been a higher proportion

Table 15.4 Importance of attributes, New Zealand and Scottish sample comparisons

Importance:	New Zealand sample			Scottish sample				
Attribute	N	Mean	sd	N	Mean	sd	t-test	Sig.
Clean rooms	428	6.19	1.31	394	6.02	1.25	− 1.93	0.052
Private showers and toilets	427	5.42	1.72	382	4.47	1.97	− 7.53	0.000
Large communal rooms at budget prices	409	4.67	1.87	371	3.84	2.07	− 5.88	0.000
Self catering/cooking facilities	421	5.51	1.52	388	5.14	1.97	− 2.99	0.000
Clothes washing facilities	420	5.57	1.57	366	3.98	2.14	− 11.94	0.000
TV room	414	4.59	1.91	369	2.53	1.90	− 15.08	0.000
Study/quiet room	406	3.98	2.11	360	3.04	2.04	− 6.20	0.000
No noise rule	407	4.50	2.09	247	3.95	2.20	− 3.21	0.000
Pick up service from bus stops	405	5.09	1.77	335	2.54	2.06	− 18.09	0.000
Lots of travel information	423	5.66	1.62	372	4.47	1.91	− 9.49	0.000
Booking office for local trips	413	5.31	1.69	339	2.76	1.97	− 19.12	0.000
Close to the city centre	421	5.38	1.55	352	4.12	2.32	− 9.00	0.000

of international visitors included in the New Zealand sample (thus perhaps higher expectations of a country they may have spent a lot of time and/or money to visit). However, there is the same split between domestic and international respondents in both samples (23% domestic/ 77% international in the Scottish sample; 23% domestic/77% international in the New Zealand sample). The New Zealand respondent expectation levels may be due to the successful '100% Pure' umbrella brand developed over the last 12 years (Morgan *et al.*, 2002). The contrasts of ages within the samples may have also had an influence on the importance ratings of particular facilities; this will be discussed in more detail later in this section.

Satisfaction ratings for the same accommodation facilities will now be outlined. Again, to begin with, both samples have been combined, and their overall satisfaction levels for all 22 accommodation facilities are outlined (1 = not at all satisfied, 7 = extremely satisfied).

For the combined samples, the accommodation attributes with which respondents are most satisfied are cleanliness, the availability of additional travel information, the availability of cooking/self-catering facilities, the availability of clothes-washing facilities and the distance of the hostel from the city centre. This is reassuring, as four of these items were also rated as 'most important' by respondents. So there appears to be a match between importance and evaluations, arguably leading to a more satisfactory experience. However, it is now useful to determine how these satisfaction ratings significantly compare between the two samples. Only those attributes common to both samples are presented in Table 15.6.

There is quite a variation in the satisfaction ratings between the samples, unlike the importance ratings, where the New Zealand sample consistently exhibits higher mean scores. Table 15.6 shows the Scottish sample as having higher satisfaction with the cleanliness of rooms and cooking/self-catering facilities. Conversely, the New Zealand sample are more satisfied with the following attributes: clothes-washing facilities, TV room, pick-up service from bus stops, host of travel information available, booking office available and close to the city centre, suggesting that New Zealand hostels may be better at providing value-added 'add-ons' to the hostels, versus cooking facilities and cleanliness, which respondents may have expected.

Clarity emerges concerning these issues when the two dimensions, Importance and Satisfaction, are mapped to form a Fishbein-style matrix, summarising the salient properties of accommodation service quality in backpacker/hostel accommodation.

Table 15.5 Overall satisfaction levels for attributes (combined samples)

Rank	Attribute	N	Mean	sd
1	Staff presence (Scottish Independent Hostels)	121	5.75	1.43
2	Value for money (Scottish samples)	400	5.75	1.44
3	No-smoking rule (Scottish samples)	373	5.60	1.82
4	Clean rooms (NZ and Scottish samples)	838	5.58	1.46
5	Less rules and restrictions (Scottish Independent Hostels)	114	5.29	1.70
6	Lots of travel information (NZ and Scottish samples)	776	5.28	1.58
7	Self catering/cooking facilities (NZ and Scottish samples)	813	5.65	2.88
8	Suitable heating/air conditioning (Scottish Independent Hostels)	115	5.16	1.75
9	Clothes washing facilities (NZ and Scottish samples)	747	5.05	1.73
10	Links to adventure activities	353	5.04	1.56
11	Close to city centre (NZ and Scottish samples)	748	4.96	1.83
12	Dormitory accommodation at budget prices (NZ and Scottish samples)	770	4.93	1.67
13	Private showers and bathrooms (NZ and Scottish samples)	808	4.92	1.76
14	Single/double/twin accommodation (Scottish samples)	351	4.87	2.11
15	No noise rule after a certain time (NZ and Scottish samples)	623	4.79	1.82
16	TV room (NZ and Scottish samples)	738	4.68	1.93

17	Drying facilities (Scottish Independent Hostels)	111	4.63	2.02
18	Booking office for local trips (NZ and Scottish samples)	679	4.52	1.94
19	Private study area (both samples)	689	4.31	1.89
20	Catering for children (Scottish Independent Hostels)	87	4.20	2.16
21	Pick up/collection services (NZ and Scottish samples)	655	4.12	2.11
22	Access to Internet (Scottish Independent Hostels)	98	3.53	2.31
23	Access for disabled (Scottish Independent Hostels)	85	3.45	2.23

Table 15.6 Satisfaction with attributes by New Zealand and Scottish samples

Satisfaction: Attribute	New Zealand Sample			Scottish Sample				
	N	Mean	Sd	N	Mean	sd	t-test	Sig.
Clean rooms	417	5.26	1.51	421	5.90	1.33	6.58	0.000
Private showers and toilets	404	4.97	1.62	404	4.87	1.88	−0.82	0.412
Large communal rooms at budget prices	382	4.94	1.50	388	4.92	1.83	−0.21	0.837
Self catering/cooking facilities	405	5.31	1.44	408	5.99	3.77	3.40	0.001
Clothes washing facilities	391	5.18	1.52	356	4.90	1.93	−2.12	0.027
TV room	387	5.01	1.63	351	4.32	2.17	−4.91	0.000
Study/quiet room	348	4.35	1.81	341	4.27	1.96	−0.56	0.574
'No noise' rule	362	4.82	1.75	261	4.76	1.90	−0.40	0.689
Pick up service from bus stops	354	4.84	1.78	301	3.27	2.16	−10.17	0.000
Lots of travel information	395	5.44	1.51	381	5.12	1.64	−2.85	0.005
Booking office for local trips	375	5.12	1.63	304	3.79	2.05	−9.36	0.000
Close to the city centre	397	5.22	1.51	351	4.67	2.09	−4.13	0.000
Links to adventure activities	353	5.04	1.56					

Figure 15.1 graphs the personal constructs of the New Zealand sample. The attributes that appear in Quadrant 1 (high importance and low satisfaction) are clothes washing, booking office for local trips, and private showers and toilets. These are features that the operational managers must improve as they are highly valued, yet visitors are less than satisfied with their supply. Quadrant 2 shows those items that visitors identify as highly important to the quality of their visit as well as satisfaction with their delivery. Clean rooms is rated most highly overall. The attributes lots of travel information, clothes-washing facilities, self-catering/cooking facilities and closeness to the city centre, while falling

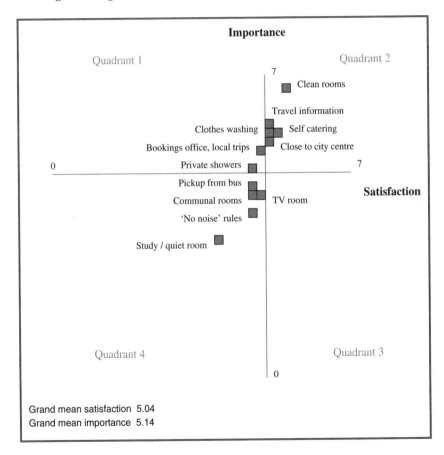

Figure 15.1 Importance versus satisfaction – New Zealand sample.

into Quadrant 2, are given mid-range satisfaction ratings even though they are identified as being important to the respondents. The third quadrant is empty. The fourth quadrant describes those attributes of service quality that are both unimportant to visitors and with which they are dissatisfied – these being pick-up service from the bus station, communal rooms, a TV room and no-noise rules. The study/quiet room is rated worst of all. These findings will be discussed in more detail later. Overall, the responses for the New Zealand sample draw a picture of moderate satisfaction for most of the accommodation attributes.

The importance/satisfaction matrix for the Scottish sample personal construct illustrates an achievement of higher levels of satisfaction overall and a wider spread of opinion as to the importance of accommodation attributes than seen above in the New Zealand sample (Figure 15.2). Perhaps this is due to its perception as a less developed locale (Duffield & Long, 1981; Fennell, 1996). The lack of links to travel infrastructure and value-added services is evident in the satisfaction ratings however. The only attribute to appear in Quadrant 1 (high importance/low satisfaction) is closeness to the city centre. Attributes in Quadrant 2 (high importance/high satisfaction) include: clean rooms and self-catering/cooking facilities as well as private showers and toilets, lots of travel information, clothes-washing facilities and no-noise rules. The latter group are given moderate satisfaction ratings. However, users of Scotland's hostels are quite satisfied with the self-catering/cooking facilities and the cleanliness of the rooms. In Quadrant 3, respondents overall are moderately satisfied with the large communal rooms at budget prices, although this is not seen as a highly important feature – perhaps reflecting a shift towards more privacy and personal conveniences. The final quadrant (4) contains attributes that are rated very poorly in terms of satisfaction. These are the study/quiet room, the provision of a booking office for local trips, pick-up service from the bus/ train station and the TV room. However, these are also not considered to be very important to occupants of Scottish backpacker hostels.

To summarise, similar and differing ratings are noted below:

- High importance/low satisfaction ratings differ between the New Zealand and Scottish samples. In the New Zealand sample visitors locate a booking office for local trips, and private showers and toilets as areas where improvement would be welcomed by patrons. Whereas for the Scottish respondents, the point of weakness is proximity to the city centre.

- High importance/high satisfaction shared by both samples are clean rooms, and lots of travel information. Self-catering/cooking facilities and clothes-washing facilities were rated at moderate satisfaction levels in both samples. However the Scottish sample emphasised more satisfaction with the self-catering/cooking facilities provided than did the New Zealand respondents. Proximity to the city centre fared better in New Zealand hostels than in Scotland, where it actually appears in the high importance, low satisfaction quadrant. Private showers and toilets are ranked as moderately high in the Scottish sample, but perform less well in New Zealand, where they too shift into the not satisfied category.

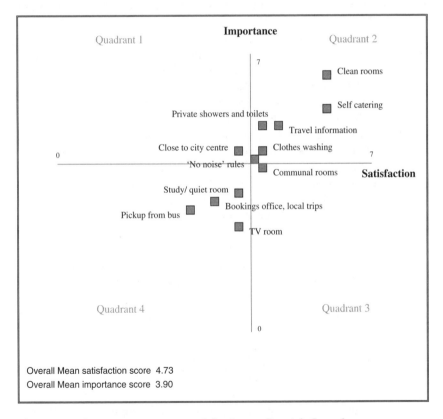

Figure 15.2 Importance versus satisfaction – Scottish Sample.

- Low importance/high satisfaction. Large communal rooms at budget prices are located in this quadrant by Scottish respondents; whereas the New Zealand sample did not have any items placed here.
- Low importance/high satisfaction. The two samples agree that pick-up from the bus/train station, quiet study room and TV room fit into this category. New Zealand respondents also locate no-noise rules and large communal rooms at budget prices here. The Scottish sample places booking office for local trips in this quadrant.

One can conclude from this information that factors of highest importance to users of backpackers/hostels are cleanliness, self-catering/cooking facilities and the provision of lots of travel information. Next on the list are clothes-washing facilities, private showers and toilets, and closeness of the accommodation to the city centre. Least important are a study/quiet room, a TV room, pick-up from the bus station, no-noise rules and large communal rooms. Satisfaction is highest with the standards of cleanliness, food preparation and laundry facilities, and the level of travel information available. These findings confirm those of Conner (2000) and Lockyer (2003, 2004) concerning the importance of cleanliness in many aspects of the service industry, and the importance of local travel information to backpackers (Pearce & Schott, 2005; Sørensen, 2003) plus the need for the redesign of facilities such as kitchens and accommodation matched to the party size and nature of guest party (Obenour *et al.*, 2006). The results also suggest a desirability for private bathrooms and toilets as identified by Cave and Ryan (2005), Mohsin and Ryan (2003) and Ryan *et al.* (2003), and also suggestions of a shift in demand for the traditional bunkroom accommodation of large communal rooms at budget prices.

The next section is a comparative analysis of the two countries in terms of the hypotheses drawn from literature – that age group (under 30s/over 30s) is a key determinant of the observable differences seen in the data. These specific age groups were chosen because they have previously been identified in the literature as being significant (Nash *et al.*, 2006).

This section begins with an outline of the significant differences between the two age groups in the New Zealand sample, regarding their importance ratings of the accommodation facilities.

The importance ratings in the New Zealand sample shown in Table 15.7 are quite evenly spread between ages. Although not significant, there are however differences between the no-noise rules and study/quiet room attributes (both of which are rated higher by the over 30s).

Table 15.7 New Zealand – importance attributes by age

New zealand – Importance	Under 30 years			Over 30 years				
	N	Mean	Sd	N	Mean	Sd	t-test	Sig.
Clean rooms	351	6.13	1.31	64	6.45	1.32	−1.81	0.072
Private showers and toilets	352	5.34	1.73	62	6.00	1.52	−2.84	0.005
Large communal rooms at budget prices	338	4.78	1.80	60	4.32	2.15	1.77	0.077
Self-catering/cooking facilities	346	5.51	1.50	62	5.69	1.49	−0.894	0.372
Washing facilities	346	5.55	1.56	61	5.79	1.51	−1.11	0.270
TV room	342	4.65	1.89	59	4.49	1.99	0.576	0.565
Study/quiet room	336	3.92	2.11	59	4.46	2.03	−1.82	0.070
'No noise' rule	331	4.45	2.06	64	4.94	2.14	−1.72	0.086
Pick up service from bus/train station	339	5.12	1.74	57	5.07	1.92	0.189	0.850
Lots of travel information	348	5.67	1.59	62	5.65	1.76	0.096	0.923
Booking office for local trips	339	5.31	1.69	62	5.39	1.68	−0.345	0.730
Close to the city centre	345	5.39	1.55	63	5.25	1.48	0.653	0.514
Links to adventure activities	331	4.95	1.76	58	4.81	1.79	0.564	0.573

Conversely, the under 30s are looking for budget communal rooms and a TV room (but again, there are no significant differences). The only significant difference between these two age groups is with the higher importance the over 30s place on private showers and toilets. This confirms the findings of Cave and Ryan (2005) and Mohsin and Ryan (2003), who argued that accommodation providers should be encouraged to remove communal sleeping facilities and install smaller rooms with en-suite amenities to appease the older travellers.

Table 15.8 displays the satisfaction ratings between the two age groups in the New Zealand sample. Both age groups appear to be equally satisfied with the accommodation facilities available in the New Zealand hostels. All means were above 4.3 (4 = satisfied). There were no significant differences between the age groups regarding their satisfaction levels.

Table 15.9 outlines the significant differences between the age groups in the Scottish sample, regarding their importance ratings of the accommodation facilities. Compared to the New Zealand sample, there are a number of significant differences between the attitudes of the two age groups regarding the importance of the accommodation facilities in the Scottish sample. Attributes significantly more important to the under 30s include a TV room, pick-up service, provision of travel information, booking office and proximity to city centre. Attributes significantly more important to the over 30s include clean rooms, no-noise rules, no-smoking policies and value for money. This may suggest that the older group is not as interested in add-ons; they appear to have a different purpose for staying at the hotel, one which requires a cheap, quiet and clean room. This purpose may be hill walking or rambling. The younger sample however appear to want to learn more about the destination and require more access to experiencing the destination. These findings may be in line with Nash *et al.*'s (2006) recommendations that the under 30s are more interested in activities and socialising with others, whether it be in the TV room or in the city centre.

Table 15.10 displays the satisfaction ratings between the two age groups, of the Scottish sample. There are also a number of significant differences between the two age groups in the Scottish sample, regarding their satisfaction of the accommodation facilities. The under 30s are significantly more satisfied with the TV room, the pick-up service, the booking office and the proximity to the city centre. This all suggests that the younger age group require added extras to their accommodation stay, specifically extras that will enable them to experience the destination they are visiting. The over 30s are more interested in the no-noise

Table 15.8 New Zealand – satisfaction attributes by age

New Zealand – Satisfaction	Under 30 years			Over 30 years				
	N	Mean	Sd	N	Mean	Sd	t-test	Sig.
Clean rooms	345	5.21	1.53	61	5.44	1.37	–1.11	0.270
Private showers and toilets	334	4.98	1.60	60	4.95	1.71	0.128	0.898
Large communal rooms at budget prices	321	4.98	1.45	52	4.87	1.65	0.538	0.591
Self-catering/cooking facilities	336	5.29	1.42	59	5.41	1.54	–0.581	0.562
Washing facilities	322	5.15	1.52	58	5.31	1.50	–0.731	0.465
TV room	329	5.02	1.62	50	4.86	1.74	0.662	0.508
Study/quiet room	294	4.33	1.82	49	4.55	1.78	–0.802	0.423
'No noise' rule	300	4.80	1.74	56	4.89	1.78	–0.365	0.715
Pick up service from bus/train station	298	4.82	1.76	51	4.84	1.94	–0.102	0.918
Lots of travel information	332	5.44	1.50	54	5.33	1.63	0.465	0.642
Booking office for local trips	316	5.09	1.63	51	5.29	1.54	–0.827	0.409
Close to the city centre	329	5.25	1.48	59	5.00	1.69	1.15	0.25
Links to adventure activities	300	5.05	1.54	46	5.00	1.70	0.189	0.85

Table 15.9 Scotland – importance attributes by age

Scotland – Importance	Under 30 years			Over 30 years				
	N	Mean	Sd	N	Mean	Sd	t-test	Sig.
Clean rooms	208	5.88	1.33	177	6.19	1.11	– 2.47	0.014
Private showers and toilets	207	4.54	1.89	166	4.36	2.04	0.857	0.392
Large communal rooms at budget prices	205	3.8	2.01	158	3.85	2.18	– 0.196	0.845
Self-catering/cooking facilities	207	5.02	1.95	173	5.24	2.01	– 1.10	0.274
Washing facilities	201	4.03	2.15	157	3.92	2.18	0.49	0.624
TV room	206	2.73	1.92	155	2.27	1.86	2.27	0.024
Study/quiet room	202	3.04	2.07	151	3.07	2.05	– 0.12	0.904
'No noise' rule	135	3.41	2.05	109	4.62	2.22	– 4.41	0.000
Pick up service from bus/train station	194	2.96	2.17	136	1.91	1.72	4.71	0.000
Lots of travel information	207	4.80	1.76	159	4.06	2.01	3.78	0.000
Booking office for local trips	195	3.16	2.01	139	2.22	1.80	4.42	0.000
Close to the city centre	200	4.59	2.19	146	3.47	2.33	4.54	0.000
Non-smoking policy	199	4.42	2.31	161	5.39	2.28	– 4.00	0.000
Single/double/twin accommodation	195	4.25	2.38	152	4.30	2.39	– 0.174	0.862
Value for money	196	5.93	1.37	167	6.22	1.11	– 2.18	0.030

Table 15.10 Scotland – satisfaction attributes by age

Scotland – Satisfaction	Under 30 years			Over 30 years				
	N	Mean	Sd	N	Mean	Sd	t-test	Sig.
Clean rooms	208	5.8	1.34	201	5.99	1.34	– 1.41	0.158
Private showers and toilets	204	4.73	1.80	188	4.96	1.99	– 1.19	0.236
Large communal rooms at budget prices	198	4.85	1.80	179	4.96	1.9	– 0.59	0.556
Self-catering/cooking facilities	203	5.67	1.53	194	5.93	1.4	– 1.75	0.081
Washing facilities	185	4.71	1.87	162	5.09	2.00	– 1.83	0.069
TV room	191	4.57	1.99	151	3.99	2.32	2.50	0.013
Study/quiet room	181	4.22	1.88	153	4.32	2.06	– 0.46	0.646
'No noise' rule	132	4.52	1.75	126	5.04	2.01	– 2.24	0.026
Pick up service from bus/train station	165	3.52	2.04	130	2.92	2.26	2.42	0.016
Lots of travel information	202	5.22	1.52	173	5.02	1.79	1.18	0.241
Booking office for local trips	168	4.13	1.99	131	3.38	2.09	3.14	0.002
Close to the city centre	193	4.86	1.96	151	4.40	2.22	2.02	0.044
Non-smoking policy	192	5.42	1.81	175	5.82	1.81	– 2.13	0.034
Single/double/twin accommodation	187	4.90	2.01	159	4.85	2.23	0.216	0.829
Value for money	201	5.49	1.51	191	5.97	1.34	– 3.33	0.001

policies, no smoking and value for money features – all specific to the actual accommodation.

Conclusion

To conclude, this chapter presents a comparative analysis of hostel accommodation users in New Zealand and Scotland. Specifically it focuses on their importance and satisfaction ratings of various hostel facilities and amenities, addressing gaps in the literature regarding: cross-country comparisons (called for by Pearce & Butler, 1993) and service quality investigations in backpacker accommodation. This research also adds to the literature by expanding our understanding of the relative position of infrastructure, value-added and accommodation-specific service attributes on two service dimensions of importance and satisfaction. It confirms the need for centrally located backpacker facilities in urban contexts and the significance of pick-up services as well as the significance of facilities designed to patrons. The research appears to contradict Riley's (1988) and Aramberri's (1991) contention that backpackers are not concerned with their amenity surroundings or value-added services. This does not appear to be the case. Patrons are able to articulate very clearly those items that are of significance, and those that are not. This research also shows the differences in attitudes between age groups, confirming previous research, such as that by Nash *et al*. (2006), Obenour *et al*. (2006) and Ross (1997).

The results of this research show clear differences between the New Zealand and Scottish samples in terms of their levels of demand, some of which may be attributable to destination maturity. The New Zealand respondents appeared to be more demanding than the Scottish respondents. The importance ratings of the accommodation facilities were consistently higher in the New Zealand sample, suggesting that respondents expect a high-quality product and service in New Zealand. The low importance ratings in the Scottish sample should be further investigated. Are visitors not placing importance on particular facilities because they do not expect to get them anyway? Do they not think that these services can be provided sufficiently within the Scottish tourism industry? Are respondents assuming that the products/services are going to be better in New Zealand? Also, when looking at the comparison between satisfaction scores of the two subsamples, it is clear that the New Zealand respondents are more satisfied with all aspects of the accommodation, except for cleanliness of the rooms and self-catering/cooking facilities. So although the Scottish hostels are achieving some high ratings, there is still a lot of room for improvement and clearly a lot can be learnt from the more developed destination – New Zealand. The Scottish hostels need to be providing more 'add-ons' to the experience, the additional extras the accommodation can provide aside from a clean room and cooking facilities. Scottish hostels should provide the visitor with information about the destination they are staying in, give them easy access to city centres and have options available to arrange local trips. These are all facilities that are highly rated by the New Zealand respondents.

Scotland is relatively new to developing its industry to suit the backpacker market; this is clear from the fact that there is still a lot of room for improving transportation networks, for example, for back-packers around Scotland. Lessons can be drawn from New Zealand to better the product/services on offer to this important niche market, and one place to start would be offering the accommodation as part of the destination experience, not just as a place to stay. For both samples, younger age groups also rated 'add-ons' as valuable to their experience; such facilities are worth developing to satisfy the younger backpacker, especially considering the high proportion of the market that they make up.

Expectations of backpacker/hostel accommodation appear to be changing from the communal, cheap, 'just a bed' option that it once was believed to be (Aramberri, 1991) to something more in line with the accommodation experience of the mainstream tourist. The quality of general accommodation and the facilities available (room service, bar facilities, entertainment, service of staff, etc.) have often been noted as important to the destination experience (Lockyer, 2002; Richard & Sundaram, 1994; Tucker & Lynch, 2004), but until now there has been no understanding of the value of facilities and amenities within backpacker and hostel accommodation.

This chapter has answered the initial question – the extent to which age is a determinant in satisfaction with backpacker accommodation. This is done by establishing the requirements for privacy, for smaller rooms and for private showers and toilets, and the level of dissatisfaction with the large communal rooms and value-added services such as pick-up services and booking offices for local trips.

However, the authors believe that this chapter has prompted several other unanswered questions, to be investigated in future research, such as: the implications for domestic/international visitor comparisons both within and between countries; the potential for comparing low-end, mid-range and high-end accommodation across the full range of attributes; and to what extent identified achievement and control needs of backpackers exert an influence on the dimensions of service quality investigated here. Finally, the issue of destination maturity also remains to be assessed regarding its role in 'explaining' visitor expectation.

Chapter 16
Conclusion: Towards a Critical Agenda for Backpacker Tourism

IRENA ATELJEVIC and KEVIN HANNAM

Introduction

In the concluding chapter of *The Global Nomad*, Richards and Wilson (2004c) asked a fundamental question of what the study of backpacker tourism is and how it can be viewed. This collection has generally reaffirmed their observations of recognising two key perspectives that pull the contributions into often opposite directions: one being more interested in the symbolic nature of backpacker travel as a particular subculture; and one more industry- and market-orientated. Again, as Wilson and Richards argue in this volume, we would agree that these two trajectories can be generally divided along epistemological lines. The former being aligned with more interpretive and critical perspectives of social scientists and the latter with the observations of business and management scholars who may be trying to satisfy the knowledge demands of the tourism industry. Indeed, in this volume we might note that some chapters veer more to critical social science (for example, Hottola, this volume) and others towards business and management (for example, Cave *et al.*, this volume). However, we need to question whether this dualism is sustainable.

Whilst Richards and Wilson (2004c: 269) have tried to bring the two together in the form of a revised backpacker conceptual research model, questions remain, however, as to whether, and if so how, these two approaches can be entwined. In (re)posing this question, however, we are very much aware that this is frequently a fundamental question that faces all forms of tourism research, as the tourism studies field continues to theorise endless forms of special interest tourism. Whilst we do not deny the importance of these different approaches, we would like to move the agenda forward by engaging with theoretical discussions of tourism as a contemporary cultural and social practice through which

247

power relations, social identities and multiple subjectivities can be addressed. In doing so, we note Franklin's (2003: 132) concern of what he terms

> *touristcentricity*. This is the notion that the subject matter focuses properly on tourists rather than the social, cultural and political milieux and socio-technical networks that produced tourism and the desire to be a tourist in the first place and which subsequently sustain a changing context for new and changing tourisms – and tourist desires and practices.

In other words, once we step beyond the modernistic dualistic framing of such binaries as the everyday/extraordinary, home/away, sacred/profane, then the study of backpacker travel and tourism may become a more exciting research context and a critical realm for understanding more broader issues of global and local politics, societies, economies, cultures and mobilities.

It is this from these premises that we undertake our discussion on the future agenda of backpacker tourism research. Two key issues have prompted our discussion. Firstly, we feel that the tourism studies field is reaching an important turning point whereby the special interest tourism approach is becoming increasingly problematic. Namely, such conceptualisations frequently suffer from ethnocentrism, overgeneralisations, functionalism and an obsession with developing typologies, as well as a saturation with idiosyncratic case study empiricism. Secondly, we recognise that the overviews of gaps and future research directions as provided by many authors in *The Global Nomad* still remain very much relevant.

The increasing number of contributions, including this collection as well as the special issue of the journal *Tourism Recreation Research* in 2006, reveal further heterogeneity and the dynamic nature of backpacker phenomena. Hence, the difficult task of a more systematic overview relating the various social contexts and the magnitude and style of backpacking (Cohen, 2004) is becoming ever more urgent. In other words, many gaps remain to be filled, particularly with respect to issues of the impacts and involvement of backpacker tourism on and with both destinations and identities.

However, our ambitions and concerns here are somewhat different. We call for an engagement with more poststructuralist investigations and new theoretical discussions that have recently begun to penetrate the tourism studies field. In doing so, we want to show how the backpacker tourism phenomenon is a rich context through which many critical questions of political, theoretical and methodological natures can be addressed.

Firstly, our brief overview of different perspectives influencing the field will show how the recent backpacker tourism literature provides an example that illustrates the historical evolution of the tourism studies field. Secondly, in an attempt to critically question the structures, power bases and historical stories associated with tourism theory and practice we will discuss the most recent critical turn in tourism studies, which potentially offers new theoretical lenses and ontological departure points of how we can analyse backpacker tourism. In doing so, we go on to attempt to specifically analyse backpacker tourism within the recent theoretical connections made between discourses of tourism and mobilities.

Critical Thinking

Ateljevic and Doorne (2004) identified three distinctive phases and trajectories that have formed the body of the (mostly) English-speaking backpacker tourism research literature over the last 35 years. Their detailed overview of the major contributions gives us a framework from which to deconstruct the major perspectives that have influenced the development of this field.

In the first phase of the 1970s, the growth of international tourism from the West to 'the exoticised periphery' was firstly captured by sociologists and anthropologists who became interested in tourism as a social and cultural phenomenon. An emphasis on tourists' freedom and mobility was encapsulated by the early conceptualisation of the 'drifter', whose travel style articulated a quasipolitical statement against the growing political dominance and cultural homogeneity of the Western developed world. The images associated with the phenomenon became synonymous with associations of drug culture and anarchic values, yet simultaneously embodied an often nostalgic search for meaningful cultural existence.

The second phase of backpacker tourism research, which emerged in late 1980s and early 1990s, articulated a shift in this type of travel from drifting as a less marketed concept to backpacking as an overt marketing tool, with the terminology of the 'free independent traveller' and 'backpacker' entering the tourism academic and industry jargon in favour of previous descriptions. The economic and management vocabulary on backpacker tourism developed to produce insights as to yet another important market niche, as a reflection of tourism studies gaining greater status as primarily a business and management field (Tribe, 1997). This, again, mirrored the greater penetration by the tourism industry to peripheral places and marginal environments in both the developing and developed world and the growing recognition of the broader economic significance of tourism. With the growth of inter-disciplinary tourism programmes based predominantly within business schools, the need for practical relevance has only increased, resulting in more industry-oriented studies in the 1990s. The desire to market, manage and increasingly predict (backpacker) tourist behaviour goes some way to explain the relative dominance of the quasipositivistic tourism studies field up until the turn of the last century.

Parallel to this trend, however, a number of social scientists have continued to observe and study (backpacker) tourism from an expanding number of their own disciplinary perspectives. In other words, the study of backpacker tourism has continued to be perceived and translated in relation to its symbolic configurations of (post)modernity. This, in turn, has led to a third phase of theoretical hybridity.

Despite the cacophony of voices that often speak to different audiences disseminated over numerous tourism and non-tourism journals and books, a double trajectory can be observed that is currently characteristic to the overall tourism studies field. On the one hand backpacking continues to be considered in fairly management-orientated terms. On the other hand, in an attempt to critically question the persistent process of ethnocentricism and hegemony, some academics are increasingly embracing the deconstructionist discourses offered by poststructuralism and postcolonialism in the analyses of backpacker tourism. Essentially, the latter trajectory does away with grand theorisa-tions about society and culture, and tries to acknowledge the complex web of sociocultural relations within the highly distorted power geometries of the global politicocultural economy. This move also acknowledges the everyday power of agency and resistance within the structural relations, which has been critically analysed in the so-called 'critical' turn in both tourism studies and earlier in geography (Ateljevic *et al.*, 2005; 2007; Shurmer-Smith & Hannam, 1994).

Indeed, in various responses to broader social science debates, it has been recently argued that a wave of 'new tourism research' (Tribe, 2005) has created the 'critical turn' in tourism studies (Ateljevic *et al.*, 2005), which marks an ontological, epistemological and methodological shift (Phillimore & Goodson, 2004). Like-minded researchers are crafting space for a shared understanding of more reflexive, interpretative and critical modes of research inquiry. As Tribe (2005: 5) asserts: '... the totality of tourism studies has now developed beyond the narrow boundaries of an applied business field and has the characteristics of a fledging post-modern field of research'. This shift represents a notable move in thought, towards a broader, poststructuralist attempt to deconstruct the cultural politics of research and 'knowledge-making' in tourism academe.

Questions and debates in tourism studies surrounding ontology, epistemology, methodology and reflexivity have been central within this critical turn, reflecting elements of what Denzin and Lincoln (2000: 24; 2005) have called 'new age where messy, uncertain, multivoiced texts, cultural criticism, and new experimental works will become more common, as will more reflexive forms of fieldwork, analysis, and intertextual representation'. Denzin and Lincoln (2000) go on to describe a 'fractured future' – which will consist of a methodological backlash that will ask 'that the social sciences and the humanities become sites for critical conversations about democracy, race, gender, class, nation-states, globalization, freedom, and community' (Denzin & Lincoln, 2000: 3).

It is in this context that the proponents of critical tourism scholarship claim that this means 'more than simply a *way of knowing*, an ontology, it is a *way of being*, a commitment to tourism enquiry which is pro-social justice and equality and anti-oppression: it is an academy of hope' (Ateljevic *et al.*, 2007: 3). Aware of how the notion of a 'critical' or a 'new' school in tourism enquiry can be easily (mis)construed as labels create boundaries and academic schisms (Tribe, 2005), it seeks to transcend paradigmatic formations. Advocacy of critical scholarship is not about replacing one dominant school with another – in other words it is not about 'either/or' thinking. Moreover, in critical studies there has been too much emphasis on marking a difference and too little focus on making a difference (Ateljevic *et al.*, 2007) – too much attention on identifying problems without suggesting solutions. Hence the need to overcome the tired dualism between critical and managerial approaches – we need critical managerial approaches that identify problems and suggest solutions.

The critical turn, then, asks that we, as students, academic researchers, teachers and communicators, think about the impacts of our research on those that we study, the communities in which we work and live, and the various audiences with whom we engage. While reflexive practices emphasise the agency of researchers and the researched, and the dynamics of their intersubjective relationships, it is the act of interpretation and representation of knowledge that is the most *public* testament to reflexive practice. Researchers charged with this act may then be viewed as interlocutors who make choices about interpretation and forms of representation as a process of discovery of the subject, problem and of the self (Guba & Lincoln, 1985).

As part of this poststructural deconstruction of tourism, the cultural complexities of gender, race, class and ethnicity in the production and consumption of tourist spaces and experiences have become critical in our understanding of tourism phenomena. In order to capture these complexities, many different frameworks and theoretical metaphors have emerged to assist us in our research endeavours. One of the most critical has been that of embodiment in order to move us beyond the passivity of the tourist gaze (Urry, 1990) and to address the variety of theoretical concerns that were discussed by Wilson and Ateljevic (this volume). The discussion of embodiment and the creation of knowledge of the world cannot be separated from both wider notions of power as well as of the micropolitics of cultural negotiation. Following the feminist lead of Rose, hooks and Haraway, we acknowledge the impossibility of divorcing ourselves from the context that informs our (value-laden) analysis and privileges us with our social position of authoring and the associated power to be able to speak. Grosz (1995), for example, positions the body as an inscriptive surface where a researcher's positionality in terms of race, gender, age, class and sexuality creates a choreography of knowledge. In this context, Aitchison (2001: 142–143) reminds us of the extent to which the embrace of reflexivity has the capacity to challenge a Western academic compliance 'with the "cultural logic" (Jameson, 1992) of late capitalism which has manifested itself in postmodernism'. Our discussion thus proceeds with an acknowledgement that our understanding comes from specific, embodied and particular locations.

Three key implications have emerged as part of this shift, which are important for further discussions of backpacker tourism. Firstly, such a shift has created new conceptual implications, thus producing new ways of theorising that may help us to better understand the gendered and embodied nature of backpacker tourism (see Myers & Hannam, this volume). Secondly, it has also raised the most fundamental ontological questions of what backpacker tourism is and does (Franklin, 2003; 2007). Thirdly, managerial approaches are increasingly engaging with critical thinking so much so that the double trajectory becomes unsustainable in the 21st century (see for example, Jarvis & Peel, this volume). We take up these implications below in our discussion of what we might call backpacker mobilities.

Backpacker Mobilities

Mobility has become an evocative keyword for the 21st century and also a powerful discourse that creates its own effects and contexts. The concept of mobilities encompasses both the large-scale movements of people, objects, capital and information across the world, as well as the more local processes of daily transportation, movement through public space and the travel of material things within everyday life (Hannam *et al.*, 2006).

Fears of illicit mobilities and their attendant risks increasingly determine logics of governance and liability protection within both the public and private sectors. From SARS and avian influenza to train crashes, from airport expansion controversies to controlling global warming, from urban congestion charging to networked global terrorism, from emergency management in the onslaught of tsunamis and hurricanes to oil wars, issues of 'mobility' are centre-stage (Hannam *et al.*, 2006). *We need to ask: How do backpackers engage and negotiate such risks?* Niggel and Benson (this volume) begin to look at this in the context of South Africa.

Mobilities are centrally involved in reorganising institutions, generating climate change, moving risks and illnesses across the globe, altering travel, tourism and migration patterns, producing a more distant family life, transforming the social and educational life of young people, connecting distant people through so-called 'weak ties' and so on. However, such mobilities cannot be described without attention to the necessary spatial, infrastructural and institutional *moorings* that configure and enable mobilities – creating what Harvey (1989) called the 'spatial fix'. Thus the forms of detachment or 'deterritorialisation' associated with 'liquid modernity' (Bauman, 2000) are always accompanied by rhizomic attachments and reterritorialisations of various kinds (Sheller, 2004; Shurmer-Smith & Hannam, 1994). *We need to ask: What are the moorings for the contemporary backpacker?* Wilson *et al.* (this volume) begin to examine the various moorings of New Zealand backpackers in Europe whilst Wilson, Richards and MacDonnell (this volume) explore the moorings in Sydney.

There are new places and technologies that enhance the mobility of some peoples and places *even as they also* heighten the immobility of others, especially as they try to cross borders (Timothy, 2001; Verstraete, 2004; Wood & Graham, 2006). 'Differential mobility empowerments reflect structures and hierarchies of power and position by race, gender, age and class, ranging from the local to the global' (Tesfahuney, 1998: 501).

Rights to travel, for example, are highly uneven and skewed even between a single pair of countries (see Timothy, 2001). *We need to ask: What are the mobility empowerments for backpackers in the contemporary world? What are their impacts on the mobilities of others?*

Technological, social and cultural developments in public and private transportation, mobile communications, information storage and retrieval, surveillance systems and 'intelligent environments' are rapidly changing the nature of travel and of communications conducted at-a-distance. As mobile connectivity (and disconnection) begins to occur in new ways across a wide range of cyber-devices and integrated places, so we need better theorisation and research, especially to examine the interdependencies between changes in physical movement and in electronic communications, and especially in their increasing convergence (Hannam *et al.*, 2006). Moving on from the standard guidebook (see Welk, this volume), *we need to ask: How do backpackers engage with such technological developments?*

Mobilities, then, seem to involve the analysis of complex systems that are neither perfectly ordered nor anarchic (Urry, 2003). There is an 'orderly disorder' present within dynamic or complex adaptive systems, as analysed in recent formulations (Byrne, 1998; Hayles, 1999; Prigogine, 1997; Urry, 2003). How might the emerging mobilities paradigm help us to better understand backpacker tourism then? We sketch out a rough agenda below as we attempt to view backpacker tourism as part of a wider mobility system.

Firstly the analysis of backpacker tourism needs to be (re)positioned within a broader context of human mobility. For example, *we need to ask questions of how and when backpackers become migrants* (see Jarvis & Peel, this volume; Wilson *et al.*, this volume). The relations between migration, return migration, transnationalism and backpacker tourism need to be further researched. And, of course, the ways in which physical movement pertains to upward and downward social mobility is also central here. Moving between places physically or virtually can be a source of status and power for many backpackers over their life-course (Maoz, this volume; Myers & Hannam, this volume). In such a context we need to examine how backpackers negotiate their identities and their notions of citizenship, particularly in so-called contact zones at the interstices of different countries where notions of citizenship can become highly contested and multiple identities become increasingly fluid. Moreover, it is perhaps too obvious to perceive backpackers as being continually on the move, as being hypermobile, when in fact backpacking sometimes has more to do with being in places, of being relatively immobile and in the slow lane, through choice or finance. Places, technologies and 'gates' enhance the mobilities of some while reinforcing the immobilities (or demobilisation) of others. And such mobilities are also of course heavily gendered, (see Myers & Hannam, this volume; Wilson & Ateljevic, this volume).

Secondly, such studies of backpackers within the broader context of global human mobilities need to be brought together with more 'local' concerns about everyday transportation, material cultures and spatial relations (Wilson & Richards, this volume), as well as with more 'technological' concerns about mobile information and communication technologies and emerging infrastructures of security and surveillance. Social life seems full of multiple and extended connections, often across long distances, but these are organised through certain nodes. Mobilities thus entail distinct social spaces that orchestrate new forms of social life around such nodes, for example, stations, hotels, motorways, resorts, airports, leisure complexes, cosmopolitan cities, beaches, galleries, road-side parks and so on. Or connections might be enacted through less privileged spaces, on the street-corners, subway stations, buses, public plazas and back alleys. Also *contra* much transport research the time spent travelling is not dead time that people always seek to minimise. While the transport literature tends to distinguish travel from activities, the emerging mobilities paradigm posits that activities occur while on the move, that being on the move can involve sets of 'occasioned' activities. Backpacker research within the emerging mobilities paradigm would thus examine the embodied nature and experience of the different modes of travel that backpackers undertake, seeing these modes in part as forms of material and sociable dwelling-in-motion, places of and for various activities (see Crouch, 2000; Johnston, 2001; Veijola & Jokinen, 1994). These 'activities' can include specific forms of talk, work or information-gathering, but may involve simply being connected, main-taining a moving presence with others that holds the potential for many different convergences or divergences of physical presence. Not only does a mobilities perspective lead us to discard our usual notions of spatiality and scale, but it also undermines existing linear assumptions about temporality and timing, which often assume that actors are able to do only one thing at a time, and that events follow each other in a linear order (Hannam *et al.*, 2006).

Furthermore a clear distinction is often drawn between places and those travelling to such places. Places have frequently been seen as pushing or pulling people to visit. Places are often presumed to be relatively fixed, given and separate from those visiting. Instead we recognise that the notion of place, although deceptively simple, needs to be problematised (Shurmer-Smith & Hannam, 1994). The emerging mobility paradigm thus argues against the ontology of distinct 'places' and 'people'. Rather there is a complex relationality of places and persons connected through both performances (Sheller & Urry, 2004) and performativities (Knox, 2001). Crucial to the recognition of the materialities of mobilities is the re-centring of the corporeal body as an affective vehicle through which we sense place and movement, and construct emotional geographies (Bondi *et al.*, 2005; Crouch, 2000). Imaginative travel, for example, involves experiencing or anticipating in one's imagination the 'atmosphere of place'. Atmosphere is not reducible to the material infrastructures or to the discourses of representation. There is a complex sensuous relationality between the means of travel and the traveller (Rodaway, 1994). We need better maps of these sensuous, emotional geographies of backpackers (see Maoz, this volume).

Conclusion

In conclusion, in this chapter we have firstly mapped the current developments in critical thinking for backpacker tourism research. Secondly, we have tried to trace some of the theoretical constituents of the emerging field of mobilities research, and illustrate its application. Overall, we hope to have made a strong case for the importance and relevance of critical thinking for the future analysis of backpacker tourism. We put forward that the backpacker phenomenon examined in this book, being an embodied metaphor for the various mobilities in global contemporary culture, may serve as an interesting context in which other critical questions of economy, politics and society can also be discussed further.

References

Abdullah, A.S.M., Ebrahim, S., Fielding, R. and Morisky, D. (2004) Sexually transmitted infections in travellers: Implications for prevention and control. *Travel Medicine* 39, 533–538.

Abram, S., Waldren, J. and Macleod, D. (eds) (1997) *Tourists and Tourism: Identifying with People and Places*. Oxford: Berg.

Adler, J. (1985) Youth on the road: Reflections on the history of tramping. *Annals of Tourism Research* 12 (3), 335–354.

Adler, N.J. (1991) *International Dimensions of Organizational Behavior* (2nd edn). Boston: PWS-Kent.

Ahtola, O.T. (1975) The vector model of preferences: An alternative to the Fishbein model. *Journal of Marketing Research* 12, 52–59.

Aitchison, C. (2001) Theorizing other discourses of tourism, gender and culture: Can the subaltern speak (in tourism)? *Tourist Studies* 1, 133–147.

Aitchison, C. (2003) *Gender and Leisure: Social and Cultural Perspectives*. London: Routledge.

Aitchison, C. (2005) Feminist and gender perspectives in leisure and tourism research. In B. Ritchie, P. Burns and C. Palmer (eds) *Tourism Research Methods: Integrating Theory with Practice* (pp. 21–35). Wallingford: CABI.

Aitchison, C. and Reeves, C. (1998) Gendered (bed) spaces: The culture and commerce of women only tourism. In C. Aitchison and F. Jordan (eds) *Gender, Space and Identity*. Eastbourne: Leisure Studies Association.

Aitkenhead, D. (2001) Lovely girls, very cheap. *Granta* 73 (Spring), 127–150.

Alexandris, K., Dimitriadis, N. and Markata, D. (2002) Can perceptions of service quality predict behavioral intentions? An exploratory study in the hotel sector in Greece. *Managing Service Quality* 12 (4), 224–231.

Allon, F. (2002) On the beaten track: Place, locality and backpacker cultures in Sydney. *CSAA 2002 Annual Conference: Ute Culture: The Utility of Culture and the Uses of Cultural Studies*, Melbourne, Australia.

Allon, F. (2004) Backpacker heaven: The consumption and construction of tourist spaces and landscapes in Sydney. *Space and Culture* 7 (1), 49–63.

Almanza, B.A., Jaffe, W. and Lin, L.C. (1994) Use of the service attribute matrix to measure consumer satisfaction. *Hospitality Research Journal* 17 (2), 63–75.

Amin, A. and Thrift, N. (2002) *Cities: Reimaging the Urban*. Cambridge: Polity Press.

Anderskov, C. (2002) Backpacker culture: Meaning and identity making processes in the Backpacker culture among backpackers in Central America. *Research Report, Department of Ethnography and Social Anthropology*. Denmark: Arhus University.

Andrzej, H. and Buchanan, D. (2001) *Organizational Behaviour: An Introductory Text*. London: Prentice Hall.

Aramberri, J. (1991) The nature of youth tourism: Motivations, characteristics and requirements. Paper presented at the *International Conference on Youth Tourism, New Delhi*. Madrid: World Tourism Organisation.

Arnould, E.J. and Price, L. (1993) River magic: Extraordinary experience and the extended service encounter. *Journal of Consumer Research* 20, 24–45.

Ateljevic, I. and Doorne, S. (2000a) 'Staying within the fence': Lifestyle entrepreneurship in tourism. *Journal of Sustainable Tourism* 8 (5), 378–392.

Ateljevic, I. and Doorne, S. (2000b) Tourism as an escape: Long-term travelers in New Zealand. *Tourism Analysis* 5, 131–136.

Ateljevic, I. and Doorne, S. (2001) 'Nowhere left to run': A study of value boundaries and segmentation within the backpacker market of New Zealand. In J.A. Mazanec, G.I. Crouch, J.R. Brent Ritchie and A.G. Woodside (eds) *Consumer Psychology of Tourism, Hospitality and Leisure* (Vol. 2). Wallingford: CABI.

Ateljevic, I. and Doorne, S. (2004) Theoretical encounters: A review of backpacker literature. In G. Richards and J. Wilson (eds) *The Global Nomad: Backpacker Travel in Theory and Practice* (pp. 50–76). Clevedon: Channel View.

Ateljevic, I. and Doorne, S. (2005) Dialectics of authentification: Performing 'exotic otherness' in a backpacker enclave of Dali, China. *Journal of Tourism and Cultural Change* 3 (1), 1–17.

Ateljevic, I. and Harris, C. (2005) Tourism researcher: From 'otherness machine' to reflective bricoleur. Paper presented at *CAUTHE 2005: 'Sharing Tourism Knowledge'*. Alice Springs: Charles Darwin University.

Ateljevic, I., Harris, C., Wilson, E. and Collins, F. (2005) Getting 'entangled': Reflexivity and the 'critical turn' in tourism studies. *Tourism Recreation Research* 30 (2), 9–21.

Ateljevic, I., Pritchard, A. and Morgan, N. (eds) (2007) *The Critical Turn in Tourism Studies*. Amsterdam: Elsevier.

Australian Education Office (n.d.) *Study Abroad Guide to Australian Universities*. Sydney: AEO.

Australian Tourist Commission (ATC) (2002) *Exploring the International Backpacker Market in Australia: Added Value*. On WWW at http://www.tourism.australia.com/content/Research/tvic_backpacker_jun02.pdf. Accessed 6.7.07.

Australian Tourist Commission (ATC) (2004) *The backpacker market factsheet (May)*. On WWW at http://www.australia.com/. Accessed 4.7.04.

Avrahami, E. (2001) The Israeli backpackers: A study in the context of tourism and postmodern condition. PhD thesis, City University of New York.

Aziz, H. (1999) Whose culture is it anyway. *In Focus* 31, 14–15.

Barnett, T. (1999) Editorial. *In Focus* 31, 3.

Baum, A. and Singer J.E. (eds) (1980) *Advances in Environmental Psychology Volume 2: Applications of Personal Control*. Hillside: Lawrence Erlbaum.

Bauman, Z. (2000) *Liquid Modernity*. Cambridge: Polity.

Beck, R. (1992) Foreword. In S. Hall (ed.) *Ethics in Hospitality Management: A Book of Readings* (pp. ix–x). East Lansing: Educational Institute of the American Hotel and Motel Association.

Becken, S. (2001) A comparison of the energy intensity associated with two different travel styles. *Tourismus Journal* 5, 227–246.

Becken, S. and Butcher, G. (2004) Economic yields associated with different types of tourists: A pilot analysis. *Creating Tourism Knowledge CAUTHE Conference*. Brisbane: University of Queensland.

Becken, S., Frampton, C. and Simmons, D. (2001) Energy consumption patterns in the accommodation sector – The New Zealand case. *Ecological Economics* 39, 371–386.

Becken, S., Simmons, D. and Frampton, C. (2003) Segmenting tourists by their travel pattern for insights into achieving energy efficiency. *Journal of Travel Research* 42, 48–56.

Beeho, A. and Prentice, R. (1997) Conceptualising the experiences of heritage tourists: A case study of New Lanark World Heritage Village. *Tourism Management* 18 (2), 75–87.

Bell, C. (2002) The big'OE': Young New Zealand travellers as secular pilgrims. *Tourist Studies* 2 (2), 143–158.

Bellis, M.A., Hughes, K., Thomson, R. and Bennett, A. (2005) Sexual behaviour of young people in international tourist resorts. *Sexually Transmitted Infections* 80, 43–47.

Bhattacharyya, D.P. (1997) Mediating India: An analysis of a guidebook. *Annals of Tourism Research* 2 (24), 371–389.

Bigne, J.E. and Andreu, L. (2004) Emotions in segmentation: An empirical study. *Annals of Tourism Research* 31, 682–696.

Binder, J. (2004) The whole point of backpacking: Anthropological perspectives on the characteristics of backpacking. In G. Richards and J. Wilson (eds) *The Global Nomad: Backpacker Travel in Theory and Practice* (pp. 92–108). Clevedon: Channel View.

Black, P. (2000) Sex and travel: Making the links. In S. Clift and S. Carter (eds) *Tourism and Sex* (pp. 250–263). London: Continuum.

Bondi, L., Smith, M. and Davidson, J. (eds) (2005) *Emotional Geographies*. London: Ashgate.

Boorstin, D.J. (1961) *The Image: A Guide to Pseudo-Events in America*. New York: Harper and Row.

Bordo, S. (1997) *Twilight Zones: The Hidden Life of Cultural Images from Plato to O.J.* Berkeley: University of California Press.

Botterill, D.T. (1991) A new social movement: Tourism concern, the first two years. *Leisure Studies* 10, 203–217.

Bourdieu, P. (1984) *Distinction: A Critique of the Judgement of Taste*. London: Routledge.

Bowie, N. (1986) Business ethics. In J. De Marco and R. Fox (eds) *New Directions in Ethics: The Challenge of Applied Ethics* (pp. 158–172). New York, Routledge and Kegan Paul.

Bradt, H. (1995) Better to travel cheaply? *The Independent on Sunday* 12 February, 49.

Breathnach, P. (1994) Gender in Irish tourism employment. In V. Kinnard and D. Hall (eds) *Tourism: A Gender Analysis*. Chichester: Wiley.

Bruner, E.M. (1991) Transformation of self in tourism. *Annals of Tourism Research* 18 (2), 238–250.

Buchanan, I. and Rossetto, A. (1997) With my swag upon my shoulder. *Occasional Paper No. 24*. Canberra: Bureau of Tourism Research.

Bureau of Tourism Research (1995) National Backpacker Tourism Development Strategy. Canberra: Australian Government Publications.

Bureau of Tourism Research (2002) International Visitor Survey. Canberra: Australian Government Publications.

Bureau of Tourism Research (2005) International Visitor Survey. Canberra: Australian Government Publications.

Bureau of Tourism Research (BTR) (2004) International Visitors in Australia December Quarter 2003. Canberra: Australian Government Publications.

Burns, P.M. and Holden, A. (1995) *Tourism: A New Perspective*. Hitchin: Prentice-Hall.

Burns, T.R. and Buckley W. (eds) (1976) *Power and Control: Social Structures and Their Transformation*. London: Sage.

Butler, R. (1980) The concept of a tourist area cycle of evolution. *Canadian Geographer* 24, 5–12.

Butler, R. (1990) The concept of the Tourist Area Cycle of evolution: Implications for the management of resources. *The Canadian Geographer* 24 (11), 5–12.

Buttle, F. and Bok, B. (1996) Hotel marketing strategy and the theory of reasoned action. *International Journal of Contemporary Hospitality Management* 8 (3), 5–31.

Byrne, D. (1998) *Complexity Theory and the Social Sciences*. London: Routledge.

Callan, R. and Lefebve, C. (1997) Classification and grading of UK lodges: Do they equate to managers' and customers' perceptions? *Tourism Management* 18 (7), 417–424.

Carr, N. (2003) University and college students' tourism. In B. Ritchie (ed.) *Managing Educational Tourism* (pp. 181–225). Clevedon: Channel View.

Carr, N. (2006) Book review of *The Global Nomad*. *Tourism Management* 27 (2), 353–355.

Carraro, C. and Leveque, F. (1999) *Voluntary Approaches in Environmental Policy*. Dordrecht: Kluwer.

Cave, J. and Ryan, C. (2004) Let the respondent speak! The use of Artificial Neural Network software to model complex realities in tourism product (development). *Proceedings of the QRIB Symposium, Albany*. Auckland: Massey University.

Cave, J. and Ryan, C. (2005) Gender in backpacking and adventure tourism. Paper presented at the *4th Symposium in Consumer Psychology of Tourism, Hospitality and Leisure*. Hautes Etudes Commerciale, Universite de Montreal, Montreal, Canada, 44 p.

Cederholm, E.A. (1999) *The Attraction of the Extraordinary – Images and Experiences Among Backpacker Tourists*. Lund: University of Lund.

Cha, S. and Jeong, D. (1998) Travel motivations of Korean pleasure travellers to Australia and New Zealand. *Pacific Tourism Review* 2, 181–190.

Chadee, D. and Cutler, J. (1996) Insights into international travel by students. *Journal of Travel Research* 22, 75–80.

Chen, P. and Kerstetter, D. (1999) International students' image of rural Pennsylvania as a travel destination. *Journal of Travel Research* 37 (3), 256–266.

Clarke, N. (2003) Free independent travellers? British working holidaymakers in Australia. Paper presented at the *RGS/IBG Annual Conference*, London.

Clarke, N. (2004) Free independent travellers? British working holiday makers in Australia. *Transactions of the Institute of British Geographers* 29 (4), 499–509.

Clarke, N. (2005) Detailing transnational lives of the middle: British working holiday makers in Sydney. *Journal of Ethnic and Migration Studies* 31 (2), 307–322.

Cleverdon, R. (2001) Introduction: Fair trade in tourism – application and experience. *International Journal of Tourism Research* 3 (5), 347–349.

Cleverdon, R. and Kalisch, A. (2000) Fair trade in tourism. *International Journal of Tourism Research* 2 (3), 171–187.

Clift, S. and Carter, S. (eds) (2000) *Tourism and Sex*. London: Continuum.

Clift, S. and Grabowski, P. (eds) (1997) *Tourism and Health*. London: Pinter.

Clift, S. and Page, S. (eds) (1996) *Health and the International Tourist*. London: Routledge.

Coalter, F. (1997) Leisure sciences and leisure studies: Different concept, same crisis? *Leisure Sciences* 19 (4), 255–268.

Cohen, E. (1972) Towards a sociology of international tourism. *Social Research* 39 (1), 164–182.

Cohen, E. (1973) Nomads from affluence: Notes on the phenomenon of drifter-tourism. *International Journal of Comparative Sociology* 14 (1), 89–103.

Cohen, E. (1979) A phenomenology of tourist experiences. *Sociology* 13, 179–201.

Cohen, E. (1982) Marginal paradises: Bungalow tourism on the islands of Southern Thailand. *Annals of Tourism Research* 9 (2), 189–228.

Cohen, E. (1984) The sociology of tourism: Approaches, issues, and findings. *Annual Review of Sociology* 10, 373–392.

Cohen, E. (1989a) Alternative tourism – A critique. In T.V. Singh, H.L. Theuns and F.M. Go (eds) *Towards Appropriate Tourism: The Case of Developing Countries* (pp. 127–142). Frankfurt am Main: Peter Lang.

Cohen, E. (1989b) 'Primitive and remote': Hill tribe trekking in Thailand. *Annals of Tourism Research* 16 (1), 30–61.

Cohen, E. (2003a) Backpacking: Diversity and change. *Tourism and Cultural Change* 1, 95–110.

Cohen, E. (2003b) Tourism and religion: A case study of visiting students in Israeli Universities. *Journal of Travel Research* 42, 36–47.

Cohen, E. (2004) Backpacking: Diversity and change. In G. Richards and J. Wilson (eds) *The Global Nomad: Backpacker Travel in Theory and Practice* (pp. 43–59). Clevedon: Channel View.

Cohen, E. (2006) Pai – A backpacker enclave in transition. *Tourism Recreation Research* 31 (3), 11–28.

Cohen, J.B., Fishbein, M. and Ahtola, O.T. (1972) The nature and uses of expectancy – Value models in consumer attitude research. *Journal of Marketing Research* 9, 456–460.

Cole, D.N. (1998) Campsite conditions in the Bob Marshall Wilderness, Montana. *I. F. a. R. E. S. Research paper*. USDA Forest Service, No. INT-312.

Cole, D.N. and Stewart, W.P. (2002) Variability of user-based evaluative standards for backcountry encounters. *Leisure Sciences* 24, 313–324.

Coleman, S. and Crang, M. (eds) (2002) *Tourism: Between Place and Performance*. Oxford: Berghahn Books.

Commonwealth Department of Tourism (1995) *National Backpacker Tourism Strategy*. Canberra: Australian Government Publishing Service.

Commonwealth Department of Tourism (1996) *Building for Backpacker Accommodation*. Canberra: Commonwealth Department of Tourism.

Conner, F.L. (2000) Travelers value cleanliness above all. *Cornell Hotel and Restaurant Administration Quarterly* 41, 6.

Contiki.com (2003) Time out: 2004–2005. *Contiki Holidays for 18–35s* [Travel Brochure].

Contiki (2005) About us. Contiki website. On WWW at http://us.contiki.com/articles/1-about-contiki. Accessed 1.06.05.

Craik, J. (1997) The culture of tourism. In C. Rojek and J. Urry (eds) *Touring Cultures: Transformations of Travel and Theory* (pp. 113–136). London: Routledge.

Crick, M. (1989) Representations of international tourism in the social sciences: Sun, sex, sights, savings, and servility. *Annual Review of Anthropology* 18, 307–344.

Croot, J. (2003) Successful Kombi Nation. *The Press* E4.

Crouch, D. (1999) Introduction. In D. Crouch (ed.) *Leisure/Tourism Geographies: Practices and Geographical Knowledge* (pp. 1–14). London: Routledge.

Crouch, D. (2000) Places around us: Embodied lay geographies in leisure and tourism. *Leisure Studies* 19, 63–76.

Crouch, D. and Desforges, L. (2003) The sensuous in the tourist encounter: Introduction: The power of the body in tourist studies. *Tourist Studies* 3 (1), 5–22.

Crouch, D., Aronsson, L. and Wahlstrom, L. (2001) Tourist encounters. *Tourist Studies* 1, 253–270.

Cummings, J. (2003) *Thailand* (10th edn). Footscray: Lonely Planet.

Cummings, J. (2005a) Personal interview by Peter Welk. 19 October.

Cummings, J. (2005b) *Thailand* (11th edn). Footscray: Lonely Planet.

Cummings, J. (2005c) Homepage. On WWW at www.joecummings.com and subsequent links. Accessed 14.11.05.

Curtin, S. and Busby, G. (1999) Sustainable destination development: The tour operator perspective. *International Journal of Tourism Research* 1 (2), 135–147.

Dahles, H. and Bras, K. (1999) *Tourism and Small Entrepreneurs: Development, National Policy and Entrepreneurial Culture: Indonesian Cases*. New York: Cognizant Communication Corporation.

D'Amore, L.J. (1992) Promoting sustainable tourism – The Canadian approach. *Tourism Management* 13, 258–262.

D'Amore, L.J. (1993) A code of ethics and guidelines for socially and environmentally responsible tourism. *Journal of Travel Research* 31 (3) 64–66.

Dann, G. (1998) The pomo promo of tourism. *Tourism, Culture and Communication* 1, 1–16.

Davidson, P. (1996) The holiday and work experiences of women with young children. *Leisure Studies* 15, 89–103.

Davies, J. and Bradbery, P. (1999) Gender advertisements and tourism brochures. Paper presented at *CAUTHE Conference*, Adelaide.

Deem, R. (1996) No time for a rest? An exploration of women's work, engendered leisure and holidays. *Time and Society* 5 (1), 5–25.

Deem, R. (1999) How do we get out of the ghetto? Strategies for research on gender and leisure for the twenty-first century. *Leisure Studies* 18 (3), 161–177.

Delport, D. (2003) See you on the Baz Bus – Reports on a unique backpackers' bus. On WWW at http://www.bazbus.com/SiteContent/newsarticle.aspx?ArticleID = 28&ArticleStructureID = 3. Accessed 6.7.07.

Denzin, N.K. (1991) *Images of Postmodern Society: Social Theory and Contemporary Cinema*. London: Sage.

Denzin, N.K. and Lincoln, Y.S. (eds) (2000) *Handbook of Qualitative Research*. London: Sage.

Denzin, N.K. and Lincoln, Y.S. (2003) *The Landscape of Qualitative Research* (2nd edn). London: Sage.

Department of Education, Science and Technology (DEST) (2002) *Higher Education Statistics*. On WWW at http://www.dest.gov.au/common_topics/publications_resources/. Accessed 6.7.07.

Department of Industry, Tourism and Resources (DITR) (2003a) *Tourism Green Paper*. AGPS: Canberra. On WWW at http://www.industry.gov.au/content/itrinternet/cmscontent.cfm?objectID = 6CAA3E62-D2DF-4340-9F4AA9CC656 3504C. Accessed 6.7.07.

Department of Industry, Tourism and Resources (DITR) (2003b) *Tourism White Paper: A Medium to Long Term Strategy for Tourism*. AGPS: Canberra.

Department of Industry, Tourism and Resources (DITR) (2004) *Tourism White Paper*. AGPS: Canberra. On WWW at http://www.industry.gov.au/content/sitemap.cfm?objectid = 48A3400C-20E0-68D8-ED0D0548296A04E7. Accessed 6.7.07.

Desforges, L. (1998) 'Checking out the planet': Global representations/local identities and youth travel. In T. Skelton and G. Valentine (eds) *Cool Places: Geographies of Youth Culture* (pp. 175–192). New York: Routledge.

Desforges, L. (2000) Travelling the world – Identity and travel biography. *Annals of Tourism Research* 27 (4), 926–945.

Dolan, B. (2002) *Ladies of the Grand Tour*. London: Flamingo.

Doorne, S. (1994) Symbiosis, integration and the backpacker tourist industry. MA Thesis, Department of Geography, Victoria University of Wellington.

Drakensberg Tourism Board (2001) *Backpackers and Backpacking in South Africa*. On WWW at http://www.drakensberg-tourism.com/backpacker-south-africa.html. Accessed 2004.

D'Sa, E. (1999) Wanted: Tourists with a social conscience. *International Journal of Contemporary Hospitality Management* 11 (2/3), 64–68.

Duffield, G. and Long, J. (1981) Tourism in the highlands and islands of Scotland: Rewards and conflicts. *Annals of Tourism Research* 8 (3), 403–431.

Duffy, R. (2002) *A Trip too Far: Ecotourism, Politics and Exploitation*. London: Earthscan.

Duncan, T. (2004) Livin' the dream: Working and playing in a ski resort. Proceedings of the Institute of British Geographers and International Geographical Union Geography of Tourism and Leisure Working Group Pre-Meeting. Loch Lomond, Scotland, August.

Dunfee, T. and Black, B. (1996) Ethical issues confronting travel agents. *Journal of Business Ethics* 15 (2), 207–217.

Dunphy, D. and Benveniste, J. (2000) Sustainable corporations. In D. Dunphy, J. Benveniste, A. Griffiths and P. Sutton (eds) *Sustainability – The Corporate Challenge of the 21st Century* (pp. 1–24). St. Leonards, NSW: Allen and Unwin.

Easthope, J. (1993) Home away from home: The recent history of overseas travel by New Zealanders to Britain, c. 1960–1975. Unpublished Honours Research Paper, Victoria University, Wellington, New Zealand.

Economic Planning Unit (EPU) (2001). *Eighth Malaysia Plan (2001–2005)*. Kuala Lumpur: Percetakaan Nasional Malaysia Berhad.

Edensor, T. (1998) *Tourists at the Taj: Performance and Meaning at a Symbolic Site*. London: Routledge.

Edensor, T. (2000) Staging tourism: Tourists as performers. *Annals of Tourism Research* 27, 322–344.

Egan, C.E. (2001) Sexual behaviours, condom use and factors influencing casual sex among backpackers and other young international travellers. *The Canadian Journal of Human Sexuality* 10 (1–2), 41–58.

Elkington, J. (1997) *Cannibals with Forks: The Triple Bottom Line of 21st Century Business*. Oxford: Capstone.

Elliott, M. (2002) Must the backpackers stay home? *The Times* December 16.

Elsrud, T. (1998) Time creation in travelling: The taking and making of time among women backpackers. *Time and Society* 7, 309–334.

Elsrud, T. (2001) Risk creation in travelling: Backpacker adventure narration. *Annals of Tourism Research* 28, 597–617.

Elsrud, T. (2005) Recapturing the adventuress: Narratives on identity and gendered positioning in backpacking. *Tourism Review International* 9 (2), 123–137.

Enloe, C. (1989) *Bananas, Beaches and Bases: Making Feminist Sense of International Politics*. Berkley: University of California Press.

Erikson, E. (1959) Identity and the life cycle: Selected papers. *Psychological Issues* 1 (1), 5–165.

Fam, K.S., Foscht, T. and Collins, R.D. (2004) Trust and the online relationship – an exploratory study from New Zealand. *Tourism Management* 25, 195–207.

Farrell, R. (1999) The pre-decision process: Backpackers and their motivations to travel. Unpublished Research Report, Auckland, New Zealand.

Featherstone, M. (1995) *Undoing Culture: Globalization, Postmodernism and Identity*. London: Sage.

Fennell, D. (1996) A tourist space-time budget in the Shetland Islands. *Annals of Tourism Research* 23, 811–829.

Fennell, D. (1999) *Ecotourism: An Introduction*. London: Routledge.

Fennell, D. and Malloy, D. (1999) Measuring the ethical nature of tourism operators. *Annals of Tourism Research* 26 (4), 908–913.

Ferns, S. (1995) Home and away. *The Evening Standard* 21 April, 20–21.

Fetterman, D. (1990) *Ethnography – Step by Step*. Newbury Park: Sage.

Field, A.M. (1999) The college student market segment: A comparative study of travel behaviours of international and domestic students at a southeastern university. *Journal of Travel Research* 37, 375–381.

Finlay, H. (ed.) (1999) *Lonely Planet South-East Asia on a Shoestring*. Hawthorn: Lonely Planet Publications.

Firth, T. and Hing, N. (1999) Backpacker hostels and their guests: Attitudes and behaviours relating to sustainable tourism. *Tourism Management* 20 (2), 251–254.

Fishbein, M. (1967) *Readings in Attitude Theory and Measurement*. New York: John Wiley.

Fleckenstein, M. and Huebsch, P. (1999) Ethics in tourism – Reality or hallucination. *Journal of Business Ethics* 19 (1), 137–142.

Font, X. (2001) Regulating the green message: The players in ecolabelling. In X. Font and R. Buckley (eds) *Tourism Ecolabelling: Certification and Promotion of Sustainable Management* (pp. 1–18). Wallingford: CABI.

Fortune Small Business (2000) Chat with *Lonely Planet* founder Tony Wheeler. On WWW at www.fortune.com/fortune/smallbusiness/marketing/articles/0,15114,359792,00.html. Accessed 9.11.05.

Foster, J. (1990) Leisure – The fourth wave. In J. Kerr (ed.) *Highlands and Islands: A Generation of Progress* (pp. 121–127). Aberdeen: Aberdeen University Press.

Foucault, M. (1980) *Power/Knowledge: Selected Interviews and Other Writings 1972–1977*, edited by Colin Gordon. London: Harvester.

Franklin, A. (2003) *Tourism: An Introduction*. London: Sage.

Franklin, A. and Crang, M. (2001) The trouble with tourism and travel theory. *Tourist Studies* 1 (1), 5–22.

Freeman, R.E. (1984) *Strategic Management: A Stakeholder Approach*. Boston: Pitman.

Friedman, M.I. and Lackey, H.G. Jr. (1991) *The Psychology of Human Control – A General Theory of Purposeful Behavior*. New York: Praeger.

Friend, T. (2005) The parachute artist: Have Tony Wheeler's guidebooks travelled too far? *The New Yorker* 18 April. On WWW at www.newyorker.com/fact/content/articles/050418fa_fact. Accessed 10.10.05.

Gallagher, M. (2002) On the cusp: A new phase in the internationalization of Australian education. Paper delivered at *Sixteenth Australian International Education Conference*, Hobart, Tasmania.

Gannon, M.J. (1994) *Understanding Global Cultures: Metaphorical Journeys Through 17 Countries*. Thousand Oaks: Sage.

Garland, A. (1997) *The Beach*. Harmondsworth: Penguin.

Garnham, R. (1993) A backpacking geography of New Zealand. Paper presented at the *New Zealand Geography Conference*. Wellington.

Gibson, H. and Yiannakis, A. (2002) Tourist roles. Needs and the lifecourse. *Annals of Tourism Research* 29 (2), 358–383.

Giddens, A. (1991) *Modernity and Self-image: Self and Society in Late Modernity*. Cambridge: Polity Press.

Giesbers, M. (2002) Backpackers: Grand Tour of Toeristenvoer? Unpublished MA Thesis, Katholieke Universiteit Brabant, Tilburg.

Gluckman, R. (1999) Lonely no more. *Far Eastern Economic Review* 162 (41), 54–56.

Gobster, P.H. (1994) The urban savanna: Reuniting ecological preference and function. *Restoration and Management Notes* 12 (1), 64–69.

Goffman, E. (1956) *The Presentation of Self in Everyday Life*. New York: Doubleday.

Goffman, E. (1963) *Behavior in Public Places: Notes on the Social Organization of Gatherings*. London: Free Press.

Goffman, E. (1974) *Frame Analysis: An Essay on the Organization of Experience*. New York: Harper.

Goodall, B. (1992) How tourists choose their holidays: An analytical framework. In B. Goodall and G. Ashworth (eds) *Marketing in the Tourism Industry: The Promotion of Destination Regions* (pp. 1–17). London: Routledge.

Goodwin, H. (1999) Backpackers good, package tourists bad? *In Focus* 31, 12–13.

Gottlieb, A. (1982) Americans' vacations. *Annals of Tourism Research* 9, 165–187.

Graburn, N. (1983) The anthropology of tourism. *Annals of Tourism Research* 10 (1), 9–33.

Gregory, M. (2002) *Backpacker Tourism in South Africa (BTSA) – The Home of Backpackers in South Africa*. On WWW at http://www.btsa.co.za. Accessed 6.7.07.

Grosz, E. (1995) *Space, Time and Perversion: The Politics of Bodies*. Sydney: Allen and Unwin.

Guba, E. and Lincoln, Y. (1985) *Naturalistic Inquiry*. London: Sage.

Gumtree (2005) *Vans for sale*. On WWW at www.gumtree.com/london_second_hand_cars_for_sale.html. Accessed 26.05.05.

Gunn, C. (1994) A perspective on the purpose and nature of tourism research methods. In J.R. Brent Ritchie and C.R. Goeldner (eds) *Travel, Tourism, and Hospitality Research* (2nd edn) (pp. 3–11). New York: John Wiley.

Hall, S. (ed.) (1992) *Ethics in Hospitality Management: A Book of Readings*. East Lansing: Educational Institute of the American Hotel and Motel Association.

Hall, C.M. and Lew, A. (1998) *Sustainable Tourism: A Geographical Perspective*. Harlow, England: Addison Wesley Longman.

Hämäläinen, P. (1991) *Yemen – A Travel Survival Kit. Guidebook*. Hawthorn: Lonely Planet Publications.

Hammersley, M. and Atkinson, P. (1995) *Ethnography: Principles in Practice*. London: Routledge.

Hammitt, W.E. and Madden, M.A. (1989) Cognitive dimensions of wilderness privacy: A field test and further explanation. *Leisure Sciences* 11, 293–301.

Hammitt, W.E. and Patterson, M.E. (1991) Coping behavior to avoid visitor encounters: Its relationship to wildland privacy. *Journal of Leisure Research* 23, 225–237.

Hammitt, W.E. and Patterson, M.E. (1993) Use patterns and solitude preferences of shelter campers in Great Smoky Mountains National Park, USA. *Journal of Environmental Management* 38, 43–53.

Hampton, M. (1996) *Economic Development Impacts of Backpacker Tourism in the Periphery: A Case Study of Lombok, Indonesia*. Portsmouth: University of Portsmouth, Department of Economics.

Hampton, M.P. (1998) Backpacker tourism and economic development. *Annals of Tourism Research* 25 (3), 639–660.

Hamzah, A. (1997) The evolution of small-scale tourism in Malaysia: Problems, opportunities and implications for sustainability. In M.J. Stabler (ed.) *Tourism and Sustainability: Principles to Practice* (pp. 199–217). Wallingford: CABI.

Hannam, K., Sheller, M. and Urry, J. (2006) Mobilities, immobilities and moorings. *Mobilities* 1 (1), 1–22.

Harron, S. and Weiler, B. (1992) Review: Ethnic tourism. In B. Weiler and C.M. Hall (eds) *Special Interest Tourism* (pp. 83–94). London: Bellhaven Press.

Harstock, N. (1990) Foucault on power. In L. Nicholson (ed.) *Feminism/Postmodernism* (pp. 157–175). London: Routledge.

Harvey, D. (1989) *The Condition of Postmodernity*. Oxford: Blackwell.

Hastings, J. (1998) Time out of time: Life crises and schooner sailing in the Pacific. *Kroeber Anthropology Society Papers* 67–68, 42–54.

Hawkins, K. and Bransgrove, T. (1998) International students in universities. *Unicorn* 24 (1), 65–70.

Hay, C. and Strykert, R. (1982) *Down Under*. On Business as Usual: CBS.

Hayles, N.K. (1999) *How We Became Posthuman*. Chicago: University of Chicago Press.

Heenan, B. (1979) Population. *Pacific Viewpoint* 20 (2), 95–102.

Hegarty, J. (1992) Towards establishing a new paradigm for tourism and hospitality development. *International Journal of Hospitality Management* 11 (4), 309–317.

Helbert, L. (2002) 'The Beach' – A Correct Critique of Backpackers? Unpublished Graduate Thesis, Sheffield Hallam University, Sheffield, UK.

Helson, R. and Wink, P. (1992) Personality change in women from the early 40s to the early 50s. *Psychology and Aging* 7 (1), 46–55.

Henderson, K.A. (1994) Perspectives of analysing gender, women and leisure. *Journal of Leisure Research* 26, 119–137.

Henderson, K.A., Bialeschki, M.D., Shaw, S.M., and Freysinger, V.J. (1996). Both gains and gaps: Feminist perspectives on women's leisure. State College, PA: Venture Publishing, Inc.

Hibbert, C. (1969) *The Grand Tour*. London: Hamlyn.

Holden, A. (2003) In need of new environmental ethics for tourism? *Annals of Tourism Research* 30 (1), 94–108.

hooks, b. (1990) *Yearning: Race, Gender and Cultural Politics*. Boston, MA: South End Press.

Hottola, P. (1999) *The Intercultural Body: Western Woman, Culture Confusion and Control of Space in the South Asian Travel Scene*. Publications of the Department of Geography, no. 7. Joensuu: University of Joensuu.

Hottola, P. (2002) Touristic encounters with the exotic West: Blondes on the screens and streets of India. *Tourism Recreation Research* 27 (1), 83–90.

Hottola, P. (2004a) Culture confusion – Intercultural adaptation in tourism. *Annals of Tourism Research* 31 (2), 447–466.

Hottola, P. (2004b) *Gender and the Body in Tourism Geography*. GEO-Working Papers, Série de Investigacão 1 (1), 1–22.

Hottola, P. (2005) The metaspatialities of control management in tourism: Backpacking in India. *Tourism Geographies* 7 (1), 1–22.

Hughes, G. (1995) The cultural construction of sustainable tourism. *Tourism Management* 16 (1), 49–59.

Hultsman, J. (1995) Just tourism: An ethical framework. *Annals of Tourism Research* 22 (3), 553–567.

Humberstone, B. and Collins, D. (1998) Ecofeminism: Risk and women's experiences of landscape. In C. Aitchison and F. Jordan (eds) *Gender, Space and Identity: Leisure, Culture and Commerce* (pp. 137–150). Brighton: Leisure Studies Association.

Hsu, C.H.C. and Sung, S. (1996) International students' travel characteristics: an exploratory study. *Journal of Travel and Tourism Marketing* 5, 277–283.

Hutnyk, J. (1996) *The Rumour of Calcutta: Tourism, Charity and the Poverty of Representation*. London: Zed Books Limited.

Huxley, L. (2004) Western backpackers and the global experience: an exploration of young people's interaction with local cultures. *Tourism Culture and Communication* 5, 37–44.

IDP (2003) *International Students in Australian Universities, Statistics*. IDP, Education Australia. On WWW at www.IDP.com. Accessed 6.7.07.

Ingram, H. (1996) Classification and grading of smaller hotels, guesthouses and bed and breakfast accommodation. *International Journal of Contemporary Hospitality Management* 8 (5), 30–34.

Inside Business (2005) *Singleton sees profits in Lonely Planet*. On WWW at http://www.abc.net.au/insidebusiness/content/2005/s1352262.htm. Accessed 14.11.05.

Jameson, F. (1992) *Postmodernism or the Cultural Logic of Late Capitalism*. London: Verso.

Jarvis, J. (1994) The Billion Dollar Backpackers: The ultimate fully independent tourists. PhD Dissertation, Monash University, Australia.

Jarvis, J. (2004) Yellow bible tourism: Backpackers in Southeast Asia. In B. West (ed.) *Down The Road: Exploring Backpackers and Independent Travel*. Australia: API Network.

Jarvis, J. and Peel, V. (2005) *The Backpacker Boom Around the Globe*. Centre for Global Movements, Monash University.

Johnsen, S. (1998) Jalan Jalan! – En Sosialantropologisk Analyse av Backpackere i Nusa Tenggara, Indonesia. PhD Thesis, University of Tromsø, Norway.

Johnston, L. (2001) (Other) bodies and tourism studies. *Annals of Tourism Research* 28 (1), 180–201.

Josselson, R. (1996) *Revising Herself – The Story of Women's Identity from College to Midlife*. Oxford: Oxford University Press.

Judd, D.R. (1999) Constructing the tourist bubble. In D.R. Judd and S. Fainstein (eds) *The Tourist City* (pp. 35–53). New Haven: Yale University Press.

Jung, C. (1976) *The Portable Jung*. New York: Penguin Books.

Kaplan, C. (2000) *Questions of Travel. Post Modern Discourses of Displacement*. Durham: Duke University Press.

Karwacki, J. and Boyd, C. (1995) Ethics and ecotourism. *Business Ethics* 4 (4), 225–232.

Keeley, P. (1995) International backpacker market in Britain. *Insight* 12, B1–15.

Keeley, P. (2001) The backpacker market in Britain. *Insight* 12, B53–66.

Kinnaird, V. and Hall, D. (1994) *Tourism: A Gender Analysis*. Chichester: Wiley.

Kinnaird, V. and Hall, D. (1996) Understanding tourism processes: A gender-aware framework. *Tourism Management* 17 (2), 95–102.

Kinnaird, V. and Hall, D. (2000) Theorizing gender in tourism research. *Tourism Recreation Research* 25 (1), 71–84.

Kivela, J., Inbakaran, R. and Reece, J. (1999) Consumer research in the restaurant environment, Part 1: A conceptual model of dining satisfaction and return patronage. *International Journal of Contemporary Hospitality Management* 11 (6), 269–286.

Knox, D. (2001) Doing the Doric: The institutionalization of regional language and culture in north-east Scotland. *Social and Cultural Geography* 2 (3), 315–331.

Krippendorf, J. (1987) *The Holiday Makers: Understanding the Impact of Leisure and Travel*. Oxford: Heinemann.

Krohn, F. and Ahmed, Z. (1991) The need for developing an ethical code for the marketing of international tourism services. *Journal of Professional Services Marketing* 8 (1), 189–200.

Lahood, G. (2003) *Kombi Nation*. Arkles Entertainment.

Langer, E.J. (1983) *The Psychology of Control*. Beverly Hills: Sage.

Lansing, J. and Blood, D. (1964) *The Changing Travel Market*. Ann Arbor: Institute for Social Research.

Larson, M. and Wikström, E. (2001) Organising events: Managing conflict and consensus in a political market square. *Event Management* 7, 51–65.

Lash, S. and Urry, J. (1994). *Economics of Signs and Space*. London. Sage.

Lea, J. (1993) Tourism development ethics in the Third World. *Annals of Tourism Research* 20 (4), 701–715.

Lee, A. (1999) Backpackers 'Just want sex and drugs'. *The Times* June 29, 9.

Lee-Ross, D. (1998) A practical theory of motivation applied to hotels. *International Journal of Contemporary Hospitality Management* 10 (2), 68–74.

Lee-Ross, D. (2000) Development of the service predisposition instrument. *Journal of Managerial Psychology* 15 (2), 148–157.

Lee-Ross, D. and Pryce, J. (2005) A preliminary study of service predispositions amongst hospitality workers in Australia. *Journal of Management Development* 24 (5), 410–420.

Leiper, N. (2003) *Tourism Management* (2nd edn). French's Forest, NSW: Pearson SprintPrint.

Lennox, M.J. and Nash, J. (2003) Industry self-regulation and adverse selection: A comparison across four trade association programmes. *Business Strategy and the Environment* 12, 343–356.

Let's Go (1999) *Let's Go Homepage*. On WWW at www.letsgo.com/about.htm. Accessed 18.12.99.

Let's Go (2001) Happy Birthday Let's Go. On WWW at www.letsgo.com/yellowjacket/article.php?uid = 10. Accessed 28.6.02.

Let's Go (2005) Let's Go Homepage. On WWW at www.letsgo.com and subsequent links. Accessed 10.10.05.

Lett, J. (1983) Ludic and liminoid: Aspects of charter yacht tourism in the Caribbean. *Annals of Tourism Research* 10, 35–56.

Levinson, D. (1996) *The Seasons of a Woman's Life*. New York: Alfred A. Knopf.

Litvin, S.W. (2003) Tourism and understanding: The MBA study mission. *Annals of Tourism Research* 30 (1), 79–95.

Lloyd, K. (2003) Contesting control in transitional Vietnam: The development and regulation of traveller cafes in Hanoi and Ho Chi Minh City. *Tourism Geographies* 5 (3), 350–366.

Lockyer, T. (2002) Business guests' accommodation selection: the view from both sides. *International Journal of Contemporary Hospitality Management* 14 (6), 294–300.

Lockyer, T. (2003) Hotel cleanliness – how do guests view it? Let us get specific, a New Zealand study. *International Journal of Hospitality Management* 22, 297–315.

Lockyer, T. (2004) Weekend accommodation – The challenge: What are the guests looking for? *Journal of Hospitality and Tourism Management* 11, 1–13.

Lockyer, T. (2005) The dining experience: Critical areas of guest satisfaction. *Journal of Hospitality and Tourism Management* 12, 50–64.

Loker, L. (1991) *The Backpacker Phenomenon*. Townsville, Australia: Department of Tourism, James Cook University.

Loker, L. (1993a) *The Backpacker Phenomenon II: More Answers to Further Questions*. Townsville: James Cook University of North Queensland.

Loker, L. (1993b) Tourism development ethics in the Third World. *Annals of Tourism Research* 20 (4), 701–715.

Loker, L. (1994) *Backpackers in Australia: A Motivation-based Segmentation Study*. Paper presented at the Australian National Tourism Research and Education Conference.

Loker-Murphy, L. (1996) Backpackers in Australia: A motivation-based segment study. *Journal of Travel and Tourism Marketing* 54, 23–45.

Loker-Murphy, L. and Pearce, P. (1995) Young budget travellers: Backpackers in Australia. *Annals of Tourism Research* 22, 819–843.

Lomberg, G. (2001) *The Sceptical Environmentalist: Measuring the Real State of the World*. Cambridge: Cambridge University Press.

Lonelyplanet.com (2004) *South Africa*. Lonely Planet Online. On WWW at http://lonelyplanet.com/destinations/africa/south_africa/.

Lonely Planet (2005) *Lonely Planet Homepage*. On WWW at www.lonelyplanet.com and subsequent links. Accessed 15.11.05.

Luthans, F. (1995) *Organisational Behaviour*. New York: McGraw-Hill.

MacCannell, D. (1976) *The Tourist: A New Theory of the Leisure Class*. New York: Shocken.

MacCannell, D. (1992) *Empty Meeting Grounds: The Tourist Papers*. London: Routledge.

MacCannell, D. (1999) *The Tourist: A New Theory of the Leisure Class* (3rd edn). Berkeley: University of California Press.

Madriz, E. (1998) Young groups with low economic status; Latina women. *Qualitative Inquiry* 4, 114–128.

Maffesoli, M. (1995) *The Time of the Tribes*. London: Sage.

Malloy, D. and Fennell, D. (1998) Codes of ethics and tourism: An exploratory content analysis. *Tourism Management* 19 (5), 453–461.

Mandalia, S. (1999) Getting the hump. *In Focus* 31, 16–17.

Manning, R. (1999) *Studies in Outdoor Recreation*. Oregon: Oregon State University.

Maoz, D. (2002) *India will Love Me*. Jerusalem: Keter.

Maoz, D. (2004) The conquerors and the settlers: Two groups of young Israeli backpackers in India. In G. Richards and J. Wilson (eds) *The Global Nomad: Backpacker Travel in Theory and Practice* (pp. 109–122). Clevedon: Channel View.

Maoz, D. (2005) Young adult Israeli backpackers in India. In C. Noy and E. Cohen (eds) *Israeli Backpackers: From Tourism to Rite of Passage* (pp. 159–188). New York: State University of New York Press.

Maoz, D. (2006a) The mutual gaze. *Annals of Tourism Research* 33 (1), 221–239.

Maoz, D. (2006b) Erikson on the Tour. *Tourism Recreation Research* 31 (3), 55–63.

Maoz, D. (2007) Backpackers' motivations. The role of culture and nationality. *Annals of Tourism Research* 34 (1), 122–140.

Marcus, G.E. and Fisher, M. (1986) *Anthropology and Cultural Critique: The Experimental Moment in the Human Sciences*. Chicago: University of Chicago Press.

Marginson, S. (2005) The more we change, the more we stay the same. *Campus Review* 15, 24.

Marshall, G. (1998) The meaning of ethnic identity. *Sociology Review* 10 (2), 6.

Marshment, M. (1997) Gender takes a holiday: Representation in holiday brochures. In M.T. Sinclair (ed.) *Gender, Work and Tourism* (pp. 16–34). London: Routledge.

Maslow, A. (1970) *Motivation and Personality* (2nd edn). New York: Harper and Row.

Mathieson, A. and Wall, G. (1982) *Tourism: Economic, Physical and Social Impacts*. New York: Longman.

McCarter, N. (2001) *The Big OE: Tales from New Zealand Travellers*. Auckland: Tandom Press.

McGehee, N.G., Loker-Murphy, L. and Uysal, M. (1996) The Australian international pleasure travel market: Motivations from a gendered perspective. *Journal of Tourism Studies* 7 (1), 45–57.

McGill, D. (1989) *Kiwi Baby Boomers: Growing Up in New Zealand in the 40s, 50s and 60s*. Lower Hutt: Mills Publications.

McIntosh, A. and Siggs, A. (2005) An exploration of the experiential nature of boutique accommodation. *Journal of Travel Research* 44 (1), 74–81.

McIntosh, M., Thomas, R., Peipziger, D. and Coleman, G. (2003) *Living Corporate Citizenship: Strategic Routes to Socially Responsible Business*. London: Prentice Hall/Financial Times.

McMinn, M. (1999) Postcard from Nepal. *In Focus* 31, 20.

Michener, J. (1971) *The Drifters*. New York: Random House.

Mintel (2001) *Ethical Tourism*. London: Mintel International Group Ltd.

Mitchell, R.K., Agle, B.R. and Wood, D.J. (1997) Toward a theory of stakeholder identification and salience: Defining the principle of who and what really counts. *Academy of Management Review* 22, 853–886.

Mohsin, A., McIntosh, A. and Cave, J. (2005) Expectations of the service experience offered by restaurants and cafes in Hamilton, New Zealand. *Proceedings of the CAUTHE Conference*.

Mohsin, A. and Ryan, C. (2003) Backpackers in the Northern Territory of Australia – Motives, behaviours and satisfactions. *International Journal of Tourism Research* 5 (2), 113–131.

Morgan, D.L. (1998) *The Focus Group Guide Book*. Thousand Oaks, CA: Sage.

Morgan, N., Pritchard, A. and Piggott, R. (2002) New Zealand, 100% Pure. The creation of a powerful niche destination brand. *The Journal of Brand Management* 9 (4–5), 335–354.

Moran, D.M. (1999) Interpreting tourism experiences: The case of structured backpacker tours in New Zealand. Unpublished PhD, Lincoln University, Lincoln, New Zealand.

Moran, D. (2000) Interpreting tour experiences: The case of structured backpacker tours in New Zealand. *Pacific Tourism Review* 4, 35–43.

Mowforth, M. and Munt, I. (1998) *Tourism and Sustainability: New Tourism in the Third World*. London: Routledge.

Mulgan, J. (1984) *Report on Experience* (New edn). Auckland: Oxford University Press.

Munt, I. (1994) The 'Other' postmodern tourism: Culture, travel and the middle classes. *Theory, Culture and Society* 11, 101–123.

Murphy, L.E. (2001) Exploring social interactions of backpackers. *Annals of Tourism Research* 26, 50–67.

Muzaini, H. (2006) Backpacking Southeast Asia: Strategies of 'looking local'. *Annals of Tourism Research* 33 (1), 144–161.

Nash, R., Thyne, M. and Davies, S. (2006) An investigation into customer satisfaction levels in the budget accommodation sector in Scotland: A case study of backpacker tourists and the Scottish Youth Hostels Association. *Tourism Management* 27 (3), 525–532.

Neugarten, B. (1968) The awareness of middle age. In B. Neugarten (ed.) *Middle Age and Aging: A Reader in Social Psychology.* Chicago IL: University of Chicago Press.

Newlands, K. (2004) Setting out on the road less travelled: A study of backpacker travel in New Zealand. In G. Richards and J. Wilson (eds) *The Global Nomad: Backpacker Travel in Theory and Practice* (pp. 217–236). Clevedon: Channel View.

Noronha, F. (1999) Culture shocks. *In Focus* 31, 4–5.

Noy, C. (2004a) This trip really changed me: Backpackers' narratives of self-change. *Annals of Tourism Research* 31 (1), 78–102.

Noy, C. (2004b) Israeli backpackers: Narrative, interpersonal communication, and social construction. In C. Noy and E. Cohen (eds) *Israeli Backpackers and Their Society: A View from Afar.* New York State: University of New York Press.

Noy, C. (2006) Israeli backpacking since the 1960s: Institutionalization and its effects. *Tourism Recreation Research* 33 (1), 39–54.

Obenour, W., Patterson, M., Pedersen, P. and Pearson, L. (2006) Conceptualization of a meaning-based research approach for tourism service experiences. *Tourism Management* 27 (1), 34–41.

Odin, M. and Odin, L. (1979) *Europe: By Camper Van.* Sydney: Emma Books.

Olindo, P. (1991) The old man of nature tourism: Kenya. In T. Whelan (ed.) *Nature Tourism* (pp. 23–38). Washington: Island Press.

Oppermann, M. (1995) Travel life cycle. *Annals of Tourism Research* 22 (3), 535–551.

O'Reilly, C. (2006) From drifter to gap year tourist: Mainstreaming backpacker travel. *Annals of Tourism Research* 33 (4), 998–1017.

O'Reilly, K. (2003) When is a tourist? The articulation of tourism and migration in Spain's Costa del Sol. *Tourist Studies* 3 (3), 301–317.

Page, S., Bentley, T. and Walker, L. (2005) Tourist safety in New Zealand and Scotland. *Annals of Tourism Research* 32 (1), 150–166.

Paton, B. (2000) Voluntary environmental initiatives and sustainable industry. *Business Strategy and the Environment* 9, 328–338.

Patterson, I. (2002) Baby boomers and adventure tourism: The importance of marketing the leisure experience. *World Leisure Journal* 44, 4–10.

Patterson, M.E. and Hammitt, W.E. (1990) Backcountry encounter norms, actual reported encounters, and their relationship to wilderness solitude. *Journal of Leisure Research* 22, 259–275.

Payne, D. and Dimanche, F. (1996) Towards a code of conduct for the tourism industry: An ethics model. *Journal of Business Ethics* 15 (9), 997–1007.

Pearce, D.G. and Butler, R.W. (eds) (1993) *Tourism Research: Critiques and Challenges.* London: Routledge.

Pearce, D.G. and Schott, C. (2005) Tourism distribution channels: The visitors' perspective. *Journal of Travel Research* 44, 50–63.

Pearce, P.L (1982) *The Social Psychology of Tourist Behaviour.* Oxford: Pergamon Press.

Pearce, P.L. (1990) *The Backpacker Phenomenon: Preliminary Answers to Basic Questions.* Townsville: James Cook University of North Queensland, Department of Tourism.

Pearce, P.L. (1993) Fundamentals of tourist motivation. In D.G. Pearce and R.W. Butler (eds) *Tourism Research: Critiques and Challenges* (pp. 113–134). London. Routledge.

Pearce, P.L. (2005) Great divides or subtle contours? Contrasting British, North American/Canadian and European backpackers. In B. West (ed.) *Down the Road: Exploring Backpacker Independent Travel* (pp. 131–151). Perth: Australian Research Institute.

Peel, V. (2004) Classroom tourists: Study-abroad students and Australian studies. In D. Carter, K. Darian-Smith and G. Worby (eds) *Thinking Australian Studies: Teaching Across Cultures.* Queensland: UQP.

Pettinger, R. (1996) *Introduction to Organisation Behaviour.* Oxford: Pergamon Press.

Phillimore, J. and Goodson, L. (2004) *Qualitative Research in Tourism.* London: Routledge.

Pine, B.J. II and Gilmour, J. (1999) *The Experience Economy.* Boston: Harvard Business School Press.

Power, L. (2003) Changed planet: Guidebook publisher Tony Wheeler reflects on 30 years of mapping the world. *Sydney Morning Herald*, 10/10/03. On WWW at www.smh.com.au/articles/2003/10/10/1065676145710.html. Accessed 15.11.05.

Pratt, M. (1992) *Imperial Eyes: Travel Writing and Transculturation.* London: Routledge.

Prideaux, B. and Shiga, H. (2007) Japanese backpacking: The emergence of a new market sector – A Queensland case study. *Tourism Review International* 11, 45–56.

Priest, S.H. (1996) *Doing Media Research: An Introduction.* London: Sage.

Prigogine, I. (1997) *The End of Certainty.* New York: The Free Press.

Pritchard, A. and Morgan, N.J. (1998) Tourism, patriarchy and power: Gendered destinations. *British Sociological Association, Sexual Divisions Study Group, Gender, Power and Responsibility Conference*, London, November.

Pritchard, A. and Morgan, N. (2000a) Privileging the male gaze: Gendered tourism landscapes. *Annals of Tourism Research* 27, 884–905.

Pritchard, A. and Morgan, N. (2000b) Constructing tourism landscapes: Gender, sexuality and space. *Tourism Geographies* 2 (2), 115–139.

Pruitt, D. and LaFont, S. (1995) For love and money – Romance tourism in Jamaica. *Annals of Tourism Research* 22 (2), 422–440.

Qu, H. and Ping, E.W.Y. (1999) A service performance model of Hong Kong cruise travelers' motivation factors and satisfaction. *Tourism Management* 20, 237–244.

Raento, P. and Hottola, P. (2005) Where on Earth is New York? Pedagogical lessons from Finnish geography students' knowledge of the United States. *International Research in Geographical and Environmental Education* 14 (1), 5–27.

Raiborn, C. and Payne, D. (1990) Corporate codes of conduct: A collective conscience and continuum. *Journal of Business Ethics* 9 (11), 879–889.

Reader, L. and Ridout, L. (2003) *The Rough Guide to First-Time Asia.* New York: Rough Guides.

Reinharz, S. (1992) *Feminist Methods in Social Research.* New York: Oxford University Press.

Reisinger, Y. and Turner, L.W. (2003) *Cross-cultural Behaviour in Tourism: Concepts and Analysis*. London: Butterworth-Heinemann.

Richard, M.D. and Sundaram, D.S. (1994) A model of lodging repeat choice intentions. *Annals of Tourism Research* 21, 745– 755.

Richards, G. and Hall, D. (2000) *Tourism and Sustainable Community Development*. London: Routledge.

Richards, G. and King, B. (2003) Youth travel and backpacking. *Travel and Tourism Analyst* 6, 1– 23.

Richards, G. and Wilson, J. (2003) *Today's Youth Travellers: Tomorrow's Global Nomads. New Horizons in Youth and Student Travel*. A Report for the International Student Travel Federation (ISTC) and Association of Tourism and Leisure Education (ATLAS). Amsterdam: International Student Travel Confederation (ISTC).

Richards, G. and Wilson, J. (eds) (2004a) *The Global Nomad: Backpacker Travel in Theory and Practice*. Clevedon: Channel View Publications.

Richards, G. and Wilson, J. (2004b) The global nomad: Motivations and behaviour of independent travellers worldwide. In G. Richards and J. Wilson (eds) *The Global Nomad: Backpacker Travel in Theory and Practice* (pp. 14– 42). Clevedon: Channel View.

Richards, G. and Wilson, J. (2004c) Widening perspectives in backpacker research. In G. Richards and J. Wilson (eds) *The Global Nomad: Backpacker Travel in Theory and Practice* (pp. 253– 279). Clevedon: Channel View.

Richards, G., Wilson, J. and McDonnell, I. (2004) Proposed backpacker hostel in Jacques Avenue, Bondi Beach, Sydney. Unpublished Report for the Adjani Corp Pty Ltd.

Richter, L.K. (1993) Tourism policy making in Southeast Asia. In M. Hitchcock, V. King and M.J.G. Parnwell (eds) *Tourism in Southeast Asia* (pp. 179– 199). London: Routledge.

Richter, L.K. (1994) Exploring the political role of gender in tourism research. In W.F. Theobald (ed.) *Global Tourism: The Next Decade* (pp. 146– 157). Oxford: Butterworth Heinemann.

Riley, P. (1988) Road culture of international long-term budget travellers. *Annals of Tourism Research* 15 (3), 313– 328.

Ritchie, B. and Priddle, M. (2000) International and domestic university students and tourism: The case of the Australian capital territory. Paper presented at the *Australian Tourism and Hospitality research Conference*, Mt Buller, Australia, 2– 5 February.

Ritzer, G. (1996) *The McDonaldization of Society: An Investigation into the Changing Character of Contemporary Social Life* (2nd edn). Thousand Oaks: Pine Forge Press.

Roberts, J. (1996) Green consumers in the 1990s: Profile and implications for advertising. *Journal of Business Research* 36, 217– 231.

Rodaway, P. (1994) *Sensuous Geographies: Body, Sense and Place*. London: Routledge.

Rose, G. (1995) Place and identity: A sense of place. In D. Massey and P. Jess (eds) *A Place in the World? Places, Cultures and Globalisation*. Milton Keynes: Open University Press.

Ross, G.F. (1992) Tourist motivation among backpacker visitors to the wet tropics of Northern Australia. *Journal of Travel and Tourism Marketing* 1, 43– 59.

Ross, G.F. (1995) Service quality ideals and evaluations among backpackers. *Visions in Leisure and Business* 14, 24–42.

Ross, G.F. (1997) Backpacker achievement and environmental controllability as visitor motivations. *Journal of Travel and Tourism Marketing* 6 (2), 69–82.

Rough Guides (2005) *The Rough Guide to Rough Guides.* On WWW at www.roughguides.com/about/RGCOMPETITIVE.PDF. Accessed 14.11.05.

Ryan, C. (1995a) Learning about tourists from conversations: The over-55s in Majorca. *Tourism Management* 16, 207–215.

Ryan, C. (1995b) *Researching Tourist Satisfaction: Issues, Concepts, Problems.* London: Routledge.

Ryan, C. (1997) *The Tourist Experience – A New Introduction.* London: Cassell.

Ryan, C. (2002) Equity, management, power sharing and sustainability – Issues of the 'new tourism'. *Tourism Management* 23 (1), 17–26.

Ryan, C. and Cave, J. (2004) Letting the visitor speak: An analysis of destination image through the use of neural network software and PowerPoint presentation. *Creating Tourism Knowledge: Cauthe 2004.* Brisbane: The University of Queensland.

Ryan, C. and Mohsin, A. (2001) Backpackers attitudes to the 'Outback'. *Journal of Travel and Tourism Marketing* 10 (1), 69–92.

Ryan, C., Trauer, B., Cave, J., Sharma, A. and Sharma, S. (2003) Backpackers – what is the peak experience? *Tourism Recreation Research* 28 (3), 93–96.

Said, E.W. (1995) *Orientalism.* Harmondsworth: Penguin.

Saldanha, A. (2002) Music tourism and factions of bodies in Goa. *Tourist Studies* 2 (1), 43–62.

Saleh, F. and Ryan, C. (1992) Client perceptions of hotels: A multi-attribute approach. *Tourism Management* 13, 163–168.

SATOUR (2001) *Backpacking: Off the Beaten Track, South Africa Tourism (SATOUR).* On WWW at http://southafrica.net/index.cfm?SitePageID = 6001. Accessed 6.7.07.

Scheyvens, R. (2002) Backpacker tourism and Third World development. *Annals of Tourism Research* 29 (1), 144–164.

Schwepker, C. and Cornwall, T. (1991) An examination of ecologically concerned consumers and their intention to purchase ecologically packaged goods. *Journal of Public Policy and Marketing* 10 (2), 77–101.

Scottish National Party (2000) *Tourism: Scotland's Largest Industry. Scotland's Greatest Opportunity.* Edinburgh: Scottish National Party.

Scottish Office (1999) *Towards a Development Strategy for Rural Scotland: The Framework.* On WWW at http://www.royalsoced.org.uk/govt_responses/1998/rural.htm. Accessed 6.7.07.

Seligman, M. (1998) *Learned Optimism.* New York: Simon and Schuster.

Sheller, M. (2004) Demobilising and remobilising the Caribbean. In M. Sheller and J. Urry (eds) *Tourism Mobilities: Places to Play, Places in Play* (pp. 13–21). London: Routledge.

Sheller, M. and Urry, J. (eds) (2004) *Tourism Mobilities: Places to Play, Places in Play.* London: Routledge.

Shipway, R. (2000) The international backpacker market in Britain: A market waiting to happen. In J. Swarbrooke (ed.) *Motivations, Behaviour and Tourist Types, Reflections on International Tourism.* Sunderland: Business Education Publishers.

Shoemaker, S. (2000) Segmenting the mature market: 10 years later. *Journal of Travel Research* 39 (1), 11–27.

Shurmer-Smith, P. and Hannam, K. (1994) *Worlds of Desire, Realms of Power: A Cultural Geography*. London: Edward Arnold.

Simpson, K. (2003) Broad horizons? Youth travel and global citizenship. *Proceedings of the Institute of British Geographers Annual Conference GLTRG session*, London, September.

Sinclair, K. (ed.) (1961) *Distance Looks Our Way: The Effects of Remoteness on New Zealand*. Auckland: University of Auckland.

Slaughter, L. (2004) Profiling the international backpacker market in Australia. In G. Richards and J. Wilson (eds) *The Global Nomad: Backpacker Travel in Theory and Practice* (pp. 168–179). Clevedon: Channel View.

Smith, R. (2003) *South Africa Rides Tourism Wave*. On WWW at http://www.southafrica.info/plan_trip/holiday/tourism-090505.htm. Accessed 6.7.07.

Smith, V.L. (ed.) (1989) *Hosts and Guests: The Anthropology of Tourism* (2nd edn). Philadelphia: University of Pennsylvania Press.

Smith, V.L. (1990) Geographical implications of 'drifter' tourism: Boracay, Philippines. *Tourism Recreation Research* 15 (1), 34–42.

Smith, V.L (1992) Boracay, Philippines: A case study in 'alternative' tourism. In V.L. Smith and W. Eadington (eds) *Tourism Alternatives: Potentials and Problems in the Development of Tourism* (pp. 135–157). Philadelphia: University of Pennsylvania Press.

Soja, E.W. (1996) *Thirdspace: Journeys to Los Angeles and Other Real-and-Imagined Places*. Oxford: Blackwell.

Sollors, W. (ed.) (1989) *The Invention of Ethnicity*. New York: Oxford University Press.

Sørensen, A. (1999) Travellers in the periphery. Tourism Research Centre of Bornholm, Denmark, unpublished paper.

Sørensen, A. (2003) Backpacker ethnography. *Annals of Tourism Research* 30 (4), 847–867.

Speed, C. (2004) The backpacker tourist: Characteristics and contradictions. *Conference Proceedings Tourism: State of the Art II*. University of Strathclyde, Glasgow, June 2004.

Speed, C. and Harrison, T. (2004) Backpacking in Scotland: Formal public sector responses to an informal phenomenon. In G. Richards and J. Wilson (eds) *The Global Nomad: Backpacker Travel in Theory and Practice* (pp. 149–167). Clevedon: Channel View Publications.

Spreitzhofer, G. (1997) Rucksack-Rausch und Freizeitwahn: Drei Jahrzehnte Alternativtourismus in Südostasien. In C. Stock (ed.) *Trouble in Paradise – Tourismus in die Dritte Welt* (pp. 161–170). Freiburg: Izw.

Spreitzhofer, G. (1998) Backpacking tourism in South-East Asia. *Annals of Tourism Research* 25 (4), 979–983.

Spreitzhofer, G. (2002) The roaring nineties: Low-budget backpacking in South-east Asia as an appropriate alternative to third world mass tourism? *Asien, Afrika, Lateinamerika* 30 (2), 115–129.

Squire, S.J. (1994) Gender and tourist experiences: Assessing women's shared meanings for Beatrix Potter. *Leisure Studies* 13 (3), 195–209.

Stead, C.K. (1961) For the hulk of the world's between. In K. Sinclair (ed.) *Distance Looks Our Way: The Effects of Remoteness on New Zealand*. Auckland: University of Auckland.

Stein, J. and Stein, M. (1987) Psychotherapy, initiation and the middle transition. In L. Madhi, S. Foster and M. Little (eds) *Betwixt and Between: Patterns of Masculine and Feminine Initiation* (pp. 285–303). La Salle: Open Court.

Stewart, W.P. and Cole, D.N. (2001) Number of encounters and experience quality in Grand Canyon backcountry: Consistently negative and weak relationships. *Journal of Leisure Research* 33, 106–120.

Stone, G.J. and Nicol, S. (1999) Older, single female holidaymakers in the United Kingdom: Who needs them? *Journal of Vacation Marketing* 5 (1), 7–17.

Sutcliffe, W. (1997) *Are You Experienced?* Harmondsworth, England: Penguin.

Suvantola, J. (2002) *Tourist's Experience of Place*. Aldershot: Ashgate.

Swain, M. (1995) Gender in tourism. *Annals of Tourism Research* 22 (2), 247–266.

Swain, M. (2004) (Dis)embodied experience and power dynamics in tourism research. In J. Phillimore and L. Goodson (eds) *Qualitative Research in Tourism* (pp. 102–118). London: Routledge.

Swarbrooke, J. (1999) *Sustainable Tourism Management*. Wallingford, England: CABI Publishing.

Swarbrooke, J. and Horner, S. (1999) *Consumer Behaviour in Tourism*. Oxford: Butterworth-Heinemann.

Swarbrooke, J., Beard, C., Leckie, S. and Pomfret, G. (2003) *Adventure Tourism: The New Frontier*. Oxford: Butterworth-Heinemann.

Taylor, R. and Davies, D. (2004) Aspects of training and remuneration in the accommodation industry: A comparison between Australian and Singaporean providers. *Journal of European Industrial Training* 28 (6), 466–473.

Tearfund (2001) *Tourism: Putting Ethics into Practice*. On WWW at http://www.tearfund.org/homepage/index.asp and http://www.tearfund.org/enquiryzone. Accessed 11.3.03.

Teas, J. (1974) I'm studying monkeys: What do you do? Youthful travellers in Nepal. Paper presented at the Symposium on Tourism and Culture, Annual Meeting of the American Anthropological Association. California: University of California.

Ten Have, P. (1974) The counter culture on the move. *Mens en Maatschappij* 49 (3), 297–315.

Teo, P. and Leong, S. (2006) A postcolonial analysis of backpacking. *Annals of Tourism Research* 33 (1), 109–131.

Tesfahuney, M. (1998) Mobility, racism and geopolitics. *Political Geography* 17 (5), 499–515.

Thampson, C. and Mooney, M. (1998) Is it all rubbish? Incentives and impediments for waste minimisation in the accommodation industry. *Advances in Research – Proceedings of the 3rd New Zealand Tourism and Hospitality Research Conference*. Lincoln, Canterbury, New Zealand: Lincoln University.

The Baz Bus (2004) *Facts*. On WWW at http:/bazbus.com. Accessed 6.7.07.

Thyne, M., Davies, S. and Nash, R. (2004) A segmentation analysis of the backpacker market in Scotland: A case study of the Scottish youth hostel association. *Journal of Quality Assurance in Hospitality and Tourism* 5, 95–120.

Thyne, M., Lawson, R. and Todd, S. (2006) The use of conjoint analysis to assess the impact of the cross-cultural exchange between hosts and guests. *Tourism Management* 27 (2), 201–213.

Timothy, D. (2001) *Tourism and Political Boundaries.* London: Routledge.

TNT Magazine and Student Uni Travel (2003) *Backpackers Uncovered.* January. On WWW at http://www.tntmagazine.com.au. Accessed 4.7.06.

Tomory, D. (1998) *A Season in Heaven – True Tales from the Road to Kathmandu.* Hawthorn: Lonely Planet Publications.

Tomory, D. (2000) *Hello Goodnight: A Life of Goa.* Hawthorn: Lonely Planet Publications.

Top Deck (2004a) *Deckers London Club.* On WWW at http://www.topdecktravel.co.uk/deckmem.php. Accessed 11.6.05.

Top Deck (2004b) *Top Deck Travel – All About Us.* On WWW at http://www.topdecktravel.co.uk/about. Accessed 14.9.04.

Tourism New Zealand (1999) *Understanding New Zealand's Backpacker Market.* Wellington: Tourism New Zealand.

Tourism Research Council New Zealand (2004) *Understanding the Dynamics of New Zealand Tourism.* Wellington: The Ministry of Tourism.

Tourism Research Council New Zealand (2005) *Commercial Accommodation Survey, May.* Wellington: Ministry of Tourism.

Towner, J. (1985) The grand tour: A key phase in the history of tourism. *Annals of Tourism Research* 12 (3), 297–333.

Toxward, S. (1999) *Backpackers Expectations and Satisfactions: A Case Study of Northland New Zealand.* Christchurch, New Zealand: Lincoln University.

Tribe, J. (1997) The indiscipline of tourism. *Annals of Tourism Research* 24, 638–657.

Tribe, J. (2005) New tourism research. *Tourism Recreation Research* 30 (2), 5–8.

Tucker, H. and Lynch, P.A. (2004) Host–guest dating: The potential of improving the customer experience through host–guest psychographic matching. *Journal of Quality Assurance in Hospitality and Tourism* 5, 11–32.

Turner, L. and Ash, J. (1975) *The Golden Hordes – International Tourism and the Pleasure Periphery.* London: Constable.

Turner, V. (1973) The center out there: Pilgrim's goal. *History of Religion* 11, 191–230.

Turner, V. (1987) Betwixt and between: The liminal period in rites de passage. In L. Madhi, S. Foster and M. Little (eds) *Betwixt and Between: Patterns of Masculine and Feminine Initiation* (pp. 5–22). La Salle: Open Court.

University of Melbourne (2004) *Study Abroad and Exchange Program Guide.* University of Melbourne.

Uriely, N. (2001) 'Travelling Workers' and 'Working Tourists'. *International Journal of Tourism Research* 3 (1), 1–8.

Uriely, N. (2005) The tourist experience: Conceptual developments. *Annals of Tourism Research* 32 (1), 199–216.

Uriely, N., Yonay, Y. and Simchai, D. (2002) Backpacking experiences: A type and form analysis. *Annals of Tourism Research* 29, 520–538.

Urry, J. (1990) *The Tourist Gaze.* London: Sage.

Urry, J. (2002) *The Tourist Gaze* (2nd edn). London: Sage.

Urry, J. (2003) *Global Complexity.* Cambridge: Polity.

Valentine, G. (1989) The geography of women's fears. *Area* 21 (4), 22–29.

Vance, P. (2004) Backpacker transport choice: A conceptual framework applied to New Zealand. In G. Richards and J. Wilson (eds) *The Global Nomad: Backpacker Travel in Theory and Practice*. Clevedon: Channel View.

Veijola, S. and Jokinen, E. (1994) The body in tourism. *Theory, Culture and Society* 11, 125–151.

Verhelä, P. (2003) Toisen kulttuuriń kohtaaminen matkailussa-tapaus Hammamet [Intercultural encounter in tourism – case Hammamet]. In P. Hottola (ed.) *Kulttuurisia näkökulmia Tunisian matkailuun* [*Cultural Insights in Tunisian Tourism*] (pp. 98–113). Publications of the Finnish University Network for Tourism Studies no. 3. Joensuu: University of Joensuu.

Verstraete, G. (2004) Technological frontiers and the politics of mobility in the European Union. In S. Ahmed, C. Castaneda, A.-M. Fortier and M. Sheller (eds) *Uprootings/Regroundings: Questions of Home and Migration* (pp. 225–250). London: Berg.

VisitScotland (2000) *The Growth, Development and Future Prospects for the Hostels Market in Scotland*. On WWW at http://www.scotexchange.net/KnowYour-Market/kym-accom.htm. Accessed 6.8.03.

Visser, G. (2004) The developmental impacts of backpacker tourism in South Africa. *GeoJournal* 60 (3), 283–299.

Vogt, J. (1976) Wandering: Youth and travel behaviour. *Annals of Tourism Research* 4 (1), 25–40.

Wagner, U. (1977) Out of time and place: Mass tourism and charter trips. *Ethnos* 42, 38–52.

Walle, A. (1995) Business ethics and tourism: From micro to macro perspectives. *Tourism Management* 16 (4), 263–268.

Wang, N. (1999) Rethinking authenticity in tourism experience. *Annals of Tourism Research* 26 (2), 349–370.

Ward, C., Bochner, S. and Furnham, A. (2001) *The Psychology of Culture Shock* (2nd edn). London: Routledge.

Ward, C. and Kennedy, A. (1993) Where's the culture in cross-cultural transition? Comparative studies of sojourner adjustment. *Journal of Cross-Cultural Psychology* 24 (2), 221–249.

Ware, M.P. (1992) *Been There, Done That: A Study of Winter Backpackers in New Zealand*. Cambridge: University of Cambridge.

Waverley Council (2004) WWW.waverley.nsw.gov.au/into/Mdia/report.asp?article ID=104. Accessed 20.7.07.

Wayne, S. (1990) *Egypt and the Sudan Guidebook*. Hawthorn: Lonely Planet Publications.

Wearing, B. (1996) *Gender: The Pain and Pleasure of Difference*. Melbourne. Addison Wesley Longman.

Wearing, B. and Wearing, S. (1996) Refocusing the tourist experience: The 'flaneur' and the 'choraster'. *Leisure Studies* 15, 229–244.

Wearing, S., Cynn, S., Ponting, J. and McDonald, M. (2002) Converting environmental concern into ecotourism purchases: A qualitative evaluation of international backpackers in Australia. *Journal of Ecotourism* 1, 133–148.

Weaver, A. (2005) Spaces of containment and revenue capture: 'Super-sized' cruise ships as mobile tourism enclaves. *Tourism Geographies* 7 (2), 165–184.

Weber, D. (1995) From limen to border: A meditation on the legacy of Victor Turner for American cultural studies. *American Quarterly* 47, 525–536.

Weeden, C. (2001) Ethical tourism: An opportunity for competitive advantage? *Journal of Vacation Marketing* 8 (2), 141–153.

Weiermair, K. and Fuchs, M. (1999) Measuring tourist judgement on service quality. *Annals of Tourism Research* 26 (4), 1004–1021.

Weightman, B. (1987) Third World tourism landscapes. *Annals of Tourism Research* 14 (2), 227–239.

Welk, P. (2004) The beaten track: Anti-tourism as an element backpacker identity construction. In G. Richards and J. Wilson (eds) *The Global Nomad* (pp. 217–236). Clevedon: Channel View.

Welk, P. (2006) *The Shoestring Travellers – Constructions of Identity in the Backpacker Scene*. Bangkok: White Lotus.

Wen, J. (1998) Evaluation of tourism and tourist resources in China: Existing methods and their limitations. *International Journal of Social Economics* 25 (2/3/4), 467–485.

West, B. (ed.) (2005) *Down the Road: Exploring Backpacker and Independent Travel*. Perth: Australian Research Institute.

Westerhausen, K. (1997) Western travellers in Asia: A mobile subculture in search of a home. Unpublished doctoral dissertation, Murdoch University, Western Australia.

Westerhausen, K. (2002) Beyond the beach: An ethnography of modern travellers in Asia. *Studies in Asian Tourism no. 2*. Bangkok: White Lotus.

Wheat, S. (1995) Interview with a tour guide. *The Independent on Sunday* 12 February, 50–51.

Wheeler, T. (1977) *South-East Asia on a Shoestring Guidebook*. South Yarra: Lonely Planet Publications.

Wheeler, T. (1981) *South-East Asia on a Shoestring Guidebook*. South Yarra: Lonely Planet Publications.

Wheeler, T. (1999) In defence of backpackers. *In Focus* 31, 15–16.

Wheeler, T. and Wheeler, M. (2005) *Once While Travelling: The Lonely Planet Story*. Footscray: Lonely Planet Publications.

Wheeller, B. (1991) Tourism's troubled times: Responsible tourism is not the answer. *Tourism Management* 12 (2), 91–96.

Wheeller, B. (1992) Alternative tourism – A deceptive ploy. In C. Cooper and A. Lockwood (eds) *Progress in Tourism, Recreation and Hospitality Management, IV* (pp. 140–145). Chichester: John Wiley.

Wheeller, B. (1993) Sustaining the ego. *Journal of Sustainable Tourism* 1 (2), 121–129.

Wheeller, M. (1994a) Tourism marketing ethics: An introduction. *International Marketing Review* 12 (4), 38–49.

Wheeller, M. (1994b) The emergence of ethics on tourism and hospitality. In C. Cooper and A. Lockwood (eds) *Progress in Tourism, Recreation and Hospitality Management* (pp. 46–56). Chichester: John Wiley.

White, M. (2005) On the road: John Anderson's Contiki journey. *North and South* March, 48–56.

White, N. and White, P. (2004) Travel as transition. Identity and place. *Annals of Tourism Research* 31 (1), 200–218.

Whitney, D. (1989) The ethical orientations of hotel managers and hospitality students: Implications for industry, education and youthful careers. *Hospitality Education and Research Journal* 13 (3), 187–192.

Whitney, D. (1990) Ethics in the hospitality industry: With a focus on hotel managers. *International Journal of Hospitality Management* 9 (1), 59–68.

Wight, P. (1993a) Ecotourism: Ethics or eco-sell? *Journal of Travel Research* 31 (3), 3–9.

Wight, P. (1993b) Sustainable ecotourism: Balancing economic, environmental and social goals within an ethical framework. *The Journal of Tourism Studies* 4 (2), 54–66.

Wight, P. (1994) Environmentally responsible marketing of tourism. In E. Cater and G. Lowman (eds) *Ecotourism: A Sustainable Option?* (pp. 39–55). Chichester: John Wiley.

Wilcock, J. and Aaron, J. (1972) *India on $5 to $10 a day*. New York: Arthur Frommer.

wilderness.com (2004) *Getting Away From It All – But Does it Have Mobile Coverage?* http://www.hero.ac.uk/studying/wilderness_com1668.cfm. Accessed 7.04.

Wilkinson, S. (1998) Focus groups in feminist research: Power interaction and the co-construction of meaning. *Women's Studies International Forum* 21, 111–125.

Wilson, D. (1997) Paradoxes of Tourism in Goa. *Annals of Tourism Research* 24 (1), 52–75.

Wilson, E. and Little, D. (2005) A 'relative escape'? The impact of constraints on women who travel solo. *Tourism Review International* 9, 155–175.

Wilson, J., Fisher, D. and Moore, K. (2004) The New Zealand 'OE': The oxymoron of the working holiday. *Proceedings of the Institute of British Geographers and International Geographical Union Geography of Tourism and Leisure Working Group Pre-Meeting*, Loch Lomond, Scotland, August.

Wood, D. and Graham, S. (2006) Permeable boundaries in the software-sorted society: Surveillance and the differentiation of mobility. In M. Sheller and J. Urry (eds) *Mobile Technologies of the City*. London: Routledge.

World Business Council on Sustainable Development (2004) On WWW at http://www.wbcsd.ch/. Accessed 4.7.04.

World Commission on Environment and Development (WCEO) (1987) *Our Common Future*. Oxford: Oxford University Press.

World Tourism Organization (1999) *Global Code of Ethics for Tourism*. On WWW at http://www.unwto.org/code_ethics/eng/global.htm. Accessed 28.11.02.

World Tourism Organization (2004) *Indicators of Sustainable Development for Tourism Destinations: A Guidebook*. Madrid: World Tourism Organisation.

Yenckel, J. (1995) How to plan a 'green' vacation. *The Palm Beach Post*. Abstract from LexisNexis.

Index

Accommodation 140, 216, 219, 226, 227-244
Aitchison 95, 108, 252
Alcohol 75
Allon 203, 207
Anderskov 12, 90
Anthropology 10
Anxiety 10-11, 194
Aramberri 219
Asian backpackers 220
Ateljevic 2, 40, 95, 188, 249
Australia 4, 67, 114, 116, 142, 157-159, 161,
    177, 199, 202-204
Authenticity 10, 23, 29-32

Bangkok 17, 25
Bartering 66
Bell 115
Bhattacharyya 85, 90
Binder 10, 17
Bondi Beach 207-208
Boorstin 27, 29
Brundtland Report 42
Business and management 247

Carr 2
Central America 12, 40
China 103, 160
Clarke 25, 115, 199, 209
Cliff 51
Cohen 2, 10, 12, 26, 40, 41, 62, 117, 129, 158,
    168, 172, 188, 248
Community 132, 200
Comparative methodology 222
Consumption patterns 138
Control 28-29
Critical Studies 247, 249-252
Crick 58
Crouch 97
Cultural capital 10, 101, 178-179
Cultural confusion 27
Cultural difference 18, 212
Cultural encounters 29

Decision making process 11

Denzin 251
Desforges 2, 103, 124, 180
Drugs 75
D'sa 59
Duncan 25
Dunphy 45-48

Economic behaviour 65-68
Economic ethics 76-78
Economic spending 167
Economics 131, 144
Edensor 13, 98
Elsrud 4, 63, 215
Embodiment 4, 97-99, 100, 252
Enclaves 3, 5, 9-25, 29, 32, 199
Environmental ethics 71
Ethical tourism 55-68
Ethics 4, 54-81
Europe 4, 25, 114, 126
Expenditure 139, 167, 220
Experiences 12, 14-15, 25, 197

Facilities 215, 217, 231-235
Female travellers 97, 174, 180-186, 188,
    189-197
Feminist research 175
Fennell 55
Finlay 83
Firth 64
Franklin 41, 248, 252

Gallagher 160
Gastronomy 103
Gender 4, 5, 99, 152, 174, 176-178, 188 255
Giddens 178, 190
Giesbers 203
Gilmour 50
Global nomad 1, 3, 119
Goa 13, 67
Goffman 30
Grand Tour 189
Grosz 252
Groups 14
Guba 252

Guide books 82

Hampton 50
Hannam 2, 253, 255
Hanzah 132
Henderson 175
Holden 56
Home 17-18
Host–Guest interactions 2, 18
Hostels 145, 200-201, 206, 209, 210, 213,
    215-244
Hottola 3, 10, 13, 17, 26
Hughes 55
Hutnyk 63

Identity 2, 41, 131, 134, 174, 176, 184, 188, 192
Illegal hostels 200, 208
Independent travellers 10
India 10, 29, 188
Indonesia 13
Information 130
Infrastructure 5
Internet 16, 69
Israel 101, 114, 118, 188-190

Jarvis 130, 133, 252
Judd 13

Kaplan 179
Kelley 221
Kinnaird 176

Language 25
Let's Go 86
Lloyd 14
Local Authorities 210
Local contact 21
Local culture 21
Local development 50
Local interaction 74-76
Loker 64
Loker-Murphy 130, 144
Lomberg 48-49
Lonely Planet 4, 22, 29, 81, 82-94

MacCannell 26, 27, 29, 31, 33, 34
Malaysia 128-143
Management 11, 48,
Manning 40
Mass tourism 132
Material objects 4, 254
Metaspatial 26-28
Methodologies 11
Mid-life crisis 192

Migration 254
Moaz 2, 5, 10, 189, 254
Mobilities 253-256
Moorings 253
Motivation 19, 148-151, 155, 159, 164
Mowforth 65
Muzaini 2
Myers 5, 252

Narratives 2, 24, 190, 191-197
Newlands 85
New Zealand 114, 116, 215, 219, 220, 221,
    222.
North America 70, 218
Noy 2, 16

O'Reilly 2
Orientalism 31
Othering 24, 28, 31, 34, 100, 103,
Overseas experience 114

Pearce 3, 39, 62, 69, 151, 177, 218, 222
Peel 171
Performances 256
Performativities 256
Policy 211
Postcolonialism 97
Poststructuralism 95, 248
Power relations 2
Prideaux 12
Pritchard 176

Qualitative methods 179

Reisinger 27
Resident attitudes 210
Responsible tourism 61
Richards 9, 15, 19, 40, 54, 151, 177, 187, 210,
    222, 247
Riley 62, 64, 118, 151, 153, 169
Rites of passage 188
Ross 217
Routes 121
Ryan 223, 238

Saldanha 13
Satisfaction 219, 231-236
Scheyvens 50, 63, 67
Scotland 217, 221-223
Security 13, 14
Service 219
Sex 196
Singapore 25, 130
Slaughter 39

Social change 186
Social ethics 64-65, 73
Sorensen 2, 10, 82, 90, 151, 177
South Africa 40, 144-156
South America 12, 40
South East Asia 2, 10, 28, 31, 32, 113, 129
Space 15-16
Speed 4, 12, 69
Sprietzhofer 65
Sri Lanka 35
Staged authenticity 29
Stakeholders 201, 206, 208-210
Statistics 85, 146
Student travel 114, 159
Student travellers 40, 147, 159-161
Sustainability 3, 42-50, 51-53, 55-57, 81-82
Suvantola 26
Swarbrooke 57, 175

Teo & Leong 2
Thailand 2, 130
Theory 11,
Time 17
Tour 123-125

Tourism recreation research 1, 41, 248
Tourist gaze 29, 118
Transport 120, 122-123, 141, 145, 147, 255
Tribe 41, 96, 250-251
Turner 27
Turns 169
Typologies 129

Urban areas 14, 29, 133
Uriely 95, 188
Urry 27, 29, 30, 32, 252, 254

Van tours 121-123
Verhela 26
Vietnam 14
Visser 5, 40

Wearing 99, 182
Welk 4, 10, 35, 86, 172
Westerhausen 12, 13
World Tourism Organisation 45
World Wide Web 68-71

Youth Hostel Association 207